"*The 100 Most Asked Questions About God and the Bible* is essential for anyone who has ever had a question about the Bible; and let's be honest, that includes all of us. It is fascinating to see what the top one hundred questions are and encouraging to see them answered from God's Word. This book is indispensable for anyone seeking to speak truth into a culture ruled by lies."

—Pastor Jack Hibbs, Calvary Chapel Chino Hills

"*The 100 Most Asked Questions about God and the Bible*, tackling a hundred challenging questions, is brimming with wisdom and a beacon of clarity for all Christians. I love how the book flows and invites you to jump into a wide range of topics that provide solid biblical answers that will build confidence as you grow and share your faith."

—Jason Jimenez, founder and president of Stand Strong Ministries and bestselling author

"This book is an invaluable resource for anyone who is searching for biblical answers to some of the most popular questions people have about the Christian faith. It's also a great apologetic resource to use in conversations with your children and those seeking to obtain a deeper understanding of what Christians believe. I encourage all Christians to not only get a copy of this book, but more importantly, read it in depth to provide a solid foundation to their theological beliefs."

—Allen Parr, author of *Misled: 7 Lies that Distort the Gospel* and Christian YouTuber on The B.E.A.T.

"Our children have questions, and the Bible has answers. The problem is we are not always sure how to help our children find those answers. *The 100 Most Asked Questions About God and the Bible* helps solve this problem, modeling how to examine the Bible as a whole to answer challenging questions. I highly recommend that every Christian parent keep this book on hand as they seek to guide their children in the truth."

—Elizabeth Urbanowicz, founder, Foundation Worldview

T0033411

"GotQuestions.org is my go-to resource and recommendation for people who have questions about the Christian worldview. It is arguably the best collection of answers for questions in a skeptical age. That's why *The 100 Most Asked Questions About God and the Bible* is such a valuable book. No one is better equipped to collect and answer these questions than S. Michael Houdmann. If you're looking for a powerful, concise, and targeted resource to grow your faith or reach your friends, get this book!"

—J. Warner Wallace, *Dateline* featured cold-case detective, senior fellow at the Colson Center for Christian Worldview, professor of apologetics, and author

"My good friend, S. Michael Houdmann, has done all of us a huge service in writing and now making available this amazing resource: *The 100 Most Asked Questions About God and the Bible*. Anyone serious about the Bible and being ready to give reasons for their hope in Christ needs this book!"

—Mark Yarbrough, PhD; president, Dallas Theological Seminary

"S. Michael Houdmann, founder and president of GotQuestions.org, has compiled the most asked questions into an outstanding resource for Christians and for churches. Both detailed and accessible, Houdmann provides straight answers to tough questions, common confusions, and outright challenges to the faith. Covering the Old and New Testament, core Christian doctrine, ancient historical trivia, and practical applications, *The 100 Most Asked Questions About God and the Bible* consistently communicates with grace and truth. Most of all, Houdmann doesn't hold back from declaring—firmly but lovingly—the gospel of Jesus Christ. Pick up this book! It is a must for every Christian and church library!!"

—Dr. Christopher Yuan, speaker; author of *Holy Sexuality and the Gospel*, and producer of *The Holy Sexuality Project*

THE **100** MOST ASKED QUESTIONS ABOUT GOD AND THE BIBLE

THE 100 MOST ASKED QUESTIONS ABOUT GOD AND THE BIBLE

• • •

*Scripture's Answers on Sin, Salvation, Sexuality,
End Times, Heaven, and More*

S. Michael Houdmann

BETHANYHOUSE
a division of Baker Publishing Group
Minneapolis, Minnesota

© 2024 by Got Questions Ministries

Published by Bethany House Publishers
Minneapolis, Minnesota
BethanyHouse.com

Bethany House Publishers is a division of
Baker Publishing Group, Grand Rapids, Michigan

Printed in the United States of America

Library of Congress Cataloging-in-Publication Data
Names: Houdmann, S. Michael, author.
Title: The 100 most asked questions about God and the Bible / S. Michael Houdmann.
Other titles: One hundred most asked questions about God and the Bible
Description: Minneapolis, Minnesota : Bethany House Publishers, a division of Baker
    Publishing Group, [2024] | Includes bibliographical references.
Identifiers: LCCN 2023045274 | ISBN 9780764242465 (paperback) | ISBN
    9780764242793 (casebound) | ISBN 9781493445202 (ebook)
Subjects: LCSH: God (Christianity)—Miscellanea. | Bible—Miscellanea.
Classification: LCC BT103 .H685 2024 | DDC 231—dc23/eng/20231122
LC record available at https://lccn.loc.gov/2023045274

Cover Design: Darren Welch
Author Photo: © Sally Sue Dunn

Baker Publishing Group publications use paper produced from sustainable forestry practices and postconsumer waste whenever possible.

24 25 26 27 28 29 30   7 6 5 4 3 2 1

Contents

Introduction   13

SECTION 1
Questions about God   15

1. Is Jesus God? Did Jesus ever claim to be God?
2. What does the Bible teach about the Trinity?
3. What are the different names of God, and what do they mean?
4. What does it mean that Jesus is God's only begotten son?
5. If His name was Yeshua, why do we call Him Jesus?
6. What are the seven spirits of God?
7. Who is the Holy Spirit?
8. When/How do we receive the Holy Spirit?
9. What is the role of the Holy Spirit in our lives today?
10. What is the glory of God?

SECTION 2
Questions about Salvation   35

11. What is salvation? What is the Christian doctrine of salvation?
12. What is repentance, and is it necessary for salvation?

13. What does it mean to be a born-again Christian?

14. Can a Christian lose salvation?

15. Got Eternal Life? Do you know for sure that you will have eternal life in heaven with God?

16. What is the Romans Road to salvation?

17. Where do I find the age of accountability in the Bible?

SECTION 3
Questions about the Church   51

18. What does the Bible say about women pastors?

19. What is the difference between praise and worship?

20. What day is the Sabbath, Saturday or Sunday? Do Christians have to observe the Sabbath day?

21. What does the Bible say about Christian tithing? Should a Christian tithe?

22. What is the importance of Christian baptism?

23. Does the Bible record the death of the apostles? How did each of the apostles die?

SECTION 4
Questions about Theology   65

24. What does it mean that humanity is made in the image of God (*imago dei*)?

25. Why does God allow bad things to happen to good people?

26. What does it mean to have the fear of God?

27. How, why, and when did Satan fall from heaven?

28. What is the difference between Sheol, hades, hell, the lake of fire, paradise, and Abraham's bosom?

29. Did Jesus go to hell between His death and resurrection?

30. What happens after death?

31. What is the difference between the soul and the spirit of humanity?

32. Do pets go to heaven?

33. What is the gift of speaking in tongues?

34. What is the anointing? What does it mean to be anointed?

35. What is the difference between mercy and grace?

36. Calvinism vs. Arminianism—which view is correct?

37. What is the meaning of *BC* and *AD*?

SECTION 5
Questions about the End Times   89

38. What signs indicate that the end times are approaching?

39. What do the seven churches in Revelation stand for?

40. Who are the Four Horsemen of the Apocalypse?

41. What is the tribulation? How do we know the tribulation will last seven years?

42. Does the Bible prophesy a one-world government and a one-world currency in the end times?

43. Will we be able to see and know our friends and family members in heaven? Will we know each other in heaven?

SECTION 6
Questions about the Old Testament   101

44. What happened on each of the days of creation?

45. What does the Bible say about dinosaurs? Are there dinosaurs in the Bible?

46. Who was Cain's wife? Was Cain's wife his sister?

47. Why did God allow polygamy/bigamy in the Bible?

48. Who/what were the Nephilim?

49. What is the Book of Enoch, and should it be in the Bible?

50. What was the sin of Sodom and Gomorrah?

51. What is the meaning of Jacob wrestling with God?

52. Why was Moses not allowed to enter the Promised Land?

53. Why did God allow Solomon to have one thousand wives and concubines?

54. Why did God take Enoch and Elijah to heaven without them dying?

55. What does it mean to "spare the rod, spoil the child"?

56. What is Zion? What is Mount Zion? What is the biblical meaning of Zion?

SECTION 7

Questions about the New Testament   127

57. Old Testament vs. New Testament—what are the differences?

58. What is the new covenant?

59. Who were the twelve disciples/apostles of Jesus Christ?

60. What are the differences between the Sadducees and the Pharisees?

61. What does it mean to seek first the kingdom of God?

62. What is the meaning of the parable of the prodigal son?

63. What did Jesus mean when He said, "Take up [your] cross and follow me" in Matthew 16:24?

64. What was the significance of Jesus washing the feet of the disciples?

65. What was the significance of the temple veil being torn in two when Jesus died?

66. Why is the resurrection of Jesus Christ important?

67. What is the full armor of God?

SECTION 8

Questions about Religions, Cults, and Worldviews   153

68. What is the difference between Christianity and Judaism?

69. What is the difference between Catholics and Protestants?

70. What is Islam, and what do Muslims believe?

71. Why do Jews and Arabs/Muslims hate each other?

72. What is Mormonism? What do Mormons believe?

73. Who are the Jehovah's Witnesses, and what are their beliefs?

74. What is Free Masonry, and what do Free Masons believe?

75. What is the Illuminati conspiracy?

76. What is cultural relativism?

SECTION 9
Questions about Sin   177

77. What is the definition of *sin*?

78. Will God continue to forgive you if you commit the same sin over and over again?

79. What does the Bible say about drinking alcohol/wine? Is it a sin for a Christian to drink alcohol/wine?

80. What does the Bible say about tattoos?

81. Is gambling a sin? What does the Bible say about gambling?

82. What is the Christian view of suicide? What does the Bible say about suicide?

83. What does the Bible say about abortion?

84. What is blasphemy against the Holy Spirit?

85. What does the Bible say about breaking generational curses?

86. What is sanctification? What is the definition of Christian sanctification?

87. What does the Bible mean when it says "Do not judge"?

SECTION 10
Questions about Sexuality   201

88. What is sexual immorality?

89. What constitutes marriage according to the Bible?

90. What does the Bible say about homosexuality?

91. What does the Bible say about gay marriage/same sex marriage?

92. What is a Christian couple allowed to do in sex?

93. What does the Bible say about interracial marriage?

94. What does the Bible say about divorce and remarriage?

95. What is the difference between dating and courting?

96. What does the Bible say about sex before marriage?

97. What does the Bible say about oral sex?

98. Masturbation—is it a sin according to the Bible?

99. What does the Bible say about pornography?

100. What is agape love?

Notes   229

Acknowledgments   231

Introduction

Little did I know what God had in mind when I launched GotQuestions.org over twenty years ago. What my wife and I thought would be a fun hobby turned out to be something God intended to expand into one of the most impactful Christian websites in the world. Now, not only do I have my dream job, but I also get to watch God take our limited vision and use it in ways far beyond anything we could ask or imagine.

GotQuestions.org has received over seven hundred and fifty thousand personally submitted questions. Each month, the articles on GotQuestions.org are read approximately twenty million times. Over the years, our articles have been read well over two billion times. These interactions give GotQuestions.org plenty of data regarding what questions people are truly asking. We *know* what people are asking. We *know* the information people are searching for. And, after years of God refining us and the content we produce, we have improved at answering questions in an understandable and applicable way.

This book contains the top one hundred questions we have received. Some of the questions are of vital importance. Some of the questions are immensely personal. Some of the questions are fairly obscure. None of the questions are trivial.

My sincerest hope is that you will find this resource interesting, informative, biblically accurate, and worth sharing with others. May this book motivate you to continue asking questions and continue looking to God's Word for the answers.

                       —S. Michael Houdmann

SECTION 1
Questions about God

1. Is Jesus God? Did Jesus ever claim to be God?

Some who deny that Jesus is God make the claim that Jesus never said that He is God. It is correct that the Bible never records Jesus saying the precise words "I am God." This does not mean, however, that Jesus never claimed to be God.

Is Jesus God?—Jesus claimed to be God.

Take for example the words of Jesus in John 10:30, "I and the Father are one" (ESV). We need only to look at the Jews' reaction to His statement to know He was claiming to be God. They tried to stone Him for this very reason: "You, a mere man, *claim to be God*" (John 10:33, emphasis added). The Jews understood exactly what Jesus was claiming—deity. When Jesus declared "I and the Father are one," He was saying that He and the Father are of one nature and essence. John 8:58 is another example. Jesus declared, "I tell you the truth, before

Abraham was born, I AM!" (NLT). This is a reference to Exodus 3:14 when God revealed Himself as the "I AM." The Jews who heard this statement responded by taking up stones to kill Him for blasphemy, as the Mosaic law commanded (Leviticus 24:16). Their indignation showed He was claiming to be God.

Is Jesus God?—His followers declared Him to be God.

John reiterates the concept of Jesus' deity: "The Word [Jesus] was God" and "the Word became flesh" (John 1:1, 14). These verses clearly indicate that Jesus is God in the flesh. Acts 20:28 tells us, "Be shepherds of the church of God, which he bought with his own blood." Who bought the church with His own blood? Jesus Christ. And this same verse declares that God purchased His church with His own blood. Therefore, Jesus is God.

Thomas the disciple declared concerning Jesus, "My Lord and my God" (John 20:28). Jesus does not correct him. Titus 2:13 encourages us to wait for the coming of our God and Savior, Jesus Christ (see also 2 Peter 1:1). In Hebrews 1:8, the Father declares of Jesus, "But about the Son he says, 'Your throne, O God, will last forever and ever, a scepter of justice will be the scepter of your kingdom.'" The Father refers to Jesus as God, indicating that Jesus is indeed God.

In Revelation, an angel instructed the apostle John to only worship God (Revelation 19:10). Several times in Scripture Jesus receives worship (Matthew 2:11; 14:33; 28:9, 17; Luke 24:52; John 9:38). He never rebukes people for worshiping Him. If Jesus were not God, He would have told people not to worship Him, just as the angel in Revelation did. Beyond these, there are many other passages of Scripture that argue for Jesus being God.

Is Jesus God?—The reason Jesus must be God.

The most important reason that Jesus must be God is that if He is not God, His death would not have been sufficient to pay the penalty for the sins of the world (1 John 2:2). A created being, which Jesus would be if He were not God, could not pay the infinite penalty required for sin against an infinite God. Only God could pay such an infinite penalty. Only God could take on the sins of the world (2 Corinthians 5:21), die, and be resurrected, proving His victory over sin and death.

Is Jesus God? Yes. Jesus declared Himself to be God. His followers believed Him to be God. The provision of salvation only works if Jesus is God. Jesus is God incarnate, the eternal Alpha and Omega (Revelation 1:8; 22:13), and God our Savior (2 Peter 1:1).

2. What does the Bible teach about the Trinity?

The most difficult thing about the Christian concept of the Trinity is that there is no way to perfectly and completely understand it. The Trinity is a concept that is impossible for any human being to fully understand, let alone explain. God is infinitely greater than we are; therefore, we should not expect to be able to fully understand Him. The Bible teaches that the Father is God, that Jesus is God, and that the Holy Spirit is God. The Bible also teaches that there is only one God. Though we can understand some facts about the relationship of the different persons of the Trinity to one another, ultimately, it is incomprehensible to the human mind. However, this does not mean the Trinity is not true or that it is not based on the teachings of the Bible.

The Trinity is one God existing in three persons. This is not in any way suggesting three Gods. Keep in mind when studying this subject that the word *Trinity* is not found in Scripture. This is a term used to attempt to describe the triune God—three coexistent, coeternal persons who are God. Of real importance is that the concept represented by the word *Trinity* does exist in Scripture. The following is what God's Word says about the Trinity:

1. There is one God (Deuteronomy 6:4; 1 Corinthians 8:4; Galatians 3:20; 1 Timothy 2:5).

2. The Trinity consists of three persons (Genesis 1:1, 26; 3:22;
   11:7; Isaiah 6:8, 61:1; Matthew 3:16–17, 28:19; 2 Corinthians 13:14). In Genesis 1:1, the Hebrew plural noun *Elohim* is used. In Genesis 1:26; 3:22; 11:7; and Isaiah 6:8, the
   plural pronoun for *us* is used. The word *Elohim* and the pronoun *us* are plural forms, referring in the Hebrew language to
   more than two. While this is not an explicit argument for the
   Trinity, it does denote the aspect of plurality in God. The Hebrew word for *God*, *Elohim*, definitely allows for the Trinity.

   In Isaiah 48:16 and 61:1, the Son is speaking while mak-
   ing reference to the Father and the Holy Spirit. Compare
   Isaiah 61:1 to Luke 4:14–19 to see that it is the Son speaking.
   Matthew 3:16–17 describes the event of Jesus' baptism. Seen
   in this passage is God the Holy Spirit descending on God the
   Son while God the Father proclaims His pleasure in the Son.
   Matthew 28:19 and 2 Corinthians 13:14 are other examples
   of passages that present three distinct persons in the Trinity.

3. The members of the Trinity are distinguished one from an-
   other in various passages. In the Old Testament, LORD is
   distinguished from *Lord* (Genesis 19:24; Hosea 1:4). The
   LORD has a Son (Psalm 2:7, 12; Proverbs 30:2–4). The Spirit
   is distinguished from the LORD (Numbers 27:18) and from
   God (Psalm 51:10–12). God the Son is distinguished from
   God the Father (Psalm 45:6–7; cf. Hebrews 1:8–9). In the
   New Testament, Jesus speaks to the Father about sending
   a Helper, the Holy Spirit (John 14:16–17). This shows that
   Jesus did not consider Himself to be the Father or the Holy
   Spirit. Consider also the other instances when Jesus speaks
   to the Father. Was He speaking to Himself? No. He spoke to
   another person in the Trinity—the Father.

4. Each member of the Trinity is God. The Father is God (John
   6:27; Romans 1:7; 1 Peter 1:2). The Son is God (John 1:1, 14;
   Romans 9:5; Colossians 2:9; Hebrews 1:8; 1 John 5:20). The
   Holy Spirit is God (Acts 5:3–4; 1 Corinthians 3:16).

5. There is subordination within the Trinity. Scripture shows that the Holy Spirit is subordinate to the Father and the Son, and the Son is subordinate to the Father. This is an internal relationship and does not deny the deity of any person of the Trinity. This is simply something our finite minds cannot understand concerning the infinite God. Concerning the Son, see Luke 22:42; John 5:36; 20:21; and 1 John 4:14. Concerning the Holy Spirit, see John 14:16, 26; 15:26; 16:7; and especially John 16:13–14.

6. The individual members of the Trinity have different tasks. The Father is the ultimate source or cause of the universe (1 Corinthians 8:6; Revelation 4:11), divine revelation (Revelation 1:1), salvation (John 3:16–17), and Jesus' human works (John 5:17; 14:10). The Father initiates all of these things.

   The Son is the agent through whom the Father does the following works: the creation and maintenance of the universe (1 Corinthians 8:6; John 1:3; Colossians 1:16–17), divine revelation (John 1:1, 16:12–15; Matthew 11:27; Revelation 1:1), and salvation (2 Corinthians 5:19; Matthew 1:21; John 4:42). The Father does all these things through the Son, who functions as His agent.

   The Holy Spirit is the means by whom the Father does the following works: creation and maintenance of the universe (Genesis 1:2; Job 26:13; Psalm 104:30), divine revelation (John 16:12–15; Ephesians 3:5; 2 Peter 1:21), salvation (John 3:16; Titus 3:5; 1 Peter 1:2), and Jesus' works (Isaiah 61:1; Acts 10:38). Thus, the Father does all these things by the power of the Holy Spirit.

There have been many attempts to develop illustrations of the Trinity. However, none of the popular illustrations are completely accurate. The egg (or apple) fails in that the shell, white, and yolk are parts of the egg, not the egg in themselves, just as the skin, flesh, and seeds of the apple are parts of it, not the apple itself. The Father, Son, and Holy Spirit are not parts of God; each of them is God. The water illustration is somewhat better, but it still fails to adequately describe the Trinity. Liquid, vapor, and ice are forms of water. The Father, Son, and Holy Spirit are not forms of God; each of them is God. So, while these illustrations may give us a picture of the Trinity, the picture is not entirely accurate. An infinite God cannot be fully described by a finite illustration.

The doctrine of the Trinity has been a divisive issue throughout the entire history of the Christian church. While the core aspects of the Trinity are clearly presented in God's Word, some of the side issues are not as explicitly clear. The Father is God, the Son is God, and the Holy Spirit is God—but there is only one God. That is the biblical doctrine of the Trinity. Beyond that, the issues are, to a certain extent, debatable and nonessential. Rather than attempting to fully define the Trinity with our finite human minds, we would be better served by focusing on what is specifically written, on God's greatness, and on His infinitely higher nature. "Oh, the depth of the riches of the wisdom and knowledge of God! How unsearchable his judgments, and his paths beyond tracing out! Who has known the mind of the Lord? Or who has been his counselor?" (Romans 11:33–34).

3. What are the different names of God, and what do they mean?

Each of the many names of God describes a different aspect of His many-faceted character. Here are some of the better-known names of God in the Bible:

> **EL, ELOAH [el, el-oh-ah]:** God "mighty, strong, prominent" (Nehemiah 9:17; Psalm 139:19)—etymologically, *El* appears to mean "power" and "might" (Genesis 31:29). *El* is associated with other qualities, such as integrity (Numbers

23:19), jealousy (Deuteronomy 5:9), and compassion (Nehemiah 9:31), but the root idea of "might" remains.

ELOHIM [el-oh-*heem*]: God "Creator, Mighty and Strong" (Genesis 17:7; Jeremiah 31:33)—the plural form of *Eloah*. Being plural, *Elohim* accommodates the doctrine of the Trinity. From the Bible's first sentence, the superlative nature of God's power is evident as God (Elohim) speaks the world into existence (Genesis 1:1).

EL SHADDAI [el-shah-*dahy*]: "God Almighty," "The Mighty One of Jacob" (Genesis 49:24; Psalm 132:2, 5)—speaks to God's ultimate power over all.

ADONAI [ah-daw-*nahy*]: "Lord" (Genesis 15:2; Judges 6:15)—used in place of *YHWH*, which was thought by the Jews to be too sacred to be uttered by sinful men. In the Old Testament, *YHWH* is more often used in God's dealings with His people, while *Adonai* is used more when He deals with the Gentiles.

YHWH / YAHWEH / JEHOVAH [*yah*-way / ji-*hoh*-veh]: "Lord" (Deuteronomy 6:4; Daniel 9:14)—strictly speaking, the only proper name for God. Translated in English Bibles "Lord" (all capitals) to distinguish it from *Adonai*, "Lord." The revelation of the name is given to Moses: "I AM WHO I AM" (Exodus 3:14). This name specifies an immediacy, a presence. Yahweh is present, accessible, near to those who call on Him for deliverance (Psalm 107:13), forgiveness (Psalm 25:11), and guidance (Psalm 31:3).

YAHWEH-JIREH [*yah*-way-ji-reh]: "The Lord Will Provide" (Genesis 22:14)—the name memorialized by Abraham when God provided the ram to be sacrificed in place of Isaac.

YAHWEH-RAPHA [*yah*-way-raw-*faw*]: "The Lord Who Heals" (Exodus 15:26)—"I am the Lord who heals you" both in body and soul: in body, by preserving from and curing diseases, and in soul, by pardoning iniquities.

YAHWEH-NISSI [*yah*-way-nee-*see*]: "The LORD Our Banner" (Exodus 17:15), where *banner* is understood to be a rallying place. This name commemorates the desert victory over the Amalekites in Exodus 17.

YAHWEH-M'KADDESH [*yah*-way-meh-*kad*-esh]: "The LORD Who Sanctifies, Makes Holy" (Leviticus 20:8; Ezekiel 37:28)—God makes it clear that He alone, not the law, can cleanse His people and make them holy.

YAHWEH-SHALOM [*yah*-way-shah-lohm]: "The LORD Our Peace" (Judges 6:24)—the name given by Gideon to the altar he built after the Angel of the Lord assured him he would not die as he thought he would after seeing Him.

YAHWEH-ELOHIM [*yah*-way-el-oh-*him*]: "LORD God" (Genesis 2:4; Psalm 59:5)—a combination of God's unique name *YHWH* and the generic word for "God," signifying that He is the Lord who is God.

YAHWEH-TSIDKENU [*yah*-way-tzid-*kay*-noo]: "The LORD Our Righteousness" (Jeremiah 33:16)—as with *YHWH-M'Kaddesh*, it is God alone who provides righteousness to man, ultimately in the person of His Son, Jesus Christ, who became sin for us "that we might become the righteousness of God in Him" (2 Corinthians 5:21 NKJV).

YAHWEH-ROHI [*yah*-way-roh-*hee*]: "The LORD Our Shepherd" (Psalm 23:1)—after David pondered his relationship as a shepherd to his sheep, he realized that was exactly the relationship God had with him, so he declares, "The LORD is my shepherd [Yahweh-Rohi]; I shall not want" (Psalm 23:1 ESV).

YAHWEH-SHAMMAH [*yah*-way-sham-*mahw*]: "The LORD Is There" (Ezekiel 48:35)—the name ascribed to Jerusalem and the temple there, indicating that the once-departed glory of the Lord (Ezekiel 8–11) had returned (Ezekiel 44:1–4).

YAHWEH-SABAOTH [*yah*-way-sah-bah-*ohth*]: "The LORD of Hosts" (Isaiah 1:24; Psalm 46:7)—*hosts* means "hordes," both of angels and of men. He is LORD of the hosts of heaven and of the inhabitants of the earth, of Jews and Gentiles, of rich and poor, master and slave. The name is expressive of the majesty, power, and authority of God and shows that He is able to accomplish what He determines to do.

EL ELYON [el-el-*yohn*]: "Most High" (Deuteronomy 26:19)—the name is derived from the Hebrew root for "go up" or "ascend," so the implication is that which is the very highest. *El Elyon* denotes exaltation and speaks of absolute right to lordship.

EL ROI [el-roh-*ee*]: "God of Seeing" (Genesis 16:13)—the name ascribed to God by Hagar, alone and desperate in the wilderness after being driven out by Sarah (Genesis 16:1–14). When Hagar met the Angel of the Lord, she realized she had seen God Himself in a theophany. She also realized that *El Roi* saw her in her distress and testified that He is a living God who sees all.

EL-OLAM [el-oh-*lahm*]: "Everlasting God" (Psalm 90:1–3)—God's nature is without beginning or end, free from all constraints of time, and He contains within Himself the very cause of time. "From everlasting to everlasting you are God" (Psalm 90:2).

EL-GIBHOR [el-ghee-*bohr*]: "Mighty God" (Isaiah 9:6)—the name describing the Messiah, Christ Jesus, in this prophetic portion of Isaiah. As a powerful and mighty warrior, the Messiah, the Mighty God, will accomplish the destruction of God's enemies and rule with a rod of iron (Revelation 19:15).

4. What does it mean that Jesus is God's only begotten son?

The phrase "only begotten Son" occurs in John 3:16, which reads in the King James Version as, "For God so loved the world, that he gave his only begotten Son, that whosoever believeth in him should not perish, but have everlasting life." The phrase "only begotten" translates the Greek word *monogenes*. This word is variously translated into English as "only," "one and only," and "only begotten."

It's this last phrase ("only begotten" used in the KJV, NASB, and the NKJV) that causes problems. False teachers have latched on to this phrase to try to prove their false teaching that Jesus Christ isn't God; i.e., that Jesus isn't equal in essence to God as the second person of the Trinity. They see the word *begotten* and say that Jesus is a created being because only someone who had a beginning in time can be "begotten." What this fails to note is that *begotten* is an English translation of a Greek word. As such, we have to look at the original meaning of the Greek word, not transfer English meanings into the text.

So what does *monogenes* mean? According to the *Greek-English Lexicon of the New Testament and Other Early Christian Literature* (BAGD, 3rd edition), *monogenes* has two primary definitions. The first definition is "pertaining to being the only one of its kind within a specific relationship." This is its meaning in Hebrews 11:17 when the writer refers to Isaac as Abraham's "only begotten son" (KJV). Abraham had more than one son, but Isaac was the only son he had by Sarah and the only son of the covenant. Therefore, it is the uniqueness of Isaac among the other sons that allows for the use of *monogenes* in that context.

The second definition is "pertaining to being the only one of its kind or class, unique in kind." This is the meaning that is implied in John 3:16 (see also John 1:14, 18; 3:18; 1 John 4:9). John was primarily concerned with demonstrating that Jesus is the Son of God (John 20:31), and he uses *monogenes* to highlight Jesus as uniquely God's Son—sharing the same divine nature as God—as opposed to believers who are God's sons and daughters by adoption (Ephesians 1:5). Jesus is God's "one and only" Son.

The bottom line is that terms such as *Father* and *Son*, descriptive of God and Jesus, are human terms that help us understand the relationship between the different persons of the Trinity. If you can understand the relationship between a human father and a human son, then you can understand, in part, the relationship between the first and second persons of the Trinity. The analogy breaks down if you try to take it too far and teach, as some pseudo-Christian cults (such as the Jehovah's Witnesses), that Jesus was literally "begotten" as in produced or created by God the Father.

5. If His name was Yeshua, why do we call Him Jesus?

Some people claim that our Lord should not be referred to as Jesus. Instead, we should only use the name Yeshua. Some even go so far as to say that calling Him Jesus is blasphemous. Others go into great detail about how the name Jesus is unbiblical because the letter *J* is a modern invention and there was no letter *J* in Greek or Hebrew.

Yeshua is the Hebrew name, and its English spelling is "Joshua." *Iesous* is the Greek transliteration of the Hebrew name, and its English spelling is "Jesus." Thus, the names Joshua and Jesus are essentially the same; both are English pronunciations of the Hebrew and Greek names for our Lord. (For examples of how the two names are interchangeable, see Acts 7:45 and Hebrews 4:8 in the KJV. In both cases, the word *Jesus* refers to the Old Testament character Joshua.)

Changing the language of a word does not affect the meaning of the word. We call a bound and covered set of pages a book. In German, it becomes a *Buch*. In Spanish, it is a *libro*; in French, a *livre*. The language changes, but the object itself does not. As Shakespeare said, "That which we call a rose / By any other name would smell as sweet" (Romeo and Juliet, II:i). In the same way, we can refer to Jesus as Jesus, Yeshua, or *YehSou* (Cantonese) without changing His nature. In any language, His name means "The Lord Is Salvation."

As for the controversy over the letter *J*, it is much ado about nothing. It is true that the languages in which the Bible was written had no letter *J*. But that doesn't mean the Bible never refers to Jerusalem or Judah. And it doesn't mean we cannot use the spelling "Jesus." If a person speaks and reads English, it is acceptable for him to spell things in an English fashion. Spellings can change even within a language: Americans write "Savior," while the British write "Saviour." The addition of a *u* (or its subtraction, depending on your point of view) has nothing to do with whom we're talking about. Jesus is the Savior, and He is the Saviour. Jesus and Yeshua and Iesous are all referring to the same person.

The Bible nowhere commands us to only speak or write His name in Hebrew or Greek. It never even hints at such an idea. Rather, when the message of the gospel was being proclaimed on the Day of Pentecost, the apostles spoke in the languages of the "Parthians, Medes and Elamites; residents of Mesopotamia, Judea and Cappadocia, Pontus and Asia, Phrygia and Pamphylia, Egypt and the parts of Libya near Cyrene" (Acts 2:9–10). In the power of the Holy Spirit, Jesus was made known to every language group in a way they could readily understand. Spelling did not matter.

We refer to Him as Jesus because, as English-speaking people, we know of Him through English translations of the Greek New Testament. Scripture does not value one language over another, and it gives no indication that we must resort to Hebrew when addressing the Lord. The command is to call "on the name of the Lord," with the promise that we "will be saved" (Acts 2:21; Joel 2:32). Whether we call on Him in English, Korean, Hindi, or Hebrew, the result is the same: the Lord is salvation.

6. What are the seven spirits of God?

The "seven spirits of God" are mentioned several times in the book of Revelation:

- Revelation 1:4–5, "John, To the seven churches in the province of Asia: Grace and peace to you from him who is, and

who was, and who is to come, and from the seven spirits before his throne, and from Jesus Christ . . ."

- Revelation 3:1, "To the angel of the church in Sardis write:
  These are the words of him who holds the seven spirits of
  God . . ."

- Revelation 4:5, "From the throne came flashes of lightning,
  rumblings and peals of thunder. In front of the throne, seven
  lamps were blazing. These are the seven spirits of God."

- Revelation 5:6, "Then I saw a Lamb, looking as if it had been
  slain, standing at the center of the throne, encircled by the
  four living creatures and the elders. The Lamb had seven
  horns and seven eyes, which are the seven spirits of God sent
  out into all the earth."

The identity of "the seven spirits" is not explicit in these passages,
but arriving at the proper interpretation is fairly straightforward. The
"seven spirits" cannot be seven angelic beings such as seraphim or
cherubim because of the context of Revelation 1:4. John says that
"grace and peace" are coming to the churches from three sources:
"him who is, and who was, and who is to come" (verse 4), "the seven
spirits before his throne" (verse 4), and "Jesus Christ" (verse 5).
This is a depiction of the Trinity: grace and peace are given by the
Father, the Son, and the Holy Spirit, the three coequal persons of
the Godhead.

In Revelation 3:1 Jesus "holds" the seven spirits of God. In John
15:26, Jesus "sends" the Holy Spirit from the Father. Both passages
suggest the superordinate role of the Son and the subordinate role
of the Spirit.

In Revelation 4:5 the seven spirits of God are symbolized as seven
burning lamps that are before God's throne. This picture agrees with
Zechariah's vision in which he sees the Holy Spirit symbolized as "a
solid gold lampstand with a bowl at the top and seven lamps on it"
(Zechariah 4:2).

In Revelation 5:6 the seven spirits are the "seven eyes" of the Lamb, and they are "sent out into all the earth." The seven eyes speak of the Spirit's (and the Lamb's) omniscience, and the fact that He is sent into all the earth speaks of His omnipresence.

Once we identify the "seven spirits" as the Holy Spirit, the question remains, why are there seven of Him? The Bible, and especially the book of Revelation, uses the number seven to refer to perfection and completion. John's vision includes a picture of the perfect and complete Holy Spirit.

Isaiah 11:2 also references the Holy Spirit using a seven-fold description: "The Spirit of the LORD will rest on him—the Spirit of wisdom and of understanding, the Spirit of counsel and of power, the Spirit of knowledge and of the fear of the LORD." The prophecy is that the Messiah would be empowered not by seven individual spirits but by the One Spirit, described seven ways:

1. The Spirit of the LORD
2. The Spirit of wisdom
3. The Spirit of understanding
4. The Spirit of counsel
5. The Spirit of power
6. The Spirit of knowledge
7. The Spirit of the fear of the Lord

The "seven spirits of God" in the book of Revelation are thus a reference to the Holy Spirit in the perfection of His manifold ministry.

7. Who is the Holy Spirit?

There are many misconceptions about the identity of the Holy Spirit. Some view the Holy Spirit as a mystical force. Others see the Holy Spirit as an impersonal power that God makes available to followers of

Christ. What does the Bible say about the identity of the Holy Spirit? Simply put, the Bible declares that the Holy Spirit is God. The Bible also tells us that the Holy Spirit is a divine person, a being with a mind, emotions, and a will.

The fact that the Holy Spirit is God is clearly seen in many Scriptures, including Acts 5:3–4. In these verses Peter confronts Ananias as to why he lied to the Holy Spirit and tells him that he had "not lied just to human beings but to God." It is a clear declaration that lying to the Holy Spirit is lying to God.

We can also know that the Holy Spirit is God because He possesses the characteristics of God. For example, His omnipresence is seen in Psalm 139:7–8, "Where can I go from your Spirit? Where can I flee from your presence? If I go up to the heavens, you are there; if I make my bed in the depths, you are there." Then, in 1 Corinthians 2:10–11, we see the characteristic of omniscience in the Holy Spirit. "These are the things God has revealed to us by his Spirit. The Spirit searches all things, even the deep things of God. For who knows a person's thoughts except their own spirit within them? In the same way no one knows the thoughts of God except the Spirit of God."

We can know that the Holy Spirit is indeed a divine person because He possesses a mind, emotions, and a will. The Holy Spirit thinks and knows (1 Corinthians 2:10). The Holy Spirit can be grieved (Ephesians 4:30). The Spirit intercedes for us (Romans 8:26–27). He makes decisions according to His will (1 Corinthians 12:7–11). The Holy Spirit is God, the third person of the Trinity. As God, the Holy Spirit can truly function as the Comforter and Counselor that Jesus promised He would be (John 14:16, 26; 15:26).

8. When/How do we receive the Holy Spirit?

The apostle Paul clearly taught that we receive the Holy Spirit the moment we receive Jesus Christ as our Savior. First Corinthians

12:13 declares, "For we were all baptized by one Spirit into one body—whether Jews or Greeks, whether slave or free—and we were all given the one Spirit to drink" (CSB). Romans 8:9 tells us that if a person does not possess the Holy Spirit, he or she does not belong to Christ: "You, however, are not in the realm of the flesh but are in the realm of the Spirit, if indeed the Spirit of God lives in you. And if anyone does not have the Spirit of Christ, they do not belong to Christ." Ephesians 1:13–14 teaches that the Holy Spirit is the seal of salvation for all those who believe: "When you believed, you were marked in him with a seal, the promised Holy Spirit, who is a deposit guaranteeing our inheritance until the redemption of those who are God's possession—to the praise of his glory."

These three passages make it clear that the Holy Spirit is received at the moment of salvation. Paul could not say that we all were baptized by one Spirit and all given one Spirit to drink if not all of the Corinthian believers possessed the Holy Spirit. Romans 8:9 is even stronger, stating that if a person does not have the Spirit, he does not belong to Christ. Therefore, the possession of the Spirit is an identifying factor of the possession of salvation. Further, the Holy Spirit could not be the seal of salvation (Ephesians 1:13–14) if He is not received at the moment of salvation. Many passages make it known that our salvation is secured the moment we receive Christ as Savior.

The ministries of the Holy Spirit are often confused. The receiving/indwelling of the Spirit occurs at the moment of salvation. But the filling of the Spirit is an ongoing process in the Christian life. We hold that the baptism of the Spirit also occurs at the moment of salvation. Some Christians believe that the baptism of the Spirit comes subsequent to salvation.

In conclusion, how do we receive the Holy Spirit? We receive the Holy Spirit by simply receiving the Lord Jesus Christ as our Savior (John 3:5–16). When do we receive the Holy Spirit? The Holy Spirit becomes our permanent possession the moment we believe.

9. What is the role of the Holy Spirit in our lives today?

Of all the gifts given to mankind by God, there is none greater than the presence of the Holy Spirit. The Spirit has many functions, roles, and activities. First, He does a work in the hearts of all people everywhere. Jesus told the disciples that He would send the Spirit into the world to "convict the world regarding sin, and righteousness, and judgment" (John 16:8 NASB). Everyone has a "God consciousness," whether or not they admit it. The Spirit applies God's truths to people's minds to convince them by fair and sufficient arguments that they are sinners. Responding to that conviction brings us to salvation.

Once we are saved and belong to God, the Spirit takes up residence in our hearts forever, sealing us with the confirming, certifying, and assuring pledge of our eternal state as His children. Jesus said He would send the Spirit to us to be our Helper, Comforter, and Guide. "And I will ask the Father, and he will give you another Counselor to be with you forever" (John 14:16 CSB). The Greek word translated here "Counselor" means "one who is called alongside" and has the idea of someone who encourages and exhorts. The Holy Spirit takes up permanent residence in the hearts of believers (Romans 8:9; 1 Corinthians 6:19–20; 12:13). Jesus gave the Spirit as a "compensation" for His absence, to perform the functions toward us that He would have done if He had remained personally with us.

Among those functions is that of revealer of truth. The Spirit's presence within us enables us to understand and interpret God's Word. Jesus told His disciples that "when he, the Spirit of truth, comes, he will guide you into all the truth" (John 16:13). He reveals to our minds the whole counsel of God as it relates to worship, doctrine, and Christian living. He is the ultimate guide, going before, leading the way, removing obstructions, opening the understanding, and making all things plain and clear. He leads in the way we should go in all spiritual things. Without such a guide, we would be apt to fall into error. A crucial part of the truth He reveals is that Jesus is who He said He is (John 15:26; 1 Corinthians 12:3). The Spirit convinces us of Christ's deity and incarnation, His being the Messiah, His suffering and death, His resurrection and ascension, His exaltation at the right hand of God, and His role as the judge of all. He gives glory to Christ in all things (John 16:14).

Another one of the Holy Spirit's roles is that of gift-giver. First Corinthians 12 describes the spiritual gifts given to believers in order that we may function as the body of Christ on earth. All these gifts, both great and small, are given by the Spirit so that we may be His ambassadors to the world, showing forth His grace and glorifying Him.

The Spirit also functions as fruit-producer in our lives. When He indwells us, He begins the work of harvesting His fruit in our lives—love, joy, peace, patience, kindness, goodness, faithfulness, gentleness, and self-control (Galatians 5:22–23). These are not works of our flesh, which is incapable of producing such fruit, but they are products of the Spirit's presence in our lives.

The knowledge that the Holy Spirit of God has taken up residence in our lives, that He performs all these miraculous functions, that He dwells with us forever, and that He will never leave or forsake us is cause for great joy and comfort. Thank God for this precious gift—the Holy Spirit and His work in our lives!

10. What is the glory of God?

The glory of God is the beauty of His spirit. It is not an aesthetic beauty or a material beauty, but the beauty that emanates from His character, from all that He is. The glory of man—human dignity and honor—fades (1 Peter 1:24). But the glory of God, which is manifested in all His attributes together, never passes away. It is eternal.

Moses requested of God, "Now show me your glory" (Exodus 33:18). In His response, God equates His glory with "all my goodness" (verse 19). "But," God said, "you cannot see my face, for no one may see me and live" (verse 20). So, God hid Moses in "a cleft in the rock" to protect him from the fulness of God's glory as it passed by (verses 21–23). No mortal can view God's excelling splendor without being utterly overwhelmed. The glory of God puts the pride of man to shame: "Enter into the rock, and hide in the dust, from the terror of the LORD, and the glory of His majesty. The lofty looks of man shall be humbled, the haughtiness of men shall be bowed down, and the LORD alone shall be exalted in that day" (Isaiah 2:10–11, NKJV).

Often, in the Old Testament, the manifestation of God's glory was accompanied by supernatural fire, thick clouds, and a great quaking of the earth. We see these phenomena when God gave the law to Moses: "Mount Sinai was covered with smoke, because the LORD descended on it in fire. The smoke billowed up from it like smoke from a furnace, and the whole mountain trembled violently" (Exodus 19:18; see also Deuteronomy 5:24–25; 1 Kings 8:10–11; and Isaiah 6:1–4). The prophet Ezekiel's vision of the glory of God was full of fire and lightning and tumultuous sounds, after which he saw "what looked like a throne of lapis lazuli, and high above on the throne was a figure like that of a man. I saw that from what appeared to be his waist up he looked like glowing metal, as if full of fire, and that from there down he looked like fire; and brilliant light surrounded him. Like the appearance of a rainbow in the clouds on a rainy day, so was the radiance around him. This was the appearance of the likeness of the glory of the LORD" (Ezekiel 1:26–28).

In the New Testament, the glory of God is revealed in His Son, Jesus Christ: "The Word became flesh and made his dwelling among us. We have seen his glory, the glory of the one and only Son, who came from the Father, full of grace and truth" (John 1:14). Jesus came as "a light for revelation to the Gentiles, and the glory of [God's] people Israel" (Luke 2:32). The miracles that Jesus did were "signs through which he revealed his glory" (John 2:11). In Christ, the glory of God is meekly veiled, approachable, and knowable. He promises to return some day "on the clouds of heaven, with power and great glory" (Matthew 24:30).

Isaiah 43:7 says that God saved Israel for His glory—in the redeemed will be seen the distillation of God's grace, power, and faithfulness. The natural world also exhibits God's glory, revealed to all men, no matter their race, heritage, or location. As Psalm 19:1–4 says, "The heavens declare the glory of God; the skies proclaim the work of his hands. Day after day they pour forth speech; night after night they reveal knowledge. They have no speech, they use no words; no sound is heard from them. Yet their voice goes out into all the earth, their words to the ends of the world."

Psalm 73:24 calls heaven itself "glory." Sometimes Christians speak of death as being "received unto glory," a phrase borrowed from this psalm. When the Christian dies, he or she will be taken into God's presence and surrounded by God's glory and majesty. In that place, His glory will be seen clearly: "For now we see only a reflection as in a mirror; then we shall see face to face" (1 Corinthians 13:12). In the future New Jerusalem, the glory of God will be manifest: "The city does not need the sun or the moon to shine on it, for the glory of God gives it light, and the Lamb is its lamp" (Revelation 21:23).

God will not give His glory to another (Isaiah 42:8; cf. Exodus 34:14). Yet this is the very thing that people try to steal. Scripture indicts all idolaters: "Although they claimed to be wise, they became fools and exchanged the glory of the immortal God for images made to look like a mortal human being and birds and animals and reptiles" (Romans 1:22–23). Only God is eternal, and His perfect and eternal attributes of holiness, majesty, goodness, love, etc., are not to be exchanged for the imperfections and corruption of anything in this world.

SECTION 2

Questions about Salvation

11. What is salvation? What is the Christian doctrine of salvation?

Salvation is deliverance from danger or suffering. To save is to deliver or protect. The word carries the idea of victory, health, or preservation. Sometimes the Bible uses the words *saved* or *salvation* to refer to temporal, physical deliverance, such as Paul's deliverance from prison (Philippians 1:19).

More often, the word *salvation* concerns an eternal, spiritual deliverance. When Paul told the Philippian jailer what he must do to be saved, he was referring to the jailer's eternal destiny (Acts 16:30–31). Jesus equated being saved with entering the kingdom of God (Matthew 19:24–25).

What are we saved *from*? In the Christian doctrine of salvation, we are saved from "wrath," that is, from God's judgment of sin (Romans 5:9; 1 Thessalonians 5:9). Our sin has separated us from God, and the consequence of sin is death (Romans 6:23). Biblical salvation refers to our deliverance from the consequence of sin and therefore involves the removal of sin. We are saved from both the power and penalty of sin.

Who does the saving? Only God can remove sin and deliver us from sin's penalty (2 Timothy 1:9; Titus 3:5).

How does God save? In the Christian doctrine of salvation, God has rescued us through Jesus Christ (John 3:17). Specifically, it was Jesus' death on the cross and subsequent resurrection that achieved our salvation (Romans 5:10; Ephesians 1:7). Scripture is clear that salvation is the gracious, undeserved gift of God (Ephesians 2:5, 8) and is only available through faith in Jesus Christ (Acts 4:12).

How do we receive salvation? We are saved by *faith*. First, we must *hear* the gospel—the good news of Jesus' death and resurrection (Ephesians 1:13). Then we must *believe*—fully trust the Lord Jesus (Romans 1:16). This involves repentance, a changing of mind about sin and Christ (Acts 3:19), and calling on the name of the Lord (Romans 10:9–10, 13).

A definition of the Christian doctrine of salvation would be "the deliverance, by the grace of God, from eternal punishment for sin, that is granted to those who accept by faith God's conditions of repentance and faith in the Lord Jesus." Salvation is available in Jesus alone (John 14:6; Acts 4:12) by faith alone (Ephesians 2:8–9) and is dependent on God alone for provision and assurance.

12. What is repentance, and is it necessary for salvation?

Many understand the term *repentance* to mean "a turning from sin." Regretting sin and turning from it are related to repentance, but the precise meaning of the word is somewhat different. In the

Bible, the word *repent* means "to change one's mind." The Bible also tells us that true repentance will result in a change of actions (Luke 3:8–14; Acts 3:19). In summarizing his ministry, Paul declares, "I preached that they should repent and turn to God and demonstrate their repentance by their deeds" (Acts 26:20). The short biblical definition of *repentance* is "a change of mind that results in a change of action."

What, then, is the connection between repentance and salvation? The book of Acts especially focuses on repentance regarding salvation (Acts 2:38; 3:19; 11:18; 17:30; 20:21; 26:20). To repent, in relation to salvation, is to change your mind concerning sin and Jesus Christ. In Peter's sermon on the day of Pentecost (Acts chapter 2), he concludes with a call for the people to repent (Acts 2:38). Repent from what? Peter calls the people who rejected Jesus (Acts 2:36) to change their minds about that sin and to change their minds about Christ Himself, recognizing that He is indeed "Lord and Christ" (Acts 2:36 ESV). Peter calls the people to change their minds, to abhor their past rejection of Christ, and to embrace faith in Him as their Messiah and Savior.

Repentance involves recognizing that you have thought wrongly in the past and determining to think rightly in the future. The repentant person has second thoughts about the mindset he formerly embraced. There is a change of disposition and a new way of thinking about God, about sin, about holiness, and about doing God's will. True repentance is prompted by "godly sorrow," and it "leads to salvation" (2 Corinthians 7:10).

Repentance and faith can be understood as two sides of the same coin. It is impossible to place your faith in Jesus Christ as the Savior without first changing your mind about your sin, about who Jesus is, and what He has done. Whether it is repentance from willful rejection or repentance from ignorance or disinterest, it is a change of mind. Biblical repentance, in relation to salvation, is changing your mind from rejection of Christ to faith in Christ.

Repentance is not a work we do to earn salvation. No one can repent and come to God unless God pulls that person to Himself (John 6:44). Repentance is something God gives—it is only possible because of His grace (Acts 5:31; 11:18). No one can repent unless God grants repentance. All of salvation, including repentance and faith, is a result of God drawing us, opening our eyes, and changing our hearts. God's longsuffering leads us to repentance (2 Peter 3:9), as does His kindness (Romans 2:4).

While repentance is not a work that earns salvation, repentance unto salvation does result in works. It is impossible to truly change your mind without changing your actions in some way. In the Bible, repentance results in a change in behavior. That is why John the Baptist called people to "produce fruit in keeping with repentance" (Matthew 3:8). A person who has truly repented of sin and exercised faith in Christ will give evidence of a changed life (2 Corinthians 5:17; Galatians 5:19–23; James 2:14–26).

To see what repentance looks like in real life, turn to the story of Zacchaeus. Here was a man who cheated and stole and lived lavishly on his ill-gotten gains—until he met Jesus. At that point he had a radical change of mind: "Look, Lord!" said Zacchaeus. "Here and now I give half of my possessions to the poor, and if I have cheated anybody out of anything, I will pay back four times the amount" (Luke 19:8). Jesus happily proclaimed that salvation had come to Zacchaeus's house, and that even the tax collector was now "a son of Abraham" (verse 9)—a reference to Zacchaeus's faith. The cheat became a philanthropist; the thief made restitution. That's repentance, coupled with faith in Christ.

Repentance, properly defined, is necessary for salvation. Biblical repentance is changing your mind about your sin—no longer is sin something to toy with; it is something to be forsaken as you "flee from the coming wrath" (Matthew 3:7). It is also changing your mind about Jesus Christ—no longer is He to be mocked, discounted, or ignored; He is the Savior to be clung to; He is the Lord to be worshiped and adored.

13. What does it mean to be a born-again Christian?

What does it mean to be a born-again Christian? The classic passage from the Bible that answers this question is John 3:1–21. The Lord Jesus Christ is talking to Nicodemus, a prominent Pharisee and member of the Sanhedrin (the ruling body of the Jews). Nicodemus had come to Jesus at night with some questions.

As Jesus talked with Nicodemus, He said, "'Very truly I tell you, no one can see the kingdom of God unless they are born again.' 'How can someone be born when they are old?' Nicodemus asked. 'Surely they cannot enter a second time into their mother's womb to be born!' Jesus answered, 'Very truly I tell you, no one can enter the kingdom of God unless they are born of water and the Spirit. Flesh gives birth to flesh, but the Spirit gives birth to spirit. You should not be surprised at my saying, "You must be born again""" (John 3:3–7).

The phrase translated "born again" can also be translated as "born from above." Nicodemus had a real need. He needed a change of his heart—a spiritual transformation that could only come from above. New birth, being born again, is an act of God whereby eternal life is imparted to the person who believes (2 Corinthians 5:17; Titus 3:5; 1 Peter 1:3; 1 John 2:29; 3:9; 4:7; 5:1–4, 18). John 1:12–13 indicates that being "born again" also carries the idea of becoming "children of God" through trust in the name of Jesus Christ.

This question logically comes: "Why does a person need to be born again?" The apostle Paul in Ephesians 2:1 says, "And you He made alive, who were dead in trespasses and sins" (NKJV). To the Romans he wrote, "For all have sinned and fall short of the glory of God" (Romans 3:23). Sinners are spiritually dead; when they receive spiritual life through faith in Christ, the Bible likens it to a rebirth. Only those who are born again have their sins forgiven and have a relationship with God.

Twice in His conversation with Nicodemus, Jesus stressed the truth that one must be born again to enter the kingdom of God (John 3:3, 5).

Being born *once* makes us children of Adam, and we share Adam's corruption. We need a *second* birth—a spiritual birth—to make us children of God. We must be born again.

How does the new birth come to be? Ephesians 2:8–9 states, "For it is by grace you have been saved, through faith—and this not from yourselves, it is the gift of God—not by works, so that no one can boast." When one is saved, he has been born again, spiritually renewed, and is now a child of God by right of that new birth. Faith in Jesus Christ, the One who paid the penalty of sin when He died on the cross, is the means by which one is born again. "Therefore, if anyone is in Christ, the new creation has come: the old has gone, the new is here!" (2 Corinthians 5:17).

If you have never trusted in the Lord Jesus Christ as your Savior, will you consider the prompting of the Holy Spirit as He speaks to your heart? You need to be born again. Will you pray a prayer of repentance and faith and become a new creation in Christ today? "Yet to all who did receive him, to those who believed in his name, he gave the right to become children of God—children born not of natural descent, nor of human decision or a husband's will, but born of God" (John 1:12–13).

14. Can a Christian lose salvation?

First, the term *Christian* must be defined. A Christian is not a person who has said a prayer or walked down an aisle or been raised in a Christian family. While each of these things can be a part of the Christian experience, they are not what makes a Christian. A Christian is a person who has fully trusted in Jesus Christ as the only Savior and therefore possesses the Holy Spirit (John 3:16; Acts 16:31; Ephesians 2:8–9).

So, with this definition in mind, can a Christian lose salvation? It's a crucially important question. Perhaps the best way to answer it is to examine what the Bible says occurs at salvation and to study what losing salvation would entail.

A Christian is a new creation. "Therefore, if anyone is in Christ, the new creation has come: the old has gone, the new is here!" (2 Corinthians 5:17). A Christian is not simply an "improved" version of a person; a Christian is an entirely new creature. He is "in Christ." For a Christian to lose salvation, the new creation would have to be destroyed.

A Christian is redeemed. "For you know that it was not with perishable things such as silver or gold that you were redeemed from the empty way of life handed down to you from your ancestors, but with the precious blood of Christ, a lamb without blemish or defect" (1 Peter 1:18–19). The word *redeemed* refers to a purchase being made, a price being paid. We were purchased at the cost of Christ's death. For a Christian to lose salvation, God Himself would have to revoke His purchase of the individual for whom He paid with the precious blood of Christ.

A Christian is justified. "Therefore, since we have been justified through faith, we have peace with God through our Lord Jesus Christ" (Romans 5:1). To justify is to declare righteous. All those who receive Jesus as Savior are declared righteous by God. For a Christian to lose salvation, God would have to go back on His Word and "un-declare" what He had previously declared. Those absolved of guilt would have to be tried again and found guilty. God would have to reverse the sentence handed down from the divine bench.

A Christian is promised eternal life. "For God so loved the world that he gave his one and only Son, that whoever believes in him shall not perish but have eternal life" (John 3:16). Eternal life is the promise of spending forever in heaven with God. God promises that if you believe, you will have eternal life. For a Christian to lose salvation, *eternal life* would have to be redefined. The Christian is promised to live forever. Does *eternal* not mean "forever"?

A Christian is marked by God and sealed by the Spirit. "You also were included in Christ when you heard the message of truth, the gospel of your salvation. When you believed, you were marked in him with a seal, the promised Holy Spirit, who is a deposit guaranteeing our inheritance until the redemption of those who are God's possession—to the praise of his glory" (Ephesians 1:13–14). At the moment of faith, the new Christian is marked and sealed with the Spirit, who was promised to act as a deposit to *guarantee* the heavenly inheritance. The end result is that God's glory is praised. For a Christian to lose salvation, God would have to erase the mark, withdraw the Spirit, cancel the deposit, break His promise, revoke the guarantee, keep the inheritance, forgo the praise, and lessen His glory.

A Christian is guaranteed glorification. "Those he predestined, he also called; those he called, he also justified; those he justified, he also glorified" (Romans 8:30). According to Romans 5:1, justification is ours at the moment of faith. According to Romans 8:30, glorification comes with justification. All those whom God justifies are promised to be glorified. This promise will be fulfilled when Christians receive their perfect resurrection bodies in heaven. If a Christian can lose salvation, then Romans 8:30 is in error, because God could not guarantee glorification for all those whom He predestines, calls, and justifies.

A Christian cannot lose salvation. Most, if not all, of what the Bible says happens to us when we receive Christ would be invalidated if salvation could be lost. Salvation is the gift of God, and God's gifts are "irrevocable" (Romans 11:29). A Christian cannot be un-newly created. The redeemed cannot be unpurchased. Eternal life cannot be temporary. God cannot renege on His Word. Scripture says that God cannot lie (Titus 1:2).

Two common objections to the belief that a Christian cannot lose salvation concern these experiential issues: 1) What about Christians who live in a sinful, unrepentant lifestyle? 2) What about Christians who reject the faith and deny Christ? The problem with these objections is the assumption that everyone who calls himself a Christian has actually been born again. The Bible declares that a true Christian will *not* live in a state of continual, unrepentant sin (1 John 3:6). The Bible also says that anyone who departs the faith is demonstrating that he was never truly a Christian (1 John 2:19). He may have been religious, he may have put on a good show, but he was never born again by the power of God. "By their fruit you will recognize them" (Matthew 7:16). The redeemed of God belong "to him who was raised from the dead, in order that we might bear fruit for God" (Romans 7:4).

Nothing can separate a child of God from the Father's love (Romans 8:38–39). Nothing can remove a Christian from God's hand (John 10:28–29). God guarantees eternal life and maintains the salvation He has given us. The Good Shepherd searches for the lost sheep, and "when he finds it, he joyfully puts it on his shoulders and goes home" (Luke 15:5–6). The lamb is found, and the Shepherd gladly bears the burden; our Lord takes full responsibility for bringing the lost one safely home.

Jude 1:24–25 further emphasizes the goodness and faithfulness of our Savior: "To him who is able to keep you from stumbling and to present you before his glorious presence without fault and with great joy—to the only God our Savior be glory, majesty, power and authority, through Jesus Christ our Lord, before all ages, now and forevermore! Amen."

15. Got Eternal Life? Do you know for sure that you will have eternal life in heaven with God?

The Bible presents a clear path to eternal life. First, we must recognize that we have sinned against God: "For all have sinned and fall short of the glory of God" (Romans 3:23). We have all done things that are displeasing to God, which makes us deserving of punishment. Since all our sins are ultimately against an eternal God, only an eternal punishment is sufficient. "The wages of sin is death, but the gift of God is eternal life through Jesus Christ our Lord" (Romans 6:23).

However, Jesus Christ, the sinless (1 Peter 2:22), eternal Son of God became a man (John 1:1, 14) and died to pay our penalty. "God demonstrates his own love for us in this: While we were still sinners, Christ died for us" (Romans 5:8). Jesus Christ died on the cross (John 19:31–42), taking the punishment that we deserve (2 Corinthians 5:21). Three days later He rose from the dead (1 Corinthians 15:1–4), proving His victory over sin and death. "In his great mercy he has given us new birth into a living hope through the resurrection of Jesus Christ from the dead" (1 Peter 1:3).

By faith, we must change our mindset regarding Christ—who He is, what He did, and why—for salvation (Acts 3:19). If we place our faith in Him, trusting His death on the cross to pay for our sins, we will be forgiven and receive the promise of eternal life in heaven. "For God so loved the world that he gave his one and only Son, that whoever believes in him shall not perish but have eternal life" (John 3:16). "If you declare with your mouth, 'Jesus is Lord,' and believe in your heart that God raised him from the dead, you will be saved" (Romans 10:9). Faith alone in the finished work of Christ on the cross is the only true path to eternal life! "For it is by grace you have been saved, through faith—and this not from yourselves, it is the gift of God—not by works, so that no one can boast" (Ephesians 2:8–9).

If you want to accept Jesus Christ as your Savior, here is a sample prayer. Remember, saying this prayer or any other prayer will not save you. It is only trusting in Christ that can save you from sin. This prayer is simply a way to express to God your faith in Him and thank Him for providing for your salvation: "God, I know that I have sinned against you and deserve punishment. But Jesus Christ took the punishment that I deserve so that through faith in Him I could be forgiven. I place my trust in you for salvation. Thank you for your wonderful grace and forgiveness—the gift of eternal life! Amen!"

16. What is the Romans Road to salvation?

The Romans Road to salvation is a way of explaining the good news of salvation using verses from the book of Romans. The Romans Road is a simple yet powerful method of explaining why we need salvation, how God provided salvation, how we can receive salvation, and what the results of salvation are.

The first verse on the Romans Road to salvation is Romans 3:23, "For all have sinned, and come short of the glory of God" (KJV). We have all sinned. We have all done things that are displeasing to God. There is no one who is innocent. Romans 3:10–18 gives a detailed picture of what sin looks like in our lives.

The second Scripture on the Romans Road to salvation, Romans 6:23, teaches us about the consequences of sin: "For the wages of sin is death." The punishment that we have earned for our sins is death. Not just physical death, but eternal death!

The third verse on the Romans Road to salvation picks up in the middle of Romans 6:23: "But the gift of God is eternal life in Christ Jesus our Lord." Romans 5:8 declares, "But God demonstrates His own love toward us, in that while we were still sinners, Christ died for us" (NASB). Jesus Christ died for us! Jesus' death paid for the price of our sins. Jesus' resurrection proves that God accepted Jesus' death as the payment for our sins.

The fourth stop on the Romans Road to salvation is Romans 10:9, "If you confess with your mouth Jesus as Lord, and believe in your heart that God raised Him from the dead, you will be saved" (NASB). Because of Jesus' death on our behalf, all we have to do is believe in Him, trusting His death as the payment for our sins—and we will be saved! Romans 10:13 says it again, "For, 'Everyone who calls on the name of the Lord will be saved.'" Jesus died to pay the penalty for our sins and rescue us from eternal death. Salvation, the forgiveness of sins, is available to anyone who will trust in Jesus Christ as Lord and Savior.

The final aspect of the Romans Road to salvation is the result of salvation. Romans 5:1 has this wonderful message: "Therefore, since we have been justified through faith, we have peace with God through our Lord Jesus Christ." Through Jesus Christ we can have a relationship of peace with God. Romans 8:1 says, "Therefore, there is now no condemnation for those who are in Christ Jesus." Because of Jesus' death on our behalf, we will never be condemned for our sins. Finally, we have this precious promise of God from Romans 8:38–39: "For I am convinced that neither death nor life, neither angels nor demons, neither the present nor the future, nor any powers, neither height nor depth, nor anything else in all creation, will be able to separate us from the love of God that is in Christ Jesus our Lord."

17. Where do I find the age of accountability in the Bible?

The concept of the "age of accountability" is that children are not held accountable by God for their sins until they reach a certain age and that, if a child dies before reaching the age of accountability, that child will, by the grace and mercy of God, be granted entrance to heaven. Is the concept of an age of accountability biblical? Is there such a thing as an "age of innocence"?

Frequently lost in the discussion regarding the age of accountability is the fact that children, no matter how young, are not "innocent" in the sense of being sinless. The Bible tells us that even if an infant or child has not committed personal sin, all people, including infants and children, are guilty before God because of inherited and imputed sin. Inherited sin is that which is passed on from our parents. In Psalm 51:5, David wrote, "Surely I was sinful at birth, sinful from the time my mother conceived me." David recognized that even at conception he was a sinner. The sad fact that infants sometimes die demonstrates that even infants are impacted by Adam's sin, since physical and spiritual death were the results of Adam's original sin.

Each person, infant or adult, stands guilty before God; each person has offended the holiness of God. The only way God can be just and at the same time declare a person righteous is for that person to have received forgiveness by faith in Christ. Christ is the only way. John 14:6 records what Jesus said: "I am the way and the truth and the life. No one comes to the Father except through me." Also, Peter states in Acts 4:12, "Salvation is found in no one else, for there is no other name under heaven given to men by which we must be saved."

What about babies and young children who never attain the ability to make the personal choice to believe in Jesus? Some believe that those who die before reaching the age of intellectual or moral accountability are automatically saved by God's grace in Christ. The reasoning is that if someone is truly incapable of making a decision for or against Christ, then that one is extended God's mercy. Charles Spurgeon held this view: "I rejoice to know that the souls of all infants, as soon as they die, speed their way to Paradise. Think what a multitude there is of them!"[1]

The Bible does not directly address an age of accountability. One verse that may speak to the issue indirectly is Romans 1:20: "Since the creation of the world God's invisible qualities—his eternal power and divine nature—have been clearly seen, being understood from what has been made, so that people are without excuse." According to this, mankind's guilt before God is based, in part, on a rejection of what can be "clearly seen" of God's existence, eternality, and power. So, what about children who have no faculty for "clearly seeing" or reasoning about God—wouldn't their natural incapacity to observe and reason excuse them from judgment?

The age of thirteen is most commonly suggested for the age of accountability, based on the Jewish custom that a child becomes an adult at the age of thirteen. However, the Bible gives no support to the age of thirteen being a set age of accountability. The age at which a child can distinguish right from wrong and becomes capable of choosing Christ likely varies from child to child.

With the above in mind, also consider this: Christ's death is presented as sufficient for all of mankind. First John 2:2 says Jesus is "the atoning sacrifice for our sins, and not only for ours but also for the sins of the whole world." This verse is clear that Jesus' death was sufficient payment for all sins, not only the sins of those who come to Him in faith. The fact that Christ's death was sufficient for all sin would allow at least the *possibility* of God's applying that payment to those who were never capable of believing.

Some see a link between the age of accountability and the covenant relationship between the nation of Israel and the Lord. In that dispensation, a male child was brought into the covenant through circumcision, which was totally out of his control, being performed on the eighth day after birth. No other requirement was imposed on him (Exodus 12:48–50; Leviticus 12:3).

The passage cited most often in support of an age of accountability is 2 Samuel 12:21–23. The context is that King David committed adultery with Bathsheba, with a resulting pregnancy. The prophet Nathan was sent by the Lord to inform David that because of his sin, the Lord would take the child in death. David responded by grieving and praying for the child. But once the child was taken, David's mourning ended. David's servants were surprised to hear this. They said to King David, "What is this thing that you have done? You fasted and wept for the child while he was alive; but when the child died, you got up and ate food." David's response was, "While the child was still alive, I fasted and wept; for I said, 'Who knows, the LORD may be gracious to me, and the child may live.' But now he has died; why should I fast? Can I bring him back again? I am going to him, but he will not return to me" (NASB). David's words might indicate that infants who die are safe in the Lord. David could have simply been referring to the fact that his child was in the grave, but he seemed to be comforted by the knowledge. The peace he felt suggests that he believed he would see his baby son again (in heaven).

In conclusion, it is possible that God applies Christ's payment for sin to young children and others incapable of faith, but the Bible does not specifically say that He does this. Therefore, this is a subject about which we should not be dogmatic. God's extending grace to those who cannot believe would seem consistent with His character. It is our position that God does apply Christ's payment for sin to babies and those who are mentally handicapped since they are incapable of understanding their sinful state and their need for the Savior. Again, we *cannot* be dogmatic. Of this we are certain: God is loving, holy, merciful, just, and gracious. Whatever God does is always right and good, and He loves children (Matthew 19:14).

SECTION 3

Questions about the Church

18. What does the Bible say about women pastors?

There is perhaps no more hotly debated issue in the church today than that of women serving as pastors/preachers. As a result, it is important to not see this issue as men versus women. There are women who believe women should not serve as pastors and that the Bible places restrictions on the ministry of women, and there are men who believe women can serve as preachers and that there are no restrictions on women in ministry. This is not an issue of chauvinism or discrimination. It is a matter of biblical interpretation.

The Word of God proclaims, "A woman should learn in quietness and full submission. I do not permit a woman to teach or to assume authority over a man; she must be quiet" (1 Timothy 2:11–12). In the church, God assigns different roles to men and women. This is a result of the way mankind was created and the way in which sin entered the world (1 Timothy 2:13–14). God, through the apostle Paul, restricts women from serving in roles of teaching and/or having spiritual authority over men in the church. This precludes women from serving as pastors over men, since pastoring definitely includes preaching, teaching publicly, and exercising spiritual authority.

There are many objections to this view of women in pastoral ministry. A common one is that Paul restricts women from teaching because, in the first century, women were typically uneducated. However, 1 Timothy 2:11–14 nowhere mentions educational status. If education were a qualification for ministry, then the majority of Jesus' disciples would not have been qualified.

A second common objection is that Paul only restricted the women *of Ephesus* from teaching men (1 Timothy was written to Timothy, the pastor of the church in Ephesus). Ephesus was known for its temple to Artemis, and women were the authorities in that branch of paganism— therefore, the theory goes, Paul was only reacting against the female-led customs of the Ephesian idolaters, and the church needed to be different. However, the book of 1 Timothy nowhere mentions Artemis, nor does Paul mention the standard practice of Artemis worshipers as a reason for the restrictions in 1 Timothy 2:11–12.

A third objection is that Paul is only referring to husbands and wives, not men and women in general. The Greek words for "woman" and "man" in 1 Timothy 2 *could* refer to husbands and wives; however, the basic meaning of the words is broader than that. Further, the same Greek words are used in verses 8–10. Are only *husbands* to lift up holy hands in prayer without anger and disputing (verse 8)? Are only *wives* to dress modestly, have good deeds, and worship God (verses 9–10)? No. Verses 8–10 clearly refer to all men and women, not just husbands and wives. There is nothing in the context that would indicate a narrowing to husbands and wives in verses 11–14.

Yet another objection to this interpretation of women in pastoral ministry references women in positions of leadership in the Bible, specifically Miriam, Deborah, and Huldah in the Old Testament. It is true that these women were chosen by God for special service to Him and that they stand as models of faith, courage, and yes, leadership. However, the authority of women in the Old Testament is not relevant to the issue of pastors in the church. The New Testament Epistles present a new paradigm for God's people—the church, the body of Christ—and that paradigm involves an authority structure unique to the church, not for the nation of Israel or any other Old Testament entity.

Similar arguments are made using Priscilla and Phoebe in the New Testament. In Acts 18, Priscilla and Aquila are presented as faithful ministers for Christ. In verse 18, Priscilla's name is mentioned first, suggesting to some that she was more prominent in ministry than her husband. (The detail of whose name comes first is probably inconsequential, because in verses 2 and 26 the order is reversed from that of verse 18.) Did Priscilla and her husband teach the gospel of Jesus Christ to Apollos? Yes, in their home they "explained to him the way of God more adequately" (Acts 18:26). Does the Bible ever say that Priscilla pastored a church or taught publicly or became the spiritual leader of a congregation of saints? No. As far as we know, Priscilla was not involved in ministry activity in contradiction to 1 Timothy 2:11–14.

In Romans 16:1, Phoebe is called a "deacon" (or "servant") in the church and is highly commended by Paul. But, as with Priscilla, there is nothing in Scripture to indicate that Phoebe was a pastor or a teacher of men in the church. "Able to teach" is given as a qualification for elders, but not for deacons (1 Timothy 3:1–13; Titus 1:6–9).

The structure of 1 Timothy 2:11–14 makes the reason why women cannot be pastors perfectly clear. Verse 13 begins with "for," giving the "cause" of Paul's statement in verses 11–12. Why should women not teach or have authority over men? Because "Adam was formed first, then Eve. And Adam was not the one deceived; it was the woman who was deceived" (verses 13–14). God created Adam first and then created Eve to be a "helper" for Adam. The order of creation has universal application in the family (Ephesians 5:22–33) and in the church.

The fact that Eve was deceived is also given as a reason for women not serving as pastors or having spiritual authority over men (1 Timothy 2:14). This does not mean that women are gullible or that they are all more easily deceived than men. If all women were more easily deceived, why would they be allowed to teach children (who are easily deceived) and other women (who are supposedly more easily deceived)? The text simply says that women are not to teach men or have spiritual authority over men because *Eve* was deceived. God has chosen to give men the primary teaching authority in the church.

Many women excel in gifts of hospitality, mercy, teaching, evangelism, and helping/serving. Much of the ministry of the local church depends on women. Women in the church are not restricted from praying publicly or prophesying (1 Corinthians 11:5), only from having spiritual teaching authority over men. The Bible nowhere restricts women from exercising the gifts of the Holy Spirit (1 Corinthians 12). Women, just as much as men, are called to minister to others, to demonstrate the fruit of the Spirit (Galatians 5:22–23), and to proclaim the gospel to the lost (Matthew 28:18–20; Acts 1:8; 1 Peter 3:15).

God has ordained that only men are to serve in positions of spiritual teaching authority in the church. This does not imply that men are better teachers or that women are inferior or less intelligent. It is simply the way God designed the church to function. Men are to set the example in spiritual leadership—in their lives and through their words. Women are to take a less authoritative role. Women are encouraged to teach other women (Titus 2:3–5). The Bible also does not restrict women from teaching children. The only roles women are restricted from are teaching and having spiritual authority over men. This bars women from serving as pastors to men. This does not make women less important, by any means; rather, it gives them a ministry focus more in agreement with God's plan and gifts.

19. What is the difference between praise and worship?

Understanding the difference between praise and worship can bring a new depth to the way we honor the Lord. Throughout the Bible are numerous commands to praise the Lord. Angels and the heavenly hosts are commanded to praise the Lord (Psalm 89:5; 103:20; 148:2). All inhabitants of the earth are instructed to praise the Lord (Psalm 138:4; Romans 15:11). We can praise Him with singing (Isaiah 12:5; Psalm 9:11), with shouting (Psalm 33:3; 98:4), with dance (Psalm 150:4), and with musical instruments (1 Chronicles 13:8; Psalm 108:2; 150:3–5).

Praise is the joyful recounting of all God has done for us. It is closely intertwined with thanksgiving as we offer back to God appreciation for His mighty works on our behalf. Praise can be a feature of other relationships as well. We can praise our family, friends, boss, or mail carrier. Praise does not require anything of us. It is merely the truthful acknowledgment of the righteous acts of another. Since God has done many wonderful deeds, He is worthy of praise (Psalm 18:3).

Worship comes from a different place within our spirits. Worship should be reserved for God alone (Luke 4:8). Worship is the art of losing self in the adoration of another. Praise can be a part of worship, but worship goes beyond praise. Praise is easy; worship is not. Worship gets to the heart of who we are. To truly worship God, we must let go of our self-worship. We must be willing to humble ourselves before God, surrender every part of our lives to His control, and adore Him for who He is, not just what He has done. Worship is a lifestyle, not just an occasional activity. Jesus said the Father is seeking those who will worship Him "in spirit and in truth" (John 4:23 KJV).

In Scripture, praise is usually presented as boisterous, joyful, and uninhibited. God invites praise of all kinds from His creation. Jesus said that if people don't praise God, even the "stones will cry out" (Luke 19:40). When the Bible mentions worship, however, the tone changes. We read verses like "Worship the LORD in the beauty of holiness" (Psalm 96:9 KJV). And "Come, let us worship and bow down" (Psalm 95:6 KJV). Often, worship is coupled with the act of bowing or kneeling, which shows humility and contrition (2 Chronicles 29:28; Hebrews 11:21; Revelation 19:10). It is through true worship that we invite the Holy Spirit to speak to us, convict us, and comfort us. Through worship, we realign our priorities with God's and acknowledge Him once more as the rightful Lord of our lives.

Just as praise is intertwined with thanksgiving, worship is intertwined with surrender. It is impossible to worship God and anything else at the same time (Luke 4:8). The physical acts often associated with worship—bowing, kneeling, lifting hands—help to create the necessary attitude of humility required for real worship. Wise worship leaders know how to structure a worship service to allow participants to both praise and worship the Lord. Often, services begin with joyous praise songs and transition to a quieter, more introspective opportunity for worship.

Worship is an attitude of the heart. A person can go through the outward motions and not be worshiping (Psalm 51:16–17; Matthew 6:5–6). God sees the heart, and He desires and deserves sincere, heartfelt praise *and* worship.

20. What day is the Sabbath, Saturday or Sunday? Do Christians have to observe the Sabbath day?

It is often claimed that God instituted the Sabbath in Eden because of the connection between the Sabbath and creation in Exodus 20:11. Although God's rest on the seventh day (Genesis 2:3) did foreshadow a future Sabbath law, there is no biblical record of the Sabbath before the children of Israel left the land of Egypt. Nowhere in Scripture is there any hint that Sabbath-keeping was practiced from Adam to Moses.

The Word of God makes it quite clear that Sabbath observance was a special sign between God and Israel: "The Israelites are to observe the Sabbath, celebrating it for the generations to come as a lasting covenant. It will be a sign between me and the Israelites forever, for in six days the LORD made the heavens and the earth, and on the seventh day he rested and was refreshed" (Exodus 31:16–17).

In Deuteronomy 5, Moses restates the Ten Commandments to the next generation of Israelites. Here, after commanding Sabbath observance in verses 12–14, Moses gives the reason the Sabbath was given to the nation Israel: "Remember that you were slaves in Egypt and that the LORD your God brought you out of there with a mighty hand and an outstretched arm. Therefore the LORD your God has commanded you to observe the Sabbath day" (Deuteronomy 5:15).

God's intent for giving the Sabbath to Israel was not that they would remember creation, but that they would remember their Egyptian slavery and the Lord's deliverance. Note the requirements for Sabbath-keeping: a person placed under that Sabbath law could not leave his home on the Sabbath (Exodus 16:29), he could not build a fire (Exodus 35:3), and he could not cause anyone else to work (Deuteronomy 5:14). A person breaking the Sabbath law was to be put to death (Exodus 31:15; Numbers 15:32–35).

An examination of New Testament passages reveals four important points concerning the Sabbath:

1. Whenever Christ appears in His resurrected form and the day is mentioned, it is always the first day of the week (Matthew 28:1–10; Mark 16:9; Luke 24:1–15; John 20:19–26).

2. The only times the Sabbath is mentioned from Acts through Revelation, the occasion is Jewish evangelism, and the setting is usually a synagogue (Acts 13–18). Paul wrote, "To the Jews I became as a Jew, that I might win Jews" (1 Corinthians 9:20 NKJV). Paul did not go to the synagogue to fellowship with and edify the saints, but to convict and save the lost.

3. After Paul states "From now on I will go to the Gentiles" (Acts 18:6), the Sabbath is never again mentioned.

4. Instead of suggesting adherence to the Sabbath day, the remainder of the New Testament implies the opposite (including the one exception to point 3, above, found in Colossians 2:16).

Looking more closely at point 4, above, will reveal that there is no obligation for the New Testament believer to keep the Sabbath and will also show that the idea of a Sunday "Christian Sabbath" is also unscriptural. As mentioned, there is one time the Sabbath is mentioned after Paul began to focus on the Gentiles: "Therefore do not let anyone judge you by what you eat or drink, or with regard to a religious festival, a New Moon celebration or a Sabbath day. These are a shadow of the things that were to come; the reality, however, is found in Christ" (Colossians 2:16–17). The Jewish Sabbath was abolished at the cross where Christ "canceled the charge of our legal indebtedness" (Colossians 2:14).

Our freedom from Sabbath-day regulations is repeated more than once in the New Testament: "One person considers one day more sacred than another; another considers every day alike. Each of them should be fully convinced in their own mind. Whoever regards one day as special does so to the Lord" (Romans 14:5–6). "But now that you know God—or rather are known by God—how is it that you are turning back to those weak and miserable forces? Do you wish to be enslaved by them all over again? You are observing special days and months and seasons and years" (Galatians 4:9–10).

Some claim that a mandate by Emperor Constantine in AD 321 "changed" the Sabbath from Saturday to Sunday. On what day did the early church meet for worship? Scripture never mentions any Sabbath (Saturday) gatherings by believers for fellowship or worship. However, there are passages that mention the first day of the week. For instance, Acts 20:7 states that "on the first day of the week we came together to break bread." In 1 Corinthians 16:2 Paul gives this instruction: "On the first day of every week, each one of you should set aside a sum of money in keeping with your income." Since Paul designates this offering as "service" in 2 Corinthians 9:12, this collection must have been linked with the Sunday worship service of the Christian assembly. Historically, Sunday, not Saturday, was the normal meeting day for Christians in the church, and its practice dates back to the first century.

The Sabbath was given to Israel, not the church. The Sabbath is still Saturday, not Sunday, and has never been changed. The Sabbath is part of the Old Testament Law, and Christians are free from the bondage of the law (Galatians 4:1–26; Romans 6:14). Sabbath-keeping is not required of the Christian—be it Saturday or Sunday. The first day of the week, Sunday, the Lord's Day (Revelation 1:10), celebrates the new creation with Christ as our resurrected Savior. The apostle Paul said that each individual Christian should decide whether to observe a Sabbath rest: "One person considers one day more sacred than another; another considers every day alike. Each of them should be fully convinced in their own mind" (Romans 14:5). We are to worship God every day, not just on Saturday or Sunday.

21. What does the Bible say about Christian tithing? Should a Christian tithe?

Many Christians struggle with the issue of tithing. In some churches giving is overemphasized. At the same time, many Christians refuse to submit to the biblical exhortations about making offerings to the Lord. Tithing/giving is intended to be a joy and a blessing. Sadly, that is sometimes not the case in the church today.

Tithing is an Old Testament concept. The tithe was a requirement of the Law in which the Israelites were to give 10 percent of the crops they grew and the livestock they raised to the tabernacle/temple (Leviticus 27:30; Numbers 18:26; Deuteronomy 14:24; 2 Chronicles 31:5). In fact, the Old Testament Law required multiple tithes—one for the Levites, one for the use of the temple and the feasts, and one for the poor of the land—which would have pushed the total to around 23.3 percent. Some understand the Old Testament tithe as a method of taxation to provide for the needs of the priests and Levites in the sacrificial system.

After the death of Jesus Christ fulfilled the Law, the New Testament nowhere commands, or even recommends, that Christians submit to a legalistic tithe system. The New Testament nowhere designates a percentage of income a person should set aside, but only says gifts should be "in keeping with your income" (1 Corinthians 16:2). Some in the Christian church have taken the 10 percent figure from the Old Testament tithe and applied it as a recommended minimum for Christians in their giving.

Although no tithe is demanded of the Christian, the New Testament talks about the importance and benefits of giving. We are to give as we are able. Sometimes that means giving more than 10 percent; sometimes that may mean giving less. It all depends on the ability of the Christian and the needs of the body of Christ. Every Christian should diligently pray and seek God's wisdom in the matter (James 1:5). Above all, offerings should be given with pure motives and an attitude of worship to God and service to the body of Christ. "Each of you should give what you have decided in your heart to give, not reluctantly or under compulsion, for God loves a cheerful giver" (2 Corinthians 9:7).

22. What is the importance of Christian baptism?

Christian baptism is one of two ordinances that Jesus instituted for the church. Just before His ascension, Jesus said, "Go and make disciples of all nations, baptizing them in the name of the Father and of the Son and of the Holy Spirit, and teaching them to obey everything I have commanded you. And surely I am with you always, to the very end of the age" (Matthew 28:19–20). These instructions specify that the church is responsible to teach Jesus' word, make disciples, and baptize those disciples. These things are to be done everywhere ("all nations") until "the very end of the age." So, if for no other reason, baptism has importance because Jesus commanded it.

Baptism was practiced before the founding of the church. The Jews of ancient times would baptize proselytes to signify the converts' "cleansed" nature. John the Baptist used baptism to prepare the way of the Lord, requiring *everyone*, not just Gentiles, to be baptized because *everyone* needs repentance. However, John's baptism, signifying repentance, is not the same as Christian baptism, as seen in Acts 18:24–26 and 19:1–7. Christian baptism has a deeper significance.

Baptism is to be done in the name of the Father, Son, and Spirit—this is what makes it *Christian* baptism. It is through this ordinance that a person is admitted into the fellowship of the church. When we are saved, we are "baptized" by the Spirit into the body of Christ, which is the church. First Corinthians 12:13 says, "We were all baptized by one Spirit so as to form one body—whether Jews or Gentiles, slave or free—and we were all given the one Spirit to drink." Baptism by water is a "reenactment" of the baptism by the Spirit.

Christian baptism is the means by which a person makes a public profession of faith and discipleship. In the waters of baptism, a person says, wordlessly, "I confess faith in Christ; Jesus has cleansed my soul from sin, and I now have a new life of sanctification."

Christian baptism illustrates, in dramatic style, the death, burial, and resurrection of Christ. At the same time, it also illustrates our death to sin and new life in Christ. As the sinner confesses the Lord Jesus, he dies to sin (Romans 6:11) and is raised to a brand-new life (Colossians 2:12). Being submerged in the water represents death to sin, and emerging from the water represents the cleansed, holy life that follows salvation. Romans 6:4 puts it this way: "We were therefore buried with him through baptism into death in order that, just as Christ was raised from the dead through the glory of the Father, we too may live a new life."

Very simply, baptism is an outward testimony of the inward change in a believer's life. Christian baptism is an act of obedience to the Lord *after* salvation; although baptism is closely associated with salvation, it is not a requirement to be saved. The Bible shows in many places that the order of events is 1) a person believes in the Lord Jesus and 2) he is baptized. This sequence is seen in Acts 2:41: "Those who accepted [Peter's] message were baptized" (see also Acts 16:14–15).

A new believer in Jesus Christ should desire to be baptized as soon as possible. In Acts 8 Philip speaks "the good news about Jesus" to the Ethiopian eunuch, and, "as they traveled along the road, they came to some water and the eunuch said, 'Look, here is water. What can stand in the way of my being baptized?'" (verses 35–36). Right away, they stopped the chariot and Philip baptized the man.

Baptism illustrates a believer's identification with Christ's death, burial, and resurrection. Everywhere the gospel is preached and people are drawn to faith in Christ, they are to be baptized.

23. Does the Bible record the death of the apostles? How did each of the apostles die?

The only apostle whose death the Bible records is James (Acts 12:2). King Herod had James "put to death with the sword," likely a reference to beheading. The circumstances of the deaths of the other apostles are related through church tradition, so we should not put too much weight on any of the other accounts. The most commonly accepted church tradition in regard to the death of an apostle is that the apostle Peter was crucified upside-down in Rome in fulfillment of Jesus' prophecy (John 21:18). The following are the most popular "traditions" concerning the deaths of the other apostles:

Matthew suffered martyrdom in Ethiopia, killed by a sword wound. John faced martyrdom when he was boiled in a huge basin of boiling oil during a wave of persecution in Rome. However, he was miraculously delivered from death. John was then sentenced to the mines on the prison island of Patmos. He wrote his prophetic book of Revelation on Patmos. The apostle John was later freed and returned to what is now modern-day Turkey. He died as an old man, the only apostle to die peacefully.

James, the brother of Jesus (not officially an apostle), was the leader of the church in Jerusalem. He was thrown from the southeast pinnacle of the temple (over a hundred feet down) when he refused to deny his faith in Christ. When they discovered that he survived the fall, his enemies beat James to death with a club. This is thought to be the same pinnacle where Satan had taken Jesus during the temptation.

Bartholomew, also known as Nathanael, was a missionary to Asia. He witnessed in present-day Turkey and was martyred for his preaching in Armenia, being flayed to death by a whip. Andrew was crucified on an X-shaped cross in Greece. After seven soldiers whipped Andrew severely, they tied his body to the cross with cords to prolong his agony. His followers reported that, when he was led toward the cross, Andrew saluted it in these words: "I have long desired and expected this happy hour. The cross has been consecrated by the body of Christ hanging on it." He continued to preach to his tormentors for two days until he died. The apostle Thomas was stabbed with a spear in India during one of his missionary trips to establish the church there. Matthias, the apostle chosen to replace the traitor Judas Iscariot, was stoned and then beheaded. The apostle Paul was tortured and then beheaded by the evil emperor Nero in Rome in AD 67. There are traditions regarding the other apostles as well, but none with any reliable historical or traditional support.

It is not so important how the apostles died. What is important is the fact that they were all willing to die for their faith. If Jesus had not been resurrected, the disciples would have known it. People will not die for something they know to be a lie. The fact that all of the apostles were willing to die horrible deaths, refusing to renounce their faith in Christ, is tremendous evidence that they had truly witnessed the resurrection of Jesus Christ.

SECTION 4
Questions about Theology

24. What does it mean that humanity is made in the image of God (*imago dei*)?

On the last day of creation, God said, "Let us make mankind in our image, in our likeness" (Genesis 1:26). Thus, He finished His work with a "personal touch." God formed Adam from the dust and gave him life by sharing His own breath (Genesis 2:7). Accordingly, humanity is unique among all God's creations, having both a material body and an immaterial soul/spirit. Humanity is made in the image of God to resemble God, relate to God, and reflect God morally, mentally, and socially.

Having the "image" or "likeness" of God means, in the simplest terms, that we were made to resemble God. Adam did not resemble

God in the sense of God's having flesh and blood. Scripture says that "God is spirit" (John 4:24) and therefore exists without a body. However, Adam's body did mirror the life of God insofar as it was created in perfect health and was not subject to death.

The image of God (Latin, *imago dei*) refers to the immaterial part of humanity. It sets human beings apart from the animal world, fits them for the dominion God intended them to have over the earth (Genesis 1:28), and enables them to commune with their Maker. It is a likeness mentally, morally, and socially.

Mentally, humanity was created as a rational, volitional agent. In other words, human beings can reason and choose. This is a reflection of God's intellect and freedom. Anytime someone invents a machine, writes a book, paints a landscape, enjoys a symphony, calculates a sum, or names a pet, he or she is proclaiming the fact that we are made in God's image.

Morally, humanity was created in righteousness and perfect innocence, a reflection of God's holiness. God saw all He had made (humanity included) and called it "very good" (Genesis 1:31). Our conscience or "moral compass" is a vestige of that original state. Whenever someone writes a law, recoils from evil, praises good behavior, or feels guilty, he or she is confirming the fact that we are made in God's own image.

Socially, humanity was created for fellowship. This reflects God's triune nature and His love. In Eden, humanity's primary relationship was with God (Genesis 3:8 implies fellowship with God), and God made the first woman because it was not good for the man to be alone (Genesis 2:18). Every time someone marries, makes a friend, hugs a child, or attends church, he or she is demonstrating the fact that we are made in the likeness of God.

Part of being made in God's image is that Adam had the capacity to make free choices. Although they were given a righteous nature, Adam and Eve made an evil choice to rebel against their Creator. In so doing, they marred the image of God within themselves and passed that damaged likeness on to all their descendants (Romans 5:12). Today, we still bear the image of God (James 3:9), but we also bear the scars of sin. Mentally, morally, socially, and physically, we show the effects of sin.

The good news is that when God redeems an individual, He begins to restore the original image of God, creating a "new self, created to be like God in true righteousness and holiness" (Ephesians 4:24). That redemption is only available by God's grace through faith in Jesus Christ as our Savior from the sin that separates us from God (Ephesians 2:8–9). Through Christ, we are made new creations in the likeness of God (2 Corinthians 5:17) and are able to more fully reflect the character and call of God to those around us.

25. Why does God allow bad things to happen to good people?

We live in a world of pain and suffering. Everyone is affected by the harsh realities of life, and the question, "Why do bad things happen to good people?" is one of the most difficult questions in all of theology. God is sovereign, so all that happens must have at least been allowed by Him, if not directly caused by Him. At the outset, we must acknowledge that human beings, who are not eternal, infinite, or omniscient, cannot expect to fully understand God's purposes and ways.

The book of Job deals with the issue of why God allows bad things to happen to good people. Job was a righteous man (Job 1:1), yet he suffered in ways that are almost beyond belief. God allowed Satan to do everything he wanted to Job except kill him, and Satan did his worst. What was Job's reaction? "Though he slay me, yet will I hope in him" (Job 13:15). "The LORD gave and the LORD has taken away; may the name of the LORD be praised" (Job 1:21). Job did not understand why God had allowed the things He did, but he knew God was good and therefore continued to trust in Him. Ultimately, that should be our reaction as well.

Why do bad things happen to good people? As hard as it is to acknowledge, we must remember that there are no "good" people, in the absolute sense of the word. All of us are tainted by and infected with sin (Ecclesiastes 7:20; Romans 3:23; 1 John 1:8). As Jesus said, "No one is good—except God alone" (Luke 18:19). All of us feel the effects of sin in one way or another. Sometimes it's our own personal sin; other times, it's the sins of others. We live in a fallen world, and we experience the effects of the fall. One of those effects is injustice and seemingly senseless suffering.

When wondering why God would allow bad things to happen to good people, it's also good to consider these four things about the bad things that happen:

1. Bad things may happen to good people in this world, *but this world is not the end.* Christians have an eternal perspective: "We do not lose heart. Though outwardly we are wasting away, yet inwardly we are being renewed day by day. For our light and momentary troubles are achieving for us an eternal glory that far outweighs them all. So we fix our eyes not on what is seen, but on what is unseen, since what is seen is temporary, but what is unseen is eternal" (2 Corinthians 4:16–18). We will have a reward some day, and it will be glorious.

2. Bad things happen to good people, *but God uses those bad things for an ultimate, lasting good.* "We know that in all things God works for the good of those who love him, who have been called according to his purpose" (Romans 8:28). When Joseph, innocent of wrongdoing, finally came through his horrific sufferings, he was able to see God's good plan in it all (see Genesis 50:19–21).

3. Bad things happen to good people, *but those bad things equip believers for deeper ministry.* "Praise be to . . . the Father of compassion and the God of all comfort, who comforts us in all our troubles, so that we can comfort those in any trouble with the comfort we ourselves receive from God. For

just as we share abundantly in the sufferings of Christ, so also our comfort abounds through Christ" (2 Corinthians 1:3–5). Those with battle scars can better help those going through battles.

4. Bad things happen to good people, *and the worst things happened to the best Person.* Jesus was the only truly Righteous One, yet He suffered more than we can imagine. We follow in His footsteps: "If you suffer for doing good and you endure it, this is commendable before God. To this you were called, because Christ suffered for you, leaving you an example, that you should follow in his steps. 'He committed no sin, and no deceit was found in his mouth.' When they hurled their insults at him, he did not retaliate; when he suffered, he made no threats. Instead, he entrusted himself to him who judges justly" (1 Peter 2:20–23). Jesus is no stranger to our pain.

Romans 5:8 declares, "But God demonstrates his own love for us in this: While we were still sinners, Christ died for us." Despite the sinful nature of the people of this world, God still loves us. Jesus loved us enough to die to take the penalty for our sins (Romans 6:23). If we receive Jesus Christ as Savior (John 3:16; Romans 10:9), we will be forgiven and are promised an eternal home in heaven (Romans 8:1).

God allows things to happen for a reason. Whether or not we understand His reasons, we must remember that God is good, just, loving, and merciful (Psalm 89:14; 135:3; 145:8; Ephesians 2:4–5). Often, bad things happen to us that we simply cannot understand. Instead of doubting God's goodness, our reaction should be to trust Him. "Trust in the LORD with all your heart and lean not on your own understanding; in all your ways submit to him, and he will make your paths straight" (Proverbs 3:5–6). We walk by faith, not by sight.

26. What does it mean to have the fear of God?

For the unbeliever, the fear of God is the fear of the judgment of God and eternal death, which is eternal separation from God (Luke 12:5; Hebrews 10:31). For the believer, the fear of God is something much different. The believer's fear is reverence of God. Hebrews 12:28–29 is a good description of this: "Therefore, since we are receiving a kingdom that cannot be shaken, let us be thankful, and so worship God acceptably with reverence and awe, for our 'God is a consuming fire.'" This reverence and awe are exactly what the fear of God means for Christians. This is the motivating factor for us to surrender to the Creator of the Universe.

Proverbs 1:7 declares, "The fear of the LORD is the beginning of knowledge." Until we understand who God is and develop a reverential fear of Him, we cannot have true wisdom. True wisdom comes only from understanding who God is and that He is holy, just, and righteous. Deuteronomy 10:12, 20–21 records, "And now, Israel, what does the LORD your God ask of you but to fear the LORD your God, to walk in obedience to him, to love him, to serve the LORD your God with all your heart and with all your soul. . . . Fear the LORD your God and serve him. Hold fast to him and take your oaths in his name. He is the one you praise; he is your God, who performed for you those great and awesome wonders you saw with your own eyes." The fear of God is the basis for our walking in His ways, serving Him, and, yes, loving Him.

Some redefine the fear of God for believers to "respecting" Him. While respect is definitely included in the concept of fearing God, there is more to it than that. A biblical fear of God includes understanding how much God hates sin and fearing His judgment of sin—even in the life of a believer. Hebrews 12:5–11 describes God's discipline of the believer. While it is done in love (Hebrews 12:6), it is still a fearful thing. When we were children, our fear of discipline from our parents no doubt prevented some evil actions on our part. The same should be true in our relationship with God. We should fear His discipline and therefore seek to live our lives in a way that pleases Him.

Believers are not to be scared of God. We have no reason to be scared of Him. We have His promise that nothing can separate us from His love (Romans 8:38–39). We have His promise that He will never leave us or forsake us (Hebrews 13:5). Fearing God means having a reverence for Him that greatly impacts the way we live. The fear of God is respecting Him, obeying Him, submitting to His discipline, and worshiping Him in awe.

27. How, why, and when did Satan fall from heaven?

Satan's fall from heaven is symbolically described in Isaiah 14:12–14 and Ezekiel 28:12–18. While these two passages are referring specifically to the kings of Babylon and Tyre, we believe they also reference the spiritual power behind those kings, namely, Satan. These passages describe *why* Satan fell, but they do not say *when* the fall occurred. Jesus, the eternal Son of God, witnessed Satan's fall, and He mentions it in Luke 10:18: "I saw Satan fall like lightning from heaven." We know that the angels were created before the earth (Job 38:4–7). Satan fell before he tempted Adam and Eve in the garden (Genesis 3:1–14). Satan's fall, therefore, must have occurred sometime after the angels were created and before he tempted Adam and Eve in the garden of Eden. Whether Satan's fall occurred hours, days, or years before he tempted Adam and Eve in the garden, Scripture does not say.

The book of Job tells us, at least in Job's time, Satan still had access to heaven and to the throne of God. "One day the angels came to present themselves before the LORD, and Satan also came with them. The LORD said to Satan, 'Where have you come from?' Satan answered the LORD, 'From roaming throughout the earth, going back and forth on it'" (Job 1:6–7). Apparently at that time, Satan was still moving freely between heaven and earth, speaking to God directly and answering for his activities. Whether God has discontinued this access is a matter of debate. Some say Satan's access to heaven was ended at the death of Christ. Others believe Satan's access to heaven will be ended at the end-times war in heaven (Revelation 12:7–12).

Why did Satan fall from heaven? Satan fell because of pride. He desired to be God, not to be a servant of God. Notice the many "I will . . ." statements in Isaiah 14:12–15. Ezekiel 28:12–15 describes Satan as an exceedingly beautiful angel. Satan was likely the highest of all angels, the anointed cherub, the most beautiful of all of God's creations, but he was not content in his position. Instead, Satan desired to be God, to essentially kick God off His throne and take over the rule of the universe. Satan wanted to be God, and interestingly enough, that desire is what Satan tempted Adam and Eve with in the garden of Eden (Genesis 3:1–5).

How did Satan fall from heaven? Because of Satan's sin, God cast him out of heaven (Isaiah 14:15; Ezekiel 28:16–17). Heaven is no place for the wicked one. Satan fell because he was *pushed*.

28. What is the difference between sheol, hades, hell, the lake of fire, paradise, and Abraham's bosom?

The different terms used in the Bible for heaven and hell—sheol, hades, Gehenna, the lake of fire, paradise, and Abraham's bosom—are the subject of much debate and can be confusing.

The word *paradise* is used as a synonym for *heaven* (2 Corinthians 12:3–4; Revelation 2:7). When Jesus was dying on the cross and one of the thieves being crucified with Him asked Him for mercy, Jesus replied, "Truly I tell you, today you will be with me in paradise" (Luke 23:43). Jesus knew that His death was imminent and that He would soon be in heaven with His Father. In His words of comfort to the penitent thief, Jesus used *paradise* as a synonym for *heaven*, and the word has come to be associated with any place of ideal loveliness and delight.

Abraham's bosom is referred to only once in the Bible—in the story of Lazarus and the rich man (Luke 16:19–31). *Abraham's lap* was used in the Talmud as a synonym for *heaven* (*Seder Nashim, Kiddushin* 72b). The image in the story is of Lazarus reclining at a table leaning on Abraham's breast at the heavenly banquet—as John leaned on Jesus' breast at the Last Supper. The point of the story is that wicked men will see the righteous in a happy state, while they themselves are in torment, and that a "great chasm" that can never be spanned exists between them (Luke 16:26). Abraham's bosom is obviously a place of peace, rest, and joy—in other words, paradise.

In the Hebrew Scriptures, the word used to describe the realm of the dead is *sheol*. It simply means "the place of the dead" or "the place of departed souls/spirits." The New Testament Greek equivalent to *sheol* is *hades*, which is also a general reference to "the place of the dead." Sheol/hades is divided into a place of blessing (where Lazarus was in Luke 16) and a place of torment (where the rich man was in Luke 16). Sheol also seems to be a temporary place where souls are kept as they await the final resurrection. The souls of the righteous, at death, go directly into the presence of God—the part of sheol called "heaven," "paradise," or "Abraham's bosom" (Luke 23:43; 2 Corinthians 5:8; Philippians 1:23).

The Greek word *gehenna* is used in the New Testament for "hell" (see Matthew 5:29; 23:33). The word is derived from the Hebrew word *ge-hinnom*, which designated a valley south of Jerusalem—a repulsive place where trash and refuse were burned. Jesus referenced Gehenna as a symbol of the place of judgment after death.

The lake of fire, mentioned only in Revelation 19:20 and 20:10, 14–15, is the final hell, the place of eternal punishment for all unrepentant rebels, both angelic and human (Matthew 25:41). It is described as a place of burning sulfur, and those in it experience eternal, unspeakable agony of an unrelenting nature (Luke 16:24; Mark 9:45–46). Those who have rejected Christ and are in the temporary abode of the dead in hades/sheol have the lake of fire as their final destination.

But those whose names are written in the Lamb's Book of Life should have no fear of this terrible fate. By faith in Christ and His blood shed on the cross for our sins, we are destined to live eternally in the presence of God.

29. Did Jesus go to hell between His death and resurrection?

There is a great deal of confusion regarding this question. The concept that Jesus went to hell after His death on the cross comes primarily from the Apostles' Creed, which states, "He descended into hell." There are also a few Scripture passages that, depending on how they are translated, describe Jesus going to "hell." In studying this issue, it is important to first understand what the Bible teaches about the realm of the dead.

In the Hebrew Scriptures, the word used to describe the realm of the dead is *sheol*. It simply means "the place of the dead" or "the place of departed souls/spirits." The New Testament Greek equivalent of *sheol* is *hades*, which also refers to "the place of the dead." The New Testament indicates that sheol/hades is a temporary place, where souls are kept as they await the final resurrection and judgment. Revelation 20:11–15 makes a clear distinction between hades and the lake of fire. The lake of fire is the permanent and final place of judgment for the lost. Hades, then, is a temporary place. Many people refer to both hades and the lake of fire as "hell," and this causes confusion. Jesus did not go to a place of torment after His death, but He did go to hades.

Sheol/hades is a realm with two divisions—a place of blessing and a place of judgment (Matthew 11:23; 16:18; Luke 10:15; 16:23; Acts 2:27–31). The abodes of the saved and the lost are both generally called "hades" in the Bible. The abode of the saved is also called

"Abraham's bosom" (KJV) or "Abraham's side" (NIV) in Luke 16:22 and "paradise" in Luke 23:43. The abodes of the saved and the lost are separated by a "great chasm" (Luke 16:26). When Jesus died, He went to the blessed side of sheol, or paradise. (Some believe, based on a particular interpretation of Ephesians 4:8–10, that Jesus took believers with Him from sheol to another place of bliss that we now call heaven. More likely, Ephesians 4 refers to the ascension of Christ.) All the unbelieving dead go to the cursed side of hades to await the final judgment. All the believing dead go to the blessed side of hades to await the resurrection. Did Jesus go to sheol/hades? Yes, according to Jesus' own words, He went to sheol (Matthew 12:39–40)—the blessed side of sheol.

Some of the confusion has arisen from such passages as Psalm 16:10–11 as translated in the King James Version: "For thou wilt not leave my soul in hell; neither wilt thou suffer thine Holy One to see corruption. Thou wilt show me the path of life." "Hell" is not a correct translation in this verse. A correct reading would be "the grave" or "sheol." Jesus said to the thief beside Him, "Today you will be with me in paradise" (Luke 23:43); He did not say, "I will see you in hell." Jesus' body was in the tomb; His soul/spirit went to be with the blessed in sheol/hades. Unfortunately, in many versions of the Bible, translators are not consistent, or specific, in how they translate the Hebrew and Greek words for "sheol," "hades," and "hell."

Some have the viewpoint that Jesus went to "hell" or the suffering side of sheol/hades in order to further be punished for our sins. This idea is completely unbiblical. It was the death of Jesus on the cross that sufficiently provided for our redemption. It was His shed blood that effected our own cleansing from sin (1 John 1:7–9). As He hung there on the cross, He took the sin burden of the whole human race upon Himself. He became sin for us: "God made him who had no sin to be sin for us, so that in him we might become the righteousness of God" (2 Corinthians 5:21). This imputation of sin helps us understand Christ's struggle in the garden of Gethsemane with the cup that He asked to pass from Him (Matthew 26:39).

As Jesus neared death, He said, "It is finished" (John 19:30). His suffering in our place was completed. His soul/spirit went to hades (the place of the dead). Jesus did not go to "hell" or the suffering side of hades; He went to "Abraham's side" or the blessed side of hades. Jesus' suffering ended the moment He died. The payment for sin was paid. He then awaited the resurrection of His body and His return to glory in His ascension. Did Jesus go to hell? No. Did Jesus go to sheol/hades? Yes.

30. What happens after death?

Within the Christian faith, there is a significant amount of confusion regarding what happens after death. Some hold that after death everyone "sleeps" until the final judgment, after which everyone will be sent to heaven or hell. Others believe that at the moment of death people are instantly judged and sent to their eternal destinations. Still others claim that when people die, their souls/spirits are sent to a temporary heaven or hell to await the final resurrection, the final judgment, and the finality of their eternal destination. So, what exactly does the Bible say happens after death?

First, for the believer in Jesus Christ, the Bible tells us that after death believers' souls/spirits are taken to heaven, because their sins were forgiven when they received Christ as Savior (John 3:16, 18, 36). For believers, death means being "away from the body and at home with the Lord" (2 Corinthians 5:6–8). However, passages such as 1 Corinthians 15:50–54 and 1 Thessalonians 4:13–17 describe believers being resurrected and given glorified bodies. If believers go to be with Christ immediately after death, what is the purpose of this resurrection? It seems that while the souls/spirits of believers go to be with Christ immediately at death, the physical body remains in the grave "sleeping." At the resurrection of believers, the physical body is resurrected, glorified, and reunited with the soul/spirit. This reunited and glorified body-soul-spirit will be the state of existence for believers for eternity in the new heavens and new earth (Revelation 21–22).

Second, for those who do not receive Jesus Christ as Savior, death means everlasting punishment. However, similar to the destiny of believers, it seems that unbelievers also go to a temporary holding place to await their final resurrection, judgment, and eternal destiny. Luke 16:22–23 describes a rich man being tormented immediately after death. Revelation 20:11–15 describes all the unbelieving dead being resurrected, judged at the great white throne, and cast into the lake of fire. Unbelievers, then, are not sent to hell (the lake of fire) immediately after death, but they are rather sent to a temporary realm of judgment and anguish. The rich man cried out, "I am in agony in this fire" (Luke 16:24).

After death, a person resides in either a place of comfort or in a place of torment. These realms act as a temporary "heaven" and a temporary "hell" until the resurrection. At that point, the soul is re-united with the body, but no one's eternal destiny will change. The first resurrection is for the "blessed and holy" (Revelation 20:6)—everyone who is in Christ—and those who are part of the first resurrection will enter the millennial kingdom and, ultimately, the new heaven and new earth (Revelation 21:1). The other resurrection happens after Christ's millennial kingdom, and it involves a judgment on the wicked and unbelieving "according to what they had done" (Revelation 20:13). These, whose names are not in the book of life, will be sent to the lake of fire to experience the "second death" (Revelation 20:14–15). The new earth and the lake of fire—these two destinations are final and eternal. People go to one or the other, based entirely on whether they have trusted Jesus Christ for salvation (Matthew 25:46; John 3:36).

31. What is the difference between the soul and the spirit of humanity?

The soul and the spirit are the two primary immaterial parts ascribed to humanity in Scripture. Discerning the precise differences between the two can be confusing. The word *spirit* refers only to the immaterial facet of humanity. Human beings have a spirit, but we are not spirits. However, in Scripture, only believers are said to be spiritually alive (1 Corinthians 2:11; Hebrews 4:12; James 2:26); unbelievers are spiritually dead (Ephesians 2:1–5; Colossians 2:13). In Paul's writing, the spiritual is pivotal to the life of the believer (1 Corinthians 2:14; 3:1; Ephesians 1:3; 5:19; Colossians 1:9; 3:16). The spirit is the element in humanity that gives us the ability to have an intimate relationship with God. The word *spirit* refers to the immaterial part of humanity that "connects" with God, who Himself is spirit (John 4:24).

The word *soul* can refer to both the immaterial and material aspects of humanity. Humans *have* a spirit but *are* souls. In its most basic sense, the word *soul* means "life"; beyond this essential meaning, the Bible speaks of the soul in many contexts. One of these is in relation to humanity's basic selfishness (e.g., Luke 12:19). Human beings have a sinful nature, and our souls are tainted with sin. The soul, as the life essence of the body, is removed at the time of physical death (Genesis 35:18 NKJV). The soul, as with the spirit, is the center of many spiritual and emotional experiences (Job 30:25; Psalm 43:5; Jeremiah 13:17). The word *soul* can refer to the whole person, whether alive on earth or in the afterlife (see Revelation 6:9).

The soul and the spirit are connected, but separable (Hebrews 4:12). The soul is the essence of humanity's being; it is who we are. The spirit is the immaterial part of humanity that connects with God.

32. Do pets go to heaven?

The Bible does not give any explicit teaching on whether pets/animals have souls, or spirits, or whether pets/animals will be in heaven. However, we can use general biblical principles to develop some clarity on the subject. The Bible states that both man (Genesis 2:7) and animals (Genesis 1:30; 6:17; 7:15, 22) have the "breath of life"; that is, both man and animals are living beings. The primary difference between human beings and animals is that humanity is made in the image and likeness of God (Genesis 1:26–27), while animals are not. Being made in the image and likeness of God means that human beings are like God in some ways; they are capable of spirituality; they have a mind, emotion, and will; and part of their being continues after death. If pets/animals do have a "soul" (or spirit or immaterial aspect), it must therefore be of a different and lesser "quality." This difference possibly means that pet/animal "souls" do not continue in existence after death.

Another factor to consider regarding whether pets will be in heaven is that animals are a part of God's creative process in Genesis. God created the animals and said they were good (Genesis 1:25). Therefore, there is no reason why there could not be pets/animals on the new earth (Revelation 21:1). There will most definitely be animals during the millennial kingdom (Isaiah 11:6; 65:25). It is impossible to say definitively whether some of these animals might be the pets we had here on earth. We do know that God is just and that when we get to heaven, we will find ourselves in complete agreement with His decision on this issue, whatever it may be.

33. What is the gift of speaking in tongues?

The first occurrence of speaking in tongues occurred on the day of Pentecost in Acts 2:1–4. The apostles shared the gospel with the crowds, speaking to them in their own languages. The crowds were amazed: "We hear them declaring the wonders of God in our own tongues!" (Acts 2:11). The Greek word translated "tongues" literally means "languages." Therefore, the gift of tongues is speaking in a language the speaker has never learned in order to minister to someone who does speak that language. In 1 Corinthians 12–14, Paul discusses miraculous gifts, saying, "Now, brothers and sisters, if I come to you and speak in tongues, what good will I be to you, unless I bring you some revelation or knowledge or prophecy or word of instruction?" (1 Corinthians 14:6). According to the apostle Paul, and in agreement with the tongues described in Acts, speaking in tongues is valuable to the one hearing God's message in his or her own language, but it is useless to everyone else unless it is interpreted/translated.

A person with the gift of interpreting tongues (1 Corinthians 12:30) could understand what a tongues speaker was saying even though he did not know the language being spoken. The tongues interpreter would then communicate the message of the tongues speaker to everyone else, so all could understand. "For this reason the one who speaks in a tongue should pray that they may interpret what they say" (1 Corinthians 14:13). Paul's conclusion regarding tongues that were not interpreted is powerful: "But in the church I would rather speak five intelligible words to instruct others than ten thousand words in a tongue" (1 Corinthians 14:19).

Is the gift of tongues for today? First Corinthians 13:8 mentions the gift of tongues ceasing, although it connects the ceasing with the arrival of the "perfect" in 1 Corinthians 13:10 (ESV). Some point to a difference in the tense of the Greek verbs—prophecy and knowledge "will cease" and "will pass away," but tongues "will be ceased"—as evidence for tongues ceasing before the arrival of the "perfect." While a possible interpretation, this is not explicitly clear from the text. Some also point to passages such as Isaiah 28:11 and Joel 2:28–29 as evidence that speaking in tongues was a sign of God's oncoming judgment. First Corinthians 14:22 describes tongues as a "sign, not for believers but for unbelievers." Using this verse, cessationists argue that the gift of tongues was a warning to the Jews that God was going to judge Israel for rejecting Jesus Christ as Messiah. Therefore, when God did in fact judge Israel (with the destruction of Jerusalem by the Romans in AD 70), the gift of tongues no longer served its intended purpose. This view is also possible, but the primary purpose of tongues being fulfilled does not necessarily demand the gift's cessation. Scripture does not conclusively assert that the gift of speaking in tongues has ceased.

At the same time, if the gift of speaking in tongues were active in the church today, it would be performed in agreement with Scripture.

It would be a real and intelligible language (1 Corinthians 14:10). It would be for the purpose of communicating God's Word with a person of another language (Acts 2:6–12). It would be exercised in the church in agreement with the command God gave through Paul, "If anyone speaks in a tongue, two—or at the most three—should speak, one at a time, and someone must interpret. If there is no interpreter, the speaker should keep quiet in the church and speak to himself and to God" (1 Corinthians 14:27–28). It would also be in accordance with 1 Corinthians 14:33, "For God is not the author of confusion but of peace, as in all the churches of the saints" (NKJV).

God can definitely give a person the gift of speaking in tongues to enable him or her to communicate with a person who speaks another language. The Holy Spirit is sovereign in the dispersion of the spiritual gifts (1 Corinthians 12:11). Just imagine how much more productive missionaries could be if they did not have to go to language school and were instantly able to speak to people in their own language. However, God does not seem to be doing this. Tongues does not seem to occur today in the manner it did in the New Testament, despite the fact that it would be immensely useful. The majority of believers who claim to practice the gift of speaking in tongues do not do so in agreement with the Scriptures mentioned above. These facts lead to the conclusion that the gift of tongues has ceased or is at least a rarity in God's plan for the church today.

34. What is the anointing? What does it mean to be anointed?

In the Bible, anointing with oil is performed in religious ceremonies and used for grooming (Ruth 3:3; Matthew 6:17), refreshment (Luke 7:46), medicinal treatments (Luke 10:34), and burial traditions (Mark 16:1).

Ceremonial anointing in the Old Testament was a physical act involving the smearing, rubbing, or pouring of sacred oil on someone's head (or on an object) as an outward symbol that God had chosen and set apart the person (or object) for a specific holy purpose.

The Hebrew term *mashach* meant "to anoint or smear with oil." The oil used for religious anointing was carefully blended with fine spices according to a specific formula prescribed by the Lord (Exodus 30:22–32). Using this oil for any other purpose was a serious offense carrying the penalty of being "cut off" from the community (Exodus 30:33).

Kings, priests, and prophets were anointed outwardly with oil to symbolize a more profound spiritual reality—that God's presence was with them and His favor was upon them (Psalm 20:6; 28:8). While David was still a young shepherd, God told Samuel to anoint him to become king over Israel (1 Samuel 16:3). From that day forward, the Spirit of the Lord rested powerfully upon David's life (1 Samuel 16:13; Psalm 89:20).

Centuries before David's time, the Lord had instructed Moses to consecrate Aaron and his sons to serve as priests (Exodus 28:41; 30:30; Leviticus 8:30; 10:7). God authenticated their priestly ministry with the fiery glory of His presence that consumed their offerings. Holy items, including the tabernacle itself, were also set apart or consecrated by anointing for use in worship and sacrificial ceremonies (Genesis 28:18; Exodus 30:26–29; 40:9–11).

The Bible contains a literal reference to a prophet's anointing when the Lord commanded Elijah to anoint Elisha as the prophet to succeed him (1 Kings 19:16). It also includes metaphorical references to anointing to indicate that prophets were empowered and protected by the Spirit of the Lord to perform their calling (1 Chronicles 16:22; Psalm 105:15).

Anointing the head with oil was also an ancient custom of hospitality shown to honored guests. In Psalm 23:5, King David pictures himself as an esteemed guest at the Lord's table. This practice of anointing a dinner guest with oil reappears in the Gospels (Luke 7:46; Mark 14:3–9; John 12:3).

In the New Testament, Jesus Christ reveals Himself as our anointed King, Priest, and Prophet. He is God's holy and chosen Son, the Mes-

siah. In fact, *Messiah*, which literally means "anointed one," is derived from the Hebrew word for "anointed." *Christ* (*Christos* in Greek)
means "the anointed one."

Jesus declared at the launch of His ministry, "The Spirit of the Lord
is on me, because he has anointed me to proclaim good news to the
poor . . . to proclaim freedom for the prisoners and recovery of sight
for the blind, to set the oppressed free" (Luke 4:18; cf. Isaiah 61:1).
Jesus Christ fulfilled Old Testament prophecy as the Anointed One,
the chosen Messiah (Luke 4:21). He proved His anointing through
the miracles He performed and the life He sacrificed as Savior of the
world (Acts 10:38–40).

There is also a sense in which Christians today are anointed.
Through Jesus Christ, believers receive "an anointing from the Holy
One" (1 John 2:20). This anointing is not expressed in an outward
ceremony but through sharing in the gift of the Holy Spirit (Romans
8:11). At the moment of salvation, believers are indwelt by the Holy
Spirit and joined to Christ, the Anointed One. As a result, we partake
of His anointing (2 Corinthians 1:21–22). According to one scholar,
this anointing "expresses the sanctifying influences of the Holy Spirit
upon Christians who are priests and kings unto God."[1]

The New Testament also associates anointing oil with healing and
prayer. When Jesus sent out the disciples to preach the gospel, "they
cast out many demons and healed many sick people, anointing them
with olive oil" (Mark 6:13 NLT). James instructs believers to "call
the elders of the church to pray over them" when they are sick "and
anoint them with oil in the name of the Lord" for healing (James
5:14).

Those in charismatic religious circles speak of "the anointing" as
something Christians can and should be seeking. It is common for
them to speak of "anointed" preachers, sermons, ministries, songs,
etc., and to advise others to "unlock their anointing" or "walk in the
anointing." The idea is that the anointing is an outpouring of God's
power to accomplish a task through the anointed one. Charismatics claim there are corporate anointings as well as various types of

individual anointings: the five-fold anointing; the apostolic anointing; and for women, the Ruth anointing, the Deborah anointing, the Anna anointing, etc. Some even speak of a "Davidic anointing" upon musical instruments—"anointed" instruments are played by God Himself to drive away demons and take worship to a higher level than ever before. Special anointings are said to allow a person to use his spiritual gift to a "higher degree." Charismatics say that special anointings are received by "releasing one's faith."

Much of the charismatic teaching on the anointing goes beyond what Scripture says. In their hunger for signs and wonders, many charismatics seek new and ever more titillating experiences, and that requires more outpourings, more spiritual baptisms, and more anointings. But the Bible points to one anointing of the Spirit, just as it points to one baptism: "As for you, the anointing you received from him remains in you" (1 John 2:27; see also 2 Timothy 1:14). This same passage also refutes another misconception, namely that Satan can somehow steal a believer's anointing. We don't need to worry about losing the anointing we received because Scripture says it *remains.*

Another aberrant teaching concerning the anointing of the Spirit is the "*Mimshach* anointing." *Mimshach* is a Hebrew word related to *mashach* ("anoint") and found only in Ezekiel 28:14, where it is said the anointed one "covers" (NKJV) or "covers and protects" (AMP). According to some in the Word of Faith camp, the *Mimshach* anointing (which was bestowed on Lucifer before his fall) is available now to believers. Receiving this anointing will cause everything one touches to increase or expand, and the anointed one will experience greater levels of success, material gain, health, and power.

Rather than chase after a new anointing, believers should remember they *already* have the gift of the Holy Spirit. The Spirit is not given in part, He does not come in portions or doses, and He is not taken away. We have the promise that "his divine power has given us everything we need for a godly life through our knowledge of him who called us by his own glory and goodness" (2 Peter 1:3).

35. What is the difference between mercy and grace?

Mercy and grace are closely related. While the terms have similar meanings, *grace* and *mercy* are not exactly the same. Mercy has to do with kindness and compassion; it is often spoken of in the context of God not punishing us as our sins deserve. Grace includes kindness and compassion but also carries the idea of bestowing a gift or favor. It may help to view mercy as a subset of grace. In Scripture, mercy is often equated with a deliverance from judgment (e.g., Deuteronomy 4:30–31; 1 Timothy 1:13), and grace is always the extending of a blessing to the unworthy.

According to the Bible, we have all sinned (Ecclesiastes 7:20; Romans 3:23; 1 John 1:8). As a result of that sin, we all deserve death (Romans 6:23) and eternal judgment in the lake of fire (Revelation 20:12–15). Given what we deserve, every day we live is an act of God's mercy. If God gave us all what we deserve, we would all be, right now, condemned for eternity. In Psalm 51:1–2, David cries out, "Have mercy on me, O God, according to your unfailing love; according to your great compassion blot out my transgressions. Wash away all my iniquity and cleanse me from my sin." Pleading for God's mercy is asking Him to show kindness and withhold the judgment we deserve.

We deserve nothing good from God. God does not owe us any good thing. Any good we experience is a result of the grace of God (Ephesians 2:5). *Grace* is simply defined as "unmerited favor." God favors us—He shows us approval and kindness—in blessing us with good things that we do not deserve and could never earn. Common grace refers to the blessings that God bestows on all of mankind regardless of their spiritual standing before Him, while saving grace is that special blessing whereby God sovereignly bestows unmerited divine assistance upon His elect for their regeneration and sanctification.

Mercy and grace are evident in the salvation that is available through Jesus Christ. We deserved judgment, but in Christ we receive mercy from God and are delivered from judgment. In Christ we receive eternal salvation, forgiveness of sins, and abundant life (John 10:10)—all gifts of grace. Our response to the mercy and grace of God should be to fall on our knees in worship and thanksgiving. Hebrews 4:16 declares, "Let us then approach God's throne of grace with confidence, so that we may receive mercy and find grace to help us in our time of need."

36. Calvinism vs. Arminianism—which view is correct?

Calvinism and Arminianism are two systems of theology that attempt to explain the relationship between God's sovereignty and man's responsibility in the matter of salvation. Calvinism is named for John Calvin, a French theologian who lived from 1509 to 1564. Arminianism is named for Jacobus Arminius, a Dutch theologian who lived from 1560 to 1609.

Both systems can be summarized with five points. Calvinism holds to the total depravity of man while Arminianism holds to partial depravity. Calvinism's doctrine of total depravity states that every aspect of humanity is corrupted by sin; therefore, human beings are unable to come to God on their own accord. Partial depravity states that every aspect of humanity is tainted by sin, but not to the extent that human beings are unable to place faith in God of their own accord. Note: classical Arminianism rejects "partial depravity" and holds a view very close to Calvinistic "total depravity" (although the extent and meaning of that depravity are debated in Arminian circles). In general, Arminians believe there is an intermediate state between total depravity and salvation. In this state, made possible by prevenient grace, the sinner is being drawn to Christ and has the God-given ability to choose salvation.

Calvinism includes the belief that election is unconditional, while Arminianism believes in conditional election. Unconditional election is the view that God elects individuals to salvation based entirely on His will, not on anything inherently worthy in the individual or on any act performed by the individual. Conditional election states that God elects individuals to salvation based on His foreknowledge of who will believe in Christ unto salvation, thereby on the condition that the individual chooses God.

Calvinism sees the atonement as limited, while Arminianism sees it as unlimited. This is likely the most controversial of the five points. Limited atonement is the belief that Jesus only died for the elect. Unlimited atonement is the belief that Jesus died for all, but that His death is not effectual until a person receives Him by faith.

Calvinism includes the belief that God's grace is irresistible, while Arminianism says that an individual can resist the grace of God. Irresistible grace argues that when God calls a person to salvation, that person will inevitably come to salvation. Resistible grace states that God calls all to salvation, but that many people resist and reject this call.

Calvinism holds to perseverance of the saints while Arminianism holds to conditional salvation. Perseverance of the saints refers to the concept that a person who is elected by God will persevere in faith and will not permanently deny Christ or turn away from Him. Conditional salvation is the view that a believer in Christ can, of his/her own free will, turn away from Christ and thereby lose salvation. Note: many Arminians deny "conditional salvation" and instead hold to "eternal security."

So, in the Calvinism vs. Arminianism debate, who is correct? It is interesting that in the diversity of the body of Christ, there are all sorts of mixtures of Calvinism and Arminianism. There are five-point Calvinists and five-point Arminians and three-point Calvinists and two-point Arminians. Many believers arrive at some sort of mixture of the two views. Ultimately, it is our opinion that both systems fail in that they attempt to explain the unexplainable. Human beings are incapable of fully grasping a concept such as this. Yes, God is absolutely sovereign and knows all. Yes, human beings are called to make a genuine decision to place faith in Christ unto salvation. These two facts seem contradictory to us, but in the mind of God they make perfect sense.

37. What is the meaning of *BC* and *AD*?

It is commonly thought that BC stands for "before Christ" and AD stands for "after death." This is only half correct. How could the year 1 BC have been "before Christ" and AD 1 been "after death"? BC does stand for "before Christ." AD actually stands for the Latin phrase *Anno Domini*, which means "in the year of our Lord." The BC/AD dating system is not taught in the Bible. It actually was not fully implemented and accepted until several centuries after Jesus' death.

It is interesting to note that the purpose of the BC/AD dating system was to make the birth of Jesus Christ the dividing point of world history. However, when the BC/AD system was being calculated, a mistake was made in pinpointing the year of Jesus' birth. Scholars later determined that Jesus was born around 6–4 BC, not AD 1. That is not the crucial issue. The birth, life, ministry, death, and resurrection of Christ are the turning points in world history. It is fitting, therefore, that Jesus Christ is the separation of old and new. BC was "before Christ," and since His birth, we have been living "in the year of our Lord." Viewing our era as "the year of our Lord" is appropriate because He *is* Lord. Philippians 2:10–11 says, "That at the name of Jesus every knee should bow, in heaven and on earth and under the earth, and every tongue confess that Jesus Christ is Lord, to the glory of God the Father" (ESV).

In recent times, there has been a push to replace the BC and AD labels with BCE and CE, meaning "before common era" and "common era," respectively. The change is simply one of semantics—that is, AD 100 is the same as 100 CE; all that changes is the label. The advocates of the switch from BC/AD to BCE/CE say that the newer designations are better in that they are devoid of religious connotation and thus prevent offending other cultures and religions that may not see Jesus as Lord. The irony, of course, is that what distinguishes BCE from CE is still the life and times of Jesus Christ.

SECTION 5
Questions about the End Times

38. What signs indicate that the end times are approaching?

In Matthew 24:5–8 Jesus gives us some important clues for discerning the approach of the end times: "Many will come in my name, claiming, 'I am the Messiah,' and will deceive many. You will hear of wars and rumors of wars, but see to it that you are not alarmed. Such things must happen, but the end is still to come. Nation will rise against nation, and kingdom against kingdom. There will be famines and earthquakes in various places. All these are the beginning of birth pains." An increase in false messiahs, an increase in warfare, and increases in famines, plagues, and natural disasters—these are signs of the end times. In this passage, though, we are given a warning: we are not to be deceived because these events are only the beginning of birth pains; the end is still to come.

Some interpreters point to every earthquake, every political upheaval, and every attack on Israel as a sure sign that the end times are rapidly approaching. While the events may signal the approach of the last days, they are not necessarily indicators that the end times have arrived. The apostle Paul warned that the last days would bring a marked increase in false teaching: "The Spirit clearly says that in later times some will abandon the faith and follow deceiving spirits and things taught by demons" (1 Timothy 4:1). The last days are described as "terrible times" because of the increasingly evil character of man and people who actively "oppose the truth" (2 Timothy 3:1–9; see also 2 Thessalonians 2:3).

Other possible signs of the end times include a rebuilding of a Jewish temple in Jerusalem, increased hostility toward Israel, and advances toward a one-world government. The most prominent sign of the end times, however, is the nation of Israel itself. In 1948, Israel was recognized as a sovereign state, essentially for the first time since 605 BC, when the Babylonians took control of Judah. God promised Abraham that his posterity would have Canaan as "an everlasting possession" (Genesis 17:8), and Ezekiel prophesied a physical and spiritual resuscitation of Israel (Ezekiel 37). Having Israel as a nation in its own land is important in light of end-times prophecy because of Israel's prominence in eschatology (Daniel 10:14; 11:41; Revelation 11:8).

With these signs in mind, we can be wise and discerning regarding the expectation of the end times. We should not, however, interpret any of these singular events as a clear indication of the soon arrival of the end times. God has given us enough information that we can be prepared, and that is what we are called to be as our hearts cry out, "Come, Lord Jesus" (Revelation 22:20).

39. What do the seven churches in Revelation stand for?

The seven churches described in Revelation 2–3 are seven literal churches at the time that John the apostle was writing Revelation. Though they were literal churches in Asia Minor at that time, there is also spiritual significance for churches and believers today. The first purpose of the letters was to communicate with the literal churches and meet their needs. The second purpose was to reveal seven different types of individuals/churches throughout history and instruct them in God's truth.

A possible third purpose is to use the seven churches to foreshadow seven different periods in the history of the Church. The problem with this view is that each church displays characteristics that could fit the Church at any time of history. So, although there may be some truth to the seven churches representing seven eras, there is far too much speculation in this regard. Our focus should be on the messages God is giving us through the seven churches.

The seven churches are as follows:

1. Ephesus (Revelation 2:1–7)—the church that had forsaken its first love (2:4).
2. Smyrna (Revelation 2:8–11)—the church that would suffer persecution (2:10).
3. Pergamum (Revelation 2:12–17)—the church that needed to repent (2:16).
4. Thyatira (Revelation 2:18–29)—the church that had a false prophetess (2:20).
5. Sardis (Revelation 3:1–6)—the church that had fallen asleep (3:2).
6. Philadelphia (Revelation 3:7–13)—the church that had endured patiently (3:10).
7. Laodicea (Revelation 3:14–22)—the church with lukewarm faith (3:16).

40. Who are the Four Horsemen of the Apocalypse?

The Four Horsemen of the Apocalypse, or simply the Four Horsemen, are described in Revelation chapter 6, verses 1–8. The Four Horsemen are symbolic depictions of different events that will take place in the end times. As an example of the Bible's influence on culture at large, the Four Horsemen of the Apocalypse have been referenced many times in literature, paintings, movies, and other media, often as portents of an imminent cataclysm or the means by which a disaster comes to pass.

The Four Horsemen correspond with the first four seals opened by the Lamb as He opens the scroll of judgment in heaven (see Revelation 5). When the Lamb opens the first seal, one of the living creatures before the heavenly throne says to John, in a voice like thunder, "Come!" (Revelation 6:1). John then records what he sees: "I looked, and there before me was a white horse! Its rider held a bow, and he was given a crown, and he rode out as a conqueror bent on conquest" (Revelation 6:2).

The first Horseman likely refers to the Antichrist. He is the false imitator of the true Christ, who is also associated with a white horse (Revelation 19:11–16). At the beginning of the tribulation, the Antichrist will be given authority ("many crowns"), and he will wage war ("a bow"), conquering all who oppose him. This description agrees with Daniel's vision of a "horn, little one" (Daniel 7:8) that rises to power and is bent on conquest: "This horn was waging war against the holy people and defeating them" (Daniel 7:21; cf. Revelation 13:7).

When the Lamb opens the second seal, the second living creature says, "Come!" (Revelation 6:3). John looks and dutifully records what he sees: "Then another horse came out, a fiery red one. Its rider was given power to take peace from the earth and to make people kill each other. To him was given a large sword" (Revelation 6:4). The second Horseman refers to terrible warfare that will break out in the end times. Those wars will include the Antichrist's rise to power, which requires the downfall of three other kings (Daniel 7:8), and possibly the Battle of Gog and Magog (Ezekiel 38–39).

The Lamb then opens the third seal, and the third living creature invites John to "Come!" (Revelation 6:5). The third Horseman then appears: "There before me was a black horse! Its rider was holding a pair of scales in his hand. Then I heard what sounded like a voice among the four living creatures, saying, 'Two pounds of wheat for a day's wages, and six pounds of barley for a day's wages, and do not damage the oil and the wine!'" (Revelation 6:5–6). The third Horseman of the Apocalypse portrays a great famine that will take place. Food is scarce, and prices are inflated beyond reason. The command to spare the oil and the wine seems to signify that the luxuries (oil and wine) will still be available during the famine, but the staples will not.

When the Lamb breaks open the fourth seal, the fourth living creature says, "Come!" (Revelation 6:7). John says, "I looked, and there before me was a pale horse! Its rider was named Death, and Hades was following close behind him. They were given power over a fourth of the earth to kill by sword, famine and plague, and by the wild beasts of the earth" (Revelation 6:8). The fourth Horseman of the Apocalypse is symbolic of death and devastation. The horse's pale color (in the original language, it's "pale green" or "yellowish green") denotes sickliness and biliousness. The fourth Horseman of the Apocalypse will bring further warfare and terrible famines along with awful plagues, diseases, and attacks by wild animals. A fourth of the world's population will die.

What is most amazing, or perhaps terrifying, is that the Four Horsemen of the Apocalypse are just precursors of even worse judgments that come later in the tribulation (Revelation chapters 8–9 and 16). For all the horror brought by the Four Horsemen, there is much more to come.

41. What is the tribulation? How do we know the tribulation will last seven years?

The tribulation is a future seven-year period when God will finish His discipline of Israel and finalize His judgment of the unbelieving world. The church, comprised of all who have trusted in the person and work of the Lord Jesus, will not be present during the tribulation (Got Questions Ministries takes a pretribulational approach to eschatology). The church will be removed from the earth in an event commonly called the rapture (1 Thessalonians 4:13–18; 1 Corinthians 15:51–53). In this way, the church is saved from the wrath to come (1 Thessalonians 5:9).

Throughout Scripture, the tribulation is associated with the day of the Lord, that time during which God personally intervenes in history to accomplish His plan (see Isaiah 2:12; 13:6–9; Joel 1:15; 2:1–31; 3:14; 1 Thessalonians 5:2). It is referred to as "tribulation . . . in the latter days" (Deuteronomy 4:30 ESV); the "great tribulation," which refers to the more intense second half of the seven-year period (Matthew 24:21 NKJV); "a time of distress" (Daniel 12:1); and "the time of Jacob's trouble" (Jeremiah 30:7 NKJV). And we have this description of the tribulation that attends the day of the Lord:

> "That day will be a day of wrath—
> a day of distress and anguish,
> a day of trouble and ruin,
> a day of darkness and gloom,
> a day of clouds and blackness—
> a day of trumpet and battle cry." (Zephaniah 1:15–16)

The tribulation will be marked by various divine judgments, celestial disturbances, natural disasters, and terrible plagues (see Revelation 6–16). In His mercy, God sets a limit on the duration of the tribulation. As Jesus said, "Those will be days of distress unequaled from the beginning, when God created the world, until now—and never to be equaled again. If the Lord had not cut short those days, no one would survive" (Mark 13:19–20).

Daniel 9:24–27 reveals the purpose and time of the tribulation. This passage speaks of 70 weeks that have been declared against "your people." Daniel's people are the Jews, the nation of Israel, and Daniel 9:24 speaks of a period of time in which God's purpose is "to finish transgression, to put an end to sin, to atone for wickedness, to bring in everlasting righteousness, to seal up vision and prophecy and to anoint the Most Holy Place." God declares that "seventy sevens" will fulfill all these things. The "sevens" are groups of years, so 70 sevens is 490 years. (Some translations refer to 70 "weeks" of years.)

In Daniel 9:25 and 26, the Messiah will be cut off after "seven sevens and sixty-two sevens" (69 total sevens), beginning with the decree to rebuild Jerusalem. In other words, 69 sevens (483 years) after the decree to rebuild is issued, the Messiah will die. Biblical historians confirm that 483 years passed from the time of the decree to rebuild Jerusalem to the time when Jesus was crucified. Most Christian scholars, regardless of their view of eschatology, have the above understanding of Daniel's 70 sevens.

God said that 70 weeks had been determined (490 years), but with the death of the Messiah, we only have 69 weeks accounted for (483 years). This leaves one seven-year period to be fulfilled "to finish transgression, to put an end to sin, to atone for wickedness, to bring in everlasting righteousness, to seal up vision and prophecy and to anoint the Most Holy Place" (Daniel 9:24). This final seven-year period is what we call the tribulation—the time when God finishes judging Israel and brings the Israelites back to Himself.

Daniel 9:27 gives a few highlights of the final week, the seven-year tribulation period: "[A ruler] will confirm a covenant with many for one 'seven.' In the middle of the 'seven' he will put an end to sacrifice and offering. And at the temple he will set up an abomination that causes desolation, until the end that is decreed is poured out on him." Jesus refers to this passage in Matthew 24:15. The ruler who confirms the covenant and then sets up the abomination is called "the beast" in Revelation 13. According to Daniel 9:27, the beast's covenant will be for seven years, but in the middle of this week (3½ years into the tribulation), the beast will break the covenant, putting a stop to the Jewish sacrifices. Revelation 13 explains that the beast will place an image of himself in the temple and require the world to worship him. Revelation 13:5 says that this will go on for 42 months, which is 3½ years (the second half of the tribulation). So, we see a covenant lasting to the middle of the "week" (Daniel 9:27 NKJV) and the beast who made the covenant demanding worship for 42 months (Revelation 13:5). Therefore, the total length of time is 84 months or 7 years.

We also have a reference to the last half of the tribulation in Daniel 7:25. There, the ruler will oppress God's people for "a time, times and half a time" (time=1 year; times=2 years; half a time=½ year; total of 3½ years). This time of oppression against the Jews is also described in Revelation 13:5–7 and is part of the great tribulation, the latter half of the seven-year tribulation when the beast, or the Antichrist, will be in power.

A further reference to the timing of events in the tribulation is found in Revelation 11:2–3, which speaks of 1,260 days and 42 months (both equaling 3½ years, using the "prophetic year" of 360 days). Also, Daniel 12:11–12 speaks of 1,290 days and 1,335 days from the midpoint of the tribulation. The additional days in Daniel 12 may include time after the tribulation for the judgment of the nations (Matthew 25:31–46) and time for the setting up of Christ's millennial kingdom (Revelation 20:4–6).

In summary, the tribulation is the seven-year period in the end times in which humanity's decadence and depravity will reach its fullness, with God judging accordingly. Also during that time, Israel will repent of their sin and receive Jesus as their Messiah, setting up a time of great blessing and restoration (Zephaniah 2:9–20; Isaiah 12; 35).

42. Does the Bible prophesy a one-world government and a one-world currency in the end times?

The Bible does not use the phrase *one-world government* or *one-world currency* in referring to the end times. It does, however, provide ample evidence to enable us to draw the conclusion that both will exist under the rule of the Antichrist in the last days.

In his apocalyptic vision in the book of Revelation, the apostle John sees the "beast," whom we identify as the Antichrist, rising out of the sea having seven heads and ten horns (Revelation 13:1). Comparing this vision to Daniel's similar one (Daniel 7:16–24), we can conclude that some sort of world governance system will be inaugurated by the beast, the most powerful "horn" (Daniel 7:21), who will "wage war against God's holy people and . . . conquer them" (Revelation 13:7). The ten-nation confederacy is also seen in the statue of Daniel 2:41–42, where the final world government consists of ten entities represented by the statue's ten toes. Whichever the ten nations are and however they come to unite, Scripture is clear that the beast will subdue three of them (Daniel 7:8), and the rest will do his bidding.

John describes the ruler of this vast empire as having power and great authority (Revelation 13:2), given to him by Satan himself. This ruler receives worship from "all the world" (Revelation 13:3–4 NKJV) and will have authority over "every tribe, people, language and nation" (Revelation 13:7). This person will truly be the leader of a one-world government that is recognized as sovereign over all other governments. We see nations today willing to give up some of their sovereignty to combat climate change; it's easy to imagine that the disasters and plagues described in Revelation 6–11 would create such a monumental crisis that the nations of the world will embrace anything and anyone who promises a solution.

Once entrenched in power, the beast (the Antichrist) and the power behind him (Satan) will move to establish absolute control. In demanding worship, Satan edges toward his goal of being like God (see Isaiah 14:12–14). To truly control people, commerce must be controlled. Revelation 13 describes how this will happen. Everyone, "great and small, rich and poor, free and slave," will be forced to receive some type of mark "on their right hands or on their foreheads" in order to buy and sell (Revelation 13:16). No doubt the majority of people in the world will receive the mark simply to survive. This new system of commerce will be universal, it will be compulsory, and it will be associated with the worship of the beast (Revelation 13:15). There is a great deal of speculation as to what form this mark will take and how it will be affixed, but the technologies available right now could accomplish it easily.

Those who are left behind after the rapture of the church will be faced with an excruciating choice—accept the mark of the beast or face starvation and horrific persecution by the Antichrist and his followers. But those who come to Christ during that time, those whose names are written in the Lamb's Book of Life (Revelation 13:8), will choose to endure, even through martyrdom.

43. Will we be able to see and know our friends and family members in heaven? Will we know each other in heaven?

Many people say the first thing they want to do when they arrive in heaven is see all their friends and loved ones who have passed on before them. That will indeed be a blessed time as believers reunite to fellowship, worship God, and enjoy the glorious wonders of heaven. One of the blessings is that we will know our friends and family members in heaven, and we will be known.

Our ability to recognize people in the afterlife is suggested in several passages of Scripture. At the transfiguration of Christ, Moses and Elijah made an appearance, and they were recognizable (Matthew 17:3–4). Though they had departed this world centuries prior, both

Moses and Elijah remained distinct persons who had not lost their identity. In Luke 16:19–31, Abraham, Lazarus, and the rich man are all recognizable after death. King Saul recognized Samuel's description given by the witch of Endor when she summoned Samuel from the realm of the dead (1 Samuel 28:8–17). And when David's young son died, David declared, "I will go to him, but he will not return to me" (2 Samuel 12:23). David's words imply that he believed he would recognize his son in heaven. In all these examples, the Bible seems to indicate that after death, we will still be recognizable to each other either by appearance or by knowing.

The Bible declares that, when we arrive in heaven, we will "be like him [Jesus], for we shall see him as he is" (1 John 3:2). Just as our earthly bodies were of the first man, Adam, so will our resurrection bodies be like Christ's glorious body (1 Corinthians 15:47; Philippians 3:21). "And just as we have borne the image of the earthly man, so shall we bear the image of the heavenly man. . . . For the perishable must clothe itself with the imperishable, and the mortal with immortality" (1 Corinthians 15:49, 53). Jesus was recognizable after His resurrection (John 20:16, 20; 21:12; 1 Corinthians 15:4–7), so it stands to reason that we also will be recognizable in our glorified bodies.

Being able to see our loved ones is a glorious aspect of heaven. What a pleasure it will be to reunite with our loved ones and worship God with them in His presence for all eternity!

SECTION 6

Questions about the Old Testament

44. What happened on each of the days of creation?

The creation account is found in Genesis 1–2. Most of God's creative work was done by speaking, an indication of the power and authority of His Word. Let us look at each day of God's creative work:

Creation Day 1 (Genesis 1:1–5)

God creates the heavens and the earth. "The heavens" refers to everything beyond the earth, outer space. The earth is made but not formed in any specific way, although water is present. God then speaks light into existence. He then separates the light from the dark and names the light "day" and the darkness "night."

Creation Day 2 (Genesis 1:6–8)

God creates the sky. The sky forms a barrier between water upon the surface and the moisture in the air. At this point earth has an atmosphere.

Creation Day 3 (Genesis 1:9–13)

God creates dry land. Continents and islands rise above the water. The large bodies of water are named "seas," and the ground is named "land." God declares that all this is good.

God creates all plant life. He creates this life to be self-sustaining: plants can reproduce. The plants are created in great diversity (many "kinds"). The land is green and teeming with plant life. God declares that this work is also good.

Creation Day 4 (Genesis 1:14–19)

God creates all the stars and heavenly bodies. The movement of these will help man track time. Two great heavenly bodies are made in relation to the earth. The first is the sun, which is the primary source of light, and the second is the moon, which reflects the light of the sun. The movement of these bodies will distinguish day from night. This work is also declared to be good by God.

Creation Day 5 (Genesis 1:20–23)

God creates all life that lives in the water, in all of its marvelous diversity. God also makes all the birds. The language of the passage allows that this may be the time God made flying insects as well; if not, they are made on day 6. All these creatures have the ability to perpetuate their species by reproduction. The creatures made on day 5 are the first creatures blessed by God. God declares this work good.

Creation Day 6 (Genesis 1:24–31)

God creates all the creatures that live on dry land. This includes every type of creature not included on previous days. God also creates man. God declares this work good.

When God was creating man, He took counsel with Himself. "God said, 'Let us make mankind in our image, in our likeness'" (Genesis 1:26). This is not an explicit revelation of the Trinity but is part of the foundation for such, as God reveals an "us" within the Godhead. God makes mankind in His own image, and thus mankind is special above all other creatures. He makes them male and female and places them in authority over the earth and over all the other creatures. God blesses them and commands them to reproduce, fill the earth, and subdue it (bring it under the rightful stewardship of mankind as authorized by God). God announces that humans and all other creatures are to eat plants alone. God will not rescind this dietary restriction until Genesis 9:3–4.

God's creative work is complete at the end of the sixth day. The entire universe in all its beauty and perfection was fully formed in these six periods labeled as "days." At the completion of His creation, God announces that it is "very good" (Genesis 1:31).

Creation Day 7 (Genesis 2:1–3)

God rests. This in no way indicates He was weary from His creative efforts; rather, it denotes that the creation is complete. He stops creating. Further, God is establishing a pattern of one day in seven to rest. The keeping of this day will eventually be a distinguishing trait of God's chosen people, Israel (Exodus 20:8–11).

Many Christians interpret these "days" of creation as literal twenty-four-hour periods, a position called Young Earth Creationism. It should be noted that certain other interpretations of these "days" suggest they were indeterminate periods of time. The Day-Age Theory and Historical Creationism are two theories that interpret the biblical data in a way that allows for an older earth. Regardless, the events and accomplishments of each "day" are the same.

45. What does the Bible say about dinosaurs? Are there dinosaurs in the Bible?

The topic of dinosaurs in the Bible is part of a larger ongoing debate within the Christian community over the age of the earth, the proper interpretation of Genesis, and how to interpret the physical evidence we find all around us. Those who believe in an older age for the earth tend to agree that the Bible does not mention dinosaurs, because, according to the old-earth paradigm, dinosaurs died out millions of years before the first man ever walked the earth, so the men who wrote the Bible could not have seen living dinosaurs.

Those who believe in a younger age for the earth tend to agree that the Bible does mention dinosaurs, though it never actually uses the word *dinosaur*. Instead, it uses the Hebrew word *tanniyn*, which is translated a few different ways in our English Bibles. Sometimes it's "sea monster," and sometimes it's "serpent." It is most commonly translated "dragon" in the King James Version. The *tanniyn* appears to have been some sort of giant reptile. These creatures are mentioned nearly thirty times in the Old Testament (e.g., Psalm 74:13; Isaiah 27:1; 51:9) and were found both on land and in the water. Another Hebrew word, *livyathan*, transliterated *leviathan*, is used six times in Scripture (e.g., Job 41:1; Psalm 104:26) and refers to some type of large, fierce sea creature. The description of leviathan in Job 41 gives the impression of a strong yet graceful, unstoppable creature against which weapons are unavailing: "Nothing on earth is its equal" (Job 41:33).

Another giant creature the Bible describes, and that Job was familiar with, is the behemoth, said to be "a prime example of God's handiwork" (Job 40:19 NLT). The behemoth is a huge plant-eating animal that dwells by the water. Its bones are like "tubes of bronze," and its limbs are like "rods of iron" (Job 40:18); its tail is likened to a cedar tree (Job 40:17). Some have tried to identify the behemoth as an elephant or a hippopotamus. Others point out that elephants and hippopotamuses have very thin tails, nothing comparable to a cedar tree. Dinosaurs like the Brachiosaurus, Apatosaurus, and Saltasaurus, on the other hand, had huge tails that could easily be compared to a cedar tree.

Nearly every ancient civilization has left some sort of art depicting giant reptilian creatures. Petroglyphs and clay figurines found in North America resemble modern depictions of dinosaurs. Rock carvings in South America depict creatures resembling Triceratops, Diplodocus, and Tyrannosaurus Rex. Roman mosaics, Mayan pottery, and Babylonian city walls all testify to man's transcultural, geographically unbounded memories of these creatures. Thirteenth-century explorer Marco Polo wrote of seeing "huge serpents" in China: "At the fore part, near the head, they have two short legs, each with three claws, as well as eyes larger than a loaf and very glaring. The jaws are wide enough to swallow a man, the teeth are large and sharp, and their whole appearance is so formidable, that neither man, nor any kind of animal can approach them without terror."[1]

So, are there dinosaurs in the Bible? The matter is far from settled. It depends on how one interprets the available evidence. If the first two chapters of Genesis are taken literally, the result is a belief in a relatively young earth and the conviction that dinosaurs and man coexisted.

If dinosaurs and human beings coexisted, what happened to the dinosaurs? The Bible does not discuss the issue, but dinosaurs likely died out sometime after the flood due to a combination of dramatic environmental shifts and being relentlessly hunted to extinction.

46. Who was Cain's wife? Was Cain's wife his sister?

The Bible does not specifically say who Cain's wife was. The only possible answer is that Cain's wife was his sister or niece or great-niece, etc. The Bible does not say how old Cain was when he killed Abel (Genesis 4:8), but they both were likely full-grown adults. Adam and

Eve surely had given birth to more children than just Cain and Abel at the time Abel was killed. They definitely had many more children later (Genesis 5:4). The fact that Cain was scared for his own life after he killed Abel (Genesis 4:14) indicates that there were likely many other children and perhaps even grandchildren of Adam and Eve living at that time. Cain's wife (Genesis 4:17) was a daughter or granddaughter of Adam and Eve.

Since Adam and Eve were the first (and only) human beings, their children would have no other choice than to intermarry. God did not forbid interfamily marriage until much later, when there were enough people to make intermarriage unnecessary (Leviticus 18:6–18). The reason that incest today often results in genetic abnormalities is that when two people of similar genetics (e.g., a brother and sister) have children together, there is a high risk of their recessive characteristics becoming dominant. When people from different families have children, it is highly unlikely that both parents will carry the same recessive traits. The human genetic code has become increasingly damaged over the centuries as genetic defects are multiplied, amplified, and passed down from generation to generation. Adam and Eve were perfectly designed by God, and their lack of genetic defects enabled them (and the first few generations of their descendants) to have a greater quality of health than we do now. When sin entered the world through Adam and Eve's disobedience to God, it brought sickness, disease, and a compromised bloodline for all their descendants. Their children had few, if any, genetic mutations; therefore, they could intermarry safely.

47. Why did God allow polygamy/bigamy in the Bible?

The question of polygamy is interesting in that most people today view polygamy as immoral. While the Bible nowhere explicitly condemns it, the Bible does reveal God's intention for marriage: one man married to one woman for life (Genesis 2:23–24; Matthew 19:4–6). The first instance of polygamy/bigamy in the Bible is that of Lamech in Genesis 4:19: "Lamech married two women." Several prominent men in the Old Testament were polygamists. Abraham, Jacob, David, Solomon, and others all had multiple wives. Solomon had seven hundred wives and three hundred concubines (essentially wives of a lower status), according to 1 Kings 11:3. What are we to make of these instances of polygamy in the Old Testament? There are three questions that need to be answered: (1) Why did God allow polygamy in the Old Testament? (2) How does God view polygamy today? and (3) Why did it change?

1. Why did God allow polygamy in the Old Testament? The Bible does not specifically say why God allowed polygamy, and we must remember that allowance is not the same as approval. As we speculate about God's permissive silence, there is at least one key factor to consider. In patriarchal societies, it was nearly impossible for an unmarried woman to provide for herself. Women were often uneducated and untrained. Women relied on their fathers, brothers, and husbands for provision and protection. Unmarried women were often subjected to prostitution and slavery.

So, God may have allowed polygamy to protect and provide for the women who otherwise may have been left destitute. A man would take multiple wives and serve as the provider and protector of all of them. While not ideal, living in a polygamist household was far better than the alternative of prostitution, slavery, or starvation. In addition to the protection/provision factor, polygamy enabled a much faster expansion of humanity, fulfilling God's command to "be fruitful and increase in number; multiply on the earth" (Genesis 9:7).

2). How does God view polygamy today? Even while recording cases of polygamy, the Bible presents monogamy as the plan that conforms most closely to God's ideal for marriage. The Bible says that God's original intention was for one man to be married to only one woman: "For this reason a man shall leave his father and mother and be joined to his wife [not wives], and they shall become one flesh [not multiple fleshes]" (Genesis 2:24 NASB). The consistent use of the singular in this verse should be noted. Later, in Deuteronomy 17:14–20, God says that the kings were not to acquire multiple wives (or horses or gold). While this cannot be interpreted as a command that kings must be monogamous, it does indicate that having multiple wives causes problems. Such problems can be clearly seen in the life of Solomon (1 Kings 11:3–4; Nehemiah 13:26).

In the New Testament, 1 Timothy 3:2, 12 and Titus 1:6 (ESV) list being "the husband of one wife" as a qualification for spiritual leadership in the church. The phrase could literally be translated "a one-woman man." However broadly or narrowly that qualification should be applied, in no sense can a polygamist be considered a "one-woman man." Is the prohibition of polygamy only for elders and deacons, the "example-setters"? No, the standard of monogamy should apply to all Christians.

Ephesians 5:22–33 speaks of the relationship between husbands and wives. When referring to a husband (singular), the passage always also refers to a wife (singular). "For the husband is the head of the wife [singular]. . . . He who loves his wife [singular] loves himself. For this reason a man will leave his father and mother and be united to his wife [singular], and the two will become one flesh. . . . Each one of you also must love his wife [singular] as he loves himself, and the wife [singular] must respect her husband [singular]." Further, if polygamy were allowable, the illustration of Christ's relationship with His Body (the Church) falls apart (Ephesians 5:32). In Colossians 3:18–19, Paul refers to husbands and wives in the plural, but in that passage it is clear that he is addressing all the husbands and wives among the Colossian believers.

3. Why did it change? It is not so much that God disallowed something He had previously allowed as it is that God restored marriage to His original plan. As seen in Genesis 2, polygamy was not God's original intent. God seems to have allowed polygamy to solve a problem, but that solution was not the ideal. In most modern societies, there is absolutely no need for polygamy. In most cultures today, women

are able to provide for and protect themselves—removing the only "positive" aspect of polygamy. Further, most modern nations outlaw polygamy. According to Romans 13:1–7, we are to obey the laws the government establishes, including laws prohibiting polygamy.

Are there some instances in which the allowance for polygamy would still apply today? Perhaps, but it is unfathomable that there would be no other solution. Due to the "one flesh" aspect of marriage, the need for oneness and harmony in marriage, and the lack of any real need for polygamy, it is our firm belief that polygamy does not honor God and is not His design for marriage.

48. Who/what were the Nephilim?

The Nephilim (translated as "fallen ones, giants") may have been the offspring of sexual relationships between the sons of God and the daughters of men in Genesis 6:1–4. There is much debate as to the identity of the Nephilim (verse 4) and the "sons of God" (verse 2), who seem to be distinct from the "human beings" in verse 1.

One theory is that the "sons of God" were fallen angels (demons) who took on physical form and mated with human females (or demons who possessed human males who then mated with human females). These unions resulted in extraordinary offspring, the Nephilim, who were "heroes of old, men of renown" (Genesis 6:4) of a giant size and, apparently, enhanced physical abilities. If demons were involved in producing the Nephilim, it is likely those demons are the ones who were judged by God and are now "kept in darkness, bound with everlasting chains for judgment on the great Day" (Jude 1:6).

Assuming the Nephilim were the spawn of demons, why would demons want to cohabit with human women and produce offspring? One speculation is that the demons were attempting to pollute the human bloodline in order to prevent the coming of the Messiah. God had promised that the Messiah would one day crush the head of the serpent, Satan (Genesis 3:15). The demons in Genesis 6 were possibly attempting to prevent the crushing of the serpent and make it impossible for a sinless "seed of the woman" to be born.

There are at least two objections to the theory that the Nephilim were demon-human hybrids: First, there is nothing in the text to expressly identify the sons of God as angels. Second, the Bible never indicates that angels are physiologically compatible with women and can procreate with them (unless Genesis 6 is the only instance).

Others have suggested that the sons of God might be fallen angels who possessed men. As in the first theory, the phrase *sons of God* could still refer to fallen angels, the difference being that the demons were using mortal men to accomplish their goals. While this view would resolve the physiological problems of the first theory, there is, again, nothing in the text to suggest demonic possession.

Another view of the Nephilim is that the statement "There were giants on the earth in those days" (Genesis 6:4 NKJV) simply means that *everyone* was big and tall and mighty. Genetically, humanity was still in a nearly pristine condition. This theory takes the view that these sons of God were simply men. This would explain why there were giants before the flood "and also afterward" (Genesis 6:4; cf. 1 Samuel 17:4–7), as primeval genetic material survived in Noah's family. The fact that Nephilim were still around sporadically after the flood is an indicator that giants like Goliath were exceptional, but not superhuman.

According to legend (the Book of Enoch and other non-biblical writings), the Nephilim were a unique race of giants and superheroes who committed acts of great evil. In the 2014 movie *Noah*, starring Russell Crowe, the Nephilim are fallen angels encased in rock. All that the Bible directly says about the Nephilim is that they were "heroes and famous warriors of ancient times" (Genesis 6:4 NLT) or "powerful men of old, the famous men" (Genesis 6:4 CSB). The Nephilim were not aliens, angels, "Watchers," or rock monsters; they were literal, physical beings.

As mentioned, there were some Nephilim after the flood, according to Genesis 6:4. When the Israelites spied out the land of Canaan, they reported back to Moses, "We saw the Nephilim there (the descendants of Anak come from the Nephilim). We seemed like grasshoppers in our own eyes, and we looked the same to them" (Numbers 13:33). Later, as Moses addressed the people of Israel before they entered Canaan, he mentioned the sons of Anak: "You are now about to cross the Jordan to go in and dispossess nations greater and stronger than you, with large cities that have walls up to the sky. The people are strong and tall—Anakites! You know about them and have heard it said: 'Who can stand up against the Anakites?'" (Deuteronomy 9:1–2). These "giants" were destroyed by the Israelites with God's help (Deuteronomy 3:10–11; 9:3; Joshua 11:21–22; 1 Samuel 17).

It's a mysterious passage, but Genesis 6:4 states that there were Nephilim in the land in the days before the flood. The passage does not explicitly say how these giants came to be. It is best to not be dogmatic on an issue the Bible says so little about and is not theologically significant in the grand scheme of things.

49. What is the Book of Enoch, and should it be in the Bible?

The Book of Enoch is any of several pseudepigraphal works that attribute themselves to Enoch, the great-grandfather of Noah; that is, Enoch son of Jared (Genesis 5:18). A piece of ancient literature is a pseudepigraphon if it makes false claims as to authorship. A pseudepigraphon will purport to have a (usually) well-known author, but its claims are unfounded.

Enoch is also one of the three people in the Bible taken up to heaven while still alive (the only others being Elijah and Jesus). We read about Enoch's translation in Genesis 5:24: "And Enoch walked with God; and he was not, for God took him" (NKJV; see also Hebrews 11:5). Most commonly, when people refer to the Book of Enoch, they mean 1 Enoch, which is wholly extant only in the Ethiopic language. The Book of Enoch is accepted as canonical by the Coptic Church in

Ethiopia and the Eritrean Orthodox Church. In addition to 1 Enoch, there are 2 Enoch (*The Book of the Secrets of Enoch*) and 3 Enoch (*The Hebrew Book of Enoch*). Fragments of the Book of Enoch in Aramaic and Hebrew were found among the Dead Sea Scrolls.

Much of the Book of Enoch is apocalyptic—it uses vivid imagery to predict doom and the final judgment of evil. There's a heavy emphasis on angelology and demonology, and a large portion of the book is devoted to filling in the backstory of Genesis 6:1–4. The Book of Enoch thus explains the origin of the Nephilim and the identity of the "sons of God," mentioned in Genesis 6:2 and 4. The result is a strange and sensationalistic piece of noncanonical literature.

In its Ethiopic form, the Book of Enoch is arranged in five sections:

Section I (chapters 1–36) has Enoch pronouncing God's judgment on the angels who cohabited with the daughters of men (see Genesis 6:1–4). In this section, two hundred angelic "Watchers" rebel against God and are cast out of heaven along with Satan. On earth, they indulge their lust and have sexual relations with human women, producing the Nephilim, a race of evil giants who terrorize the antediluvian world. Enoch sees a "chaotic and horrible" place and a fiery prison reserved for the angels who sinned (Enoch 21:3, 7).

Section II (chapters 37–71) has three parables relating apocalyptic judgments. It also contains the story of Enoch's translation into heaven (see Genesis 5:24). In this section, Enoch describes the activity of an angel named Gadreel: "He it is who showed the children of men all the blows of death, and he led astray Eve, and showed [the weapons of death to the sons of men] the shield and the coat of mail, and the sword for battle, and all the weapons of death to the children of men. And from his hand they have proceeded against those who dwell on the earth from that day and for evermore" (Enoch 69:6–7).

Section III (chapters 72–87) is primarily an explanation of the workings of the stars in their pathways, as per a vision that Enoch has.

Section IV (chapters 88–90) contains Enoch's vision of the coming flood and prophecies concerning other events yet future, including the exodus, the conquest of Canaan, the building of the temple, the fall of the northern kingdom, the destruction of Jerusalem, the final judgment, the building of the New Jerusalem, the resurrection of the saints, and the coming of the Messiah.

Section V (chapters 91–105) pronounces woes on sinners and promises blessings to the righteous. It ends with a promise of peace to the "children of uprightness" (Enoch 105:2).

The biblical book of Jude quotes from chapter 1 of the Book of Enoch in Jude 1:14–15, "Enoch, the seventh from Adam, prophesied about them: 'See, the Lord is coming with thousands upon thousands of his holy ones to judge everyone, and to convict all of them of all the ungodly acts they have committed in their ungodliness, and of all the defiant words ungodly sinners have spoken against him.'" Jude's quotation does not mean the Book of Enoch is inspired by God or that it should be in the Bible.

Jude's quote is not the only quote in the Bible from a non-biblical source. The apostle Paul quotes Epimenides in Titus 1:12, but that does not mean we should give any additional authority to Epimenides' writings. The same is true with Jude 1:14–15. Jude quoting from the Book of Enoch does not indicate the entire Book of Enoch is inspired, or even true. All it means is that this particular passage of Enoch is true. It is interesting to note that no scholars believe the Book of Enoch to have truly been written by the Enoch in the Bible. Enoch was seven generations from Adam, prior to the flood (Genesis 5:1–24). Evidently, though, the words Jude quotes were genuinely something that Enoch prophesied—or the Bible would not attribute it to him: "Enoch, the seventh from Adam, prophesied about them" (Jude 1:14). This saying of Enoch was somehow handed down through the generations and eventually recorded in the Book of Enoch.

We should treat the Book of Enoch (and the other books like it) in the same manner we do the other apocryphal writings. Some of what the Apocrypha says is true and correct, but much of it is false and historically inaccurate. If you read these books, you should consider them interesting but fallible historical documents, not as the inspired, authoritative Word of God.

50. What was the sin of Sodom and Gomorrah?

The biblical account of Sodom and Gomorrah is recorded in Genesis. Genesis 18 records the Lord and two angels coming to speak with Abraham. The Lord informed Abraham that "the outcry against Sodom and Gomorrah is so great and their sin so grievous" (Genesis 18:20). Verses 22–33 record Abraham pleading with the Lord to have mercy on Sodom and Gomorrah because of the righteous people who might be there. Abraham's nephew, Lot, and his family lived in Sodom.

Genesis 19 records the two angels, disguised as human men, visiting Sodom and Gomorrah. Lot met the angels in the city square and urged them to stay at his house. The angels agreed. The Bible then reveals the sin lurking in the Sodomites' hearts: "Before they had gone to bed, all the men from every part of the city of Sodom—both young and old—surrounded the house. They called to Lot, 'Where are the men who came to you tonight? Bring them out to us so that we can have sex with them'" (Genesis 19:4–5). The angels proceeded to blind the men surrounding the house and urge Lot and his family to flee the city. The wrath of God was about to fall. Lot and his family fled the city, and then "the LORD rained down burning sulfur on Sodom and Gomorrah—from the LORD out of the heavens. Thus he overthrew those cities and the entire plain, destroying all those living in the cities . . ." (Genesis 19:24–25).

What was the sin of Sodom and Gomorrah? According to Genesis 19, the sin involved homosexuality. The very name of that ancient city has given us the term *sodomy*, in the sense of copulation between two men, whether consensual or forced. Clearly, homosexuality was part of why God destroyed the two cities. The men of Sodom and Gomorrah wanted to perform homosexual acts on who they thought were two men.

This is not to say that homosexuality was the *only* reason why God destroyed Sodom and Gomorrah. Ezekiel 16:49–50 gives some more insight: "Now this was the sin of your sister Sodom: She and her daughters were arrogant, overfed and unconcerned; they did not help the poor and needy. They were haughty and did detestable things before me. . . ." So, the sins of Sodom included pride, apathy, complacency, idleness, and unconcern for the underprivileged.

Ezekiel 16:50 adds that a sin of Sodom was that they did "detestable things." The Hebrew word translated "detestable" refers to something that is morally disgusting. It is the same word used in Leviticus 18:22, where homosexuality is an "abomination" (NKJV). Jude 1:7 also weighs in: "Sodom and Gomorrah and the surrounding towns gave themselves up to sexual immorality and perversion." So, again, while homosexuality was not the only sin of Sodom and Gomorrah, it does appear to be the primary reason for the destruction of those cities.

Those who attempt to explain away the biblical condemnations of homosexuality claim that the sin of Sodom and Gomorrah was inhospitality. That's one of the sins—the men of Sodom and Gomorrah were certainly being inhospitable. There is probably nothing more inhospitable than homosexual gang rape. But to say God destroyed two cities and all their inhabitants simply for being inhospitable ignores some obvious details of the story.

Sodom and Gomorrah were guilty of many other sins, but homosexuality was the principal reason God poured fiery sulfur on the cities, completely destroying them and all their inhabitants. To this day, the area where Sodom and Gomorrah were located remains a desolate wasteland. Sodom and Gomorrah serve as a powerful example of how God feels about sin in general and homosexuality specifically.

51. What is the meaning of Jacob wrestling with God?

Genesis 32:22–32 recounts the puzzling story of Jacob in an all-night wrestling match. His opponent is a man who refers to himself as "God" (verse 28). Later, Jacob also refers to the man he struggled with as "God" (verse 30).

To know Jacob's story is to know his life was a never-ending struggle. Jacob's family was characterized by deep-seated hostility. Jacob was a con artist who had been conned, a liar who had been lied to, and a manipulator who had been manipulated. In many ways, he lived up to his name "Jacob," which literally means "heel-catcher" and carries the sense of "one who follows after to supplant or deceive."

God had promised Jacob that through him would come a great nation through whom the whole world would be blessed (Genesis 28:10–15). Still, Jacob was a man full of fears and anxieties. His brother, Esau, had vowed to kill him. His uncle, Laban, had cheated him for years. His two wives had an adversarial relationship with each other.

After he fled Laban's ill-treatment, Jacob and his family camped in a spot chosen for him by angels (Genesis 32:1–2). From there, he sent messengers with a gift to his estranged brother, Esau, and they returned with the news that Esau was on his way with four hundred men (Genesis 32:3–6). Fearing the worst, Jacob divided his family and herds so that if one group fell victim to Esau's men, the other group might escape. Jacob prayed for the Lord's help and then sent several caravans of lavish gifts ahead of him in hopes of pacifying Esau. Finally, Jacob sent his wives and children across the River Jabbok with all the rest of his possessions (Genesis 32:22–23).

Alone in the desert wilderness, Jacob had the ultimate restless night. A stranger visited Jacob, and they wrestled throughout the night until daybreak, at which point the stranger crippled Jacob with a blow to his hip. Even then, Jacob held on. He must have known there was something supernatural about this stranger, because he demanded a blessing from him (Genesis 32:26). The stranger then gave Jacob a new name: *Israel*, which likely means "he struggles with God" (Genesis 32:28).

The stranger gave the reason for Jacob's new name: "Because you have struggled with God and with humans and have overcome" (Genesis 32:28). Jacob asks for the stranger's name, but the man declines to give it—Jacob knew with whom he wrestled. And then Jacob receives what he wanted: a blessing (Genesis 32:29). Jacob limped for the rest of his life, but he "saw God face to face" (Genesis 32:30) and received God's blessing. In his weakness, he was strong.

The next morning, God's blessing of Jacob was evident. Esau, the brother Jacob had feared, received him gladly (Genesis 33).

In Western culture and even in our churches, we celebrate wealth, power, strength, confidence, prestige, and victory. We avoid weakness, failure, and doubt. Though we know that a measure of vulnerability, fear, and discouragement comes with life, we tend to view these as signs of failure or even a lack of faith. However, we also know that in real life, naïve optimism and the glowing accolades of glamour and success are a recipe for discontent and despair. Sooner or later, the cold, hard realism of life catches up with most of us. The story of Jacob pulls us back to reality.

Frederick Buechner characterized Jacob's divine encounter at the Jabbok River as the "magnificent defeat of the human soul at the hands of God."[2] In Jacob's story we can easily recognize our own elements of struggle: fear, darkness, loneliness, vulnerability, emptiness, exhaustion, and pain.

Even the apostle Paul experienced discouragement and fear: "We were harassed at every turn—conflicts on the outside, fears within" (2 Corinthians 7:5). But in truth, God does not want to leave us with our trials, our fears, our battles in life. What we come to learn in our conflicts is that God proffers us a corresponding divine gift. He comes to us and manifests Himself to us in our struggles. It is through Him that we can receive the power of conversion and transformation, the gifts of freedom, endurance, faith, and courage.

In the end, Jacob did what we all must do. In his weakness and fear, he faced God. Jacob was separated from all others and from his worldly possessions, and that's when he grappled all night for what was truly important. It was an exhausting struggle that left him crippled. It was only after he wrestled with God and ceased his struggling, realizing that he could not go on without Him, that he received God's blessing (Genesis 32:29).

What we learn from this remarkable incident in the life of Jacob is that our lives are never meant to be easy. This is especially true when we take it upon ourselves to wrestle with God and His will for our lives. We also learn that as Christians, despite our trials and tribulations, our strivings in this life are never devoid of God's presence, and His blessing inevitably follows the struggle, which can sometimes be messy and chaotic. Real growth experiences always involve struggle and pain.

Jacob's wrestling with God at the Jabbok that dark night reminds us of this truth: though we may fight God and His will for us, in truth, God is so very good. As believers in Christ, we may well struggle with Him through the loneliness of night, but by daybreak His blessing will come.

52. Why was Moses not allowed to enter the Promised Land?

Moses is hailed as the leader of the Exodus, the one through whom God delivered His people from Egyptian slavery. To Moses God entrusted the law. Jesus demonstrated that Moses foreshadowed His own work as the Messiah (John 3:14–15). Moses is listed in Hebrews 11 as exemplary of faith. In Deuteronomy 34 we read that God Himself buried Moses. We are also told that, "since then, no prophet has risen in Israel like Moses, whom the LORD knew face to face. . . . For no one has ever shown the mighty power or performed the awesome deeds that Moses did in the sight of all Israel" (Deuteronomy 34:10, 12). Yet Moses, for all his blessings, was not allowed to enter the Promised Land. Why not?

In Deuteronomy 32:51–52 God gives the reason that Moses was not permitted to enter the Promised Land: "This is because . . . you broke faith with me in the presence of the Israelites at the waters of Meribah Kadesh in the Desert of Zin and because you did not uphold my holiness among the Israelites. Therefore, you will see the land only from a distance; you will not enter the land I am giving to the people of Israel." God was true to His promise. He showed Moses the Promised Land but did not let him enter.

The incident at the waters of Meribah Kadesh is recorded in Numbers 20. Nearing the end of their forty years of wandering, the Israelites came to the Desert of Zin. There was no water, and the community turned against Moses and Aaron. Moses and Aaron went to the tent of meeting and prostrated themselves before God. God told Moses and Aaron to gather the assembly and speak to the rock. Water would come forth. Moses took the staff and gathered the men. Then, seemingly in anger, Moses said to them, "Listen, you rebels, must we bring you water out of this rock?" Then Moses struck the rock twice with his staff (Numbers 20:10–11). Water came from the rock, as God had promised. But God immediately told Moses and Aaron that because they failed to trust Him enough to honor Him as holy, they would not bring the children of Israel into the Promised Land (verse 12).

The punishment may seem harsh to us, but when we look closely at Moses' actions, we see several mistakes. Most obviously, Moses disobeyed a direct command from God. God had commanded Moses to speak to the rock. Instead, Moses struck the rock with his staff. Earlier, when God had brought water from a rock, He instructed Moses to strike it with a staff (Exodus 17). But God's instructions were different here. God wanted Moses to trust Him, especially after they had been in such close relationship for so many years. Moses didn't need to use force; he simply needed to obey God and know that God would be true to His promise.

Also, Moses took the credit for bringing forth the water. He asks the people gathered at the rock, "Must *we* bring you water out of this rock?" (Numbers 20:10, emphasis added). Moses seemed to be taking credit for the miracle himself (and Aaron), instead of attributing it to God. Moses did this publicly. God could not let it go unpunished and expect the Israelites to understand His holiness.

The water-giving rock is used as a symbol of Christ in 1 Corinthians 10:4. The rock was struck in Exodus 17:6, just like Christ was crucified once (Hebrews 7:27). Moses' speaking to the rock in Numbers 20 could have been meant as a picture of prayer. Jesus was "struck" once, and He continues to provide living water to those who pray in faith to Him. When Moses angrily struck the rock, he destroyed the biblical typology and in effect, crucified Christ again.

Moses' punishment for disobedience, pride, and the misrepresentation of Christ's sacrifice was steep; he was barred from entering the Promised Land (Numbers 20:12). Yet we do not see Moses complain about his punishment. Instead, he continues to faithfully lead the people and honor God.

In His holiness, God is also compassionate. He invited Moses up to Mount Nebo, where He showed His beloved prophet the Promised Land before his death. Deuteronomy 34:4–5 records, "Then the LORD said to him, 'This is the land I promised on oath to Abraham, Isaac and Jacob when I said, "I will give it to your descendants." I have let you see it with your eyes, but you will not cross over into it.' And Moses the servant of the LORD died there in Moab, as the LORD had said." Moses' failure at the rock did not negate or break his relationship with God. God continued to use the prophet and continued to love him with tenderness.

53. Why did God allow Solomon to have one thousand wives and concubines?

First Kings 11:3 states that Solomon "had seven hundred wives, princesses, and three hundred concubines" (KJV). Obviously, God allowed Solomon to have these wives, but allowance is not the same as approval. Solomon's marital decisions were in direct violation of God's law, and there were consequences.

Solomon started out well early in his life, listening to the counsel of his father, David, who told him, "Be strong, act like a man, and observe what the LORD your God requires: Walk in obedience to him, and keep his decrees and commands, his laws and regulations, as written in the Law of Moses. Do this so that you may prosper in all you do and wherever you go" (1 Kings 2:2–3). Solomon's early humility is shown in 1 Kings 3:5–9 when he requests wisdom from the Lord. Wisdom is applied knowledge; it helps us make decisions that honor the Lord and agree with the Scriptures. Solomon's book of Proverbs is filled with practical counsel on how to follow the Lord. Solomon also wrote the Song of Solomon, which presents a beautiful picture of what God intends marriage to be. So, King Solomon *knew* what was right, even if he didn't always follow the right path.

Over time, Solomon forgot his own counsel and the wisdom of Scripture. God had given clear instructions for anyone who would be king: no amassing of horses, no multiplying of wives, and no accumulating of silver and gold (Deuteronomy 17:14–20). These commands were designed to prevent the king from trusting in military might, following foreign gods, and relying on wealth instead of on God. Any survey of Solomon's life will show that he broke all three of these divine prohibitions!

Thus, Solomon's taking of many wives and concubines was in direct violation of God's Word. Just as God had predicted, "As Solomon grew old, his wives turned his heart after other gods, and his heart was not fully devoted to the LORD his God" (1 Kings 11:4). To please his wives, Solomon even got involved in sacrificing to Milcom (or Molek), a god that required "detestable" acts to be performed (1 Kings 11:7–8).

God allowed Solomon to make the choice to disobey, but Solomon's choice brought inevitable consequences. "So the LORD said to Solomon, 'Since this is your attitude and you have not kept my covenant and my decrees, which I commanded you, I will most certainly tear the kingdom away from you and give it to one of your subordinates'" (1 Kings 11:11). God showed mercy to Solomon for David's sake (verse 12), but Solomon's kingdom was eventually divided. Another chastisement upon Solomon was war with the Edomites and Aramians (verses 14–25).

Solomon was not a puppet king. God did not force him to do what was right. Rather, God laid out His will, blessed Solomon with wisdom, and expected the king to obey. In his later years, Solomon chose to disobey, and he was held accountable for his decisions.

It is instructive that toward the end of Solomon's life, God used him to write one more book, which we find in the Bible. The book of Ecclesiastes gives us the rest of the story. Solomon throughout the book tells us everything he tried in order to find fulfillment apart from God in this world, or "under the sun." This is his own testimony: "I amassed silver and gold for myself, and the treasure of kings and provinces. I acquired . . . a harem as well—the delights of a man's heart" (Ecclesiastes 2:8). But his harem did not bring happiness. Instead, "Everything was meaningless, a chasing after the wind; nothing was gained under the sun" (verse 11). At the conclusion of Ecclesiastes, we find wise counsel: "Here is the conclusion of the matter: Fear God and keep his commandments, for this is the duty of all mankind" (Ecclesiastes 12:13).

It is never God's will that anyone sin, but He does allow us to make our own choices. The story of Solomon is a powerful lesson for us that it does not pay to disobey. It is not enough to start well; we must seek God's grace to finish well too. Life without God is a dead-end street. Solomon thought that having one thousand wives and concubines would provide happiness, but whatever pleasure he derived was not worth the price he paid. A wiser Solomon concluded that his life of pleasure was "meaningless" (Ecclesiastes 12:8), and the book of Ecclesiastes ends with the warning that "God will bring every deed into judgment" (verse 14).

54. Why did God take Enoch and Elijah to heaven without them dying?

According to the Bible, Enoch and Elijah are the only two people God took to heaven without dying. Genesis 5:24 says, "Enoch walked faithfully with God; then he was no more, because God took him away." Second Kings 2:11 relates the translation of Elijah: "Suddenly a chariot of fire and horses of fire appeared and separated the two of them, and Elijah went up to heaven in a whirlwind." Enoch is described as a man who "walked faithfully with God 300 years" (Genesis 5:22–23). Elijah was perhaps the most powerful of God's prophets in the Old Testament. There are also prophecies of Elijah's return (Malachi 4:5–6).

Why did God take Enoch and Elijah? The Bible does not specifically give us the answer. Some speculate that they were taken in preparation for a role in the end times, possibly as the two witnesses in Revelation 11:3–12. This is possible but not explicitly taught in the Bible. It may be that God desired to save Enoch and Elijah from experiencing death due to their great faithfulness in serving and obeying Him. Whatever the case, God has His purposes, and while we don't always understand God's plans and purposes, we know that "His way is perfect" (Psalm 18:30).

55. What does it mean to "spare the rod, spoil the child"?

Spare the rod, spoil the child is a modern-day proverb on the wisdom of discipline. It means that if a parent refuses to discipline an unruly child, that child will grow accustomed to getting his own way and develop an air of entitlement. He will become, in the common vernacular, a spoiled brat.

Spare the rod, spoil the child is not found in Scripture, but Proverbs 13:24 expresses a similar thought: "Whoever spares the rod hates their children, but the one who loves their children is careful to discipline them." According to this bit of wisdom, withholding discipline is akin to hating one's child, and correction is a means of loving him or her. In other words, allowing a child to always do as he or she pleases is not beneficial to the child. The better, more loving action is to guide a child away from sinful ways into a more advantageous path.

Proverbs 22:15 presents discipline as an antidote to foolishness: "Folly is bound up in the heart of a child, but the rod of discipline will drive it far away." Being wise is better than being spoiled. Discipline is critical for wisdom (Proverbs 29:15), and a child who obeys his parents will be wise (Proverbs 13:1).

Spare the rod, spoil the child is usually cited in the context of spanking or other means of corporal punishment. Taken literally, both Proverbs 13:24 and the modern proverb refer to corporal punishment; however, they have application beyond physical discipline.

The primary point of the biblical proverb is that loving discipline benefits the child. Parents are sometimes tempted to think that a hands-off approach is the best way to raise children, but parents who truly love their child will provide wise and appropriate discipline (see Proverbs 3:11–12). If a child develops evil habits such as laziness and dishonesty (Proverbs 12:19, 24; 13:4), greater evil will befall. The pain of correcting bad behavior will be much less for the child now than for the adult he or she will later become.

Because everyone inherits a sin nature, everyone needs discipline. Correction is a blessing that prevents shame and undue hardship down the road. God Himself disciplines His children: "The Lord disciplines the one he loves, and he chastens everyone he accepts as his son. . . . God disciplines us for our good, in order that we may share in his holiness" (Hebrews 12:6, 10; cf. Proverbs 3:12).

To spare the rod and spoil the child is deceptive in that the spoiled child will grow up believing that sinning has no consequences. That mindset removes the moral guardrails that protect a person from harm.

To spare the rod and spoil the child is shortsighted. Failure to discipline a child ignores the immense benefit that discipline can have in later life. An athlete undergoes rigorous training in order to release his or her full potential in competition. A rosebush is heavily pruned in order to produce the best blooms. A child is disciplined in order to maximize his ability and equip him with the tools of success.

The word *rod* indicates a thin stick or switch that can inflict a small amount of physical pain with no lasting physical injury. It should go without saying that a child should never be bruised, injured, or cut by a physical corrective measure. Parents should never abuse their power and authority over their children. Discipline, physical or otherwise, should not be abusive, unfair, or administered in anger (Ephesians 6:4; Colossians 3:21). Discipline should be done in love, with purpose, and under control.

To refuse to spare the rod is to show wisdom, foresight, and love. Parents who discipline their children in this way desire to shape them into responsible adults who love and serve God (Proverbs 22:6). The goal is to build character and train the conscience.

56. What is Zion? What is Mount Zion? What is the biblical meaning of Zion?

Psalm 87:2–3 says, "The LORD loves the gates of Zion more than all the other dwellings of Jacob. Glorious things are said of you, city of God." According to this verse, *Zion* is synonymous with *city of God*, and it is a place that God loves. Zion is Jerusalem. Mount Zion is the high hill on which David built a citadel. It is on the southeast side of the city.

The word *Zion* occurs over one hundred fifty times in the Bible. It essentially means "fortification" and has the idea of being "raised up" as a "monument." Zion is described both as the city of David and the city of God. As the Bible progresses, the word *Zion* expands in scope and takes on an additional, spiritual meaning.

The first mention of Zion in the Bible is 2 Samuel 5:7: "David captured the fortress of Zion—which is the City of David." Zion was originally an ancient Jebusite fortress in the city of Jerusalem. After David's conquest of the fortress, Jerusalem became a possession of Israel. The royal palace was built there, and Zion/Jerusalem became the seat of power in Israel's kingdom.

When Solomon built the temple in Jerusalem, the meaning of *Zion* expanded further to include the temple area (Psalm 2:6; 48:2, 11–12; 132:13). This is the meaning found in the prophecy of Jeremiah 31:6, "Come, let us go up to Zion, to the LORD our God." In the Old

Testament, *Zion* is used as a name for the city of Jerusalem (Isaiah 40:9), the land of Judah (Jeremiah 31:12), and the nation of Israel as a whole (Zechariah 9:13).

The word *Zion* is also used in a theological or spiritual sense in Scripture. In the Old Testament, *Zion* refers figuratively to Israel as the people of God (Isaiah 60:14). In the New Testament, *Zion* refers to God's spiritual kingdom. We have not come to Mount Sinai, says the apostle, but "to Mount Zion, to the city of the living God, the heavenly Jerusalem" (Hebrews 12:22). Peter, quoting Isaiah 28:16, refers to Christ as the cornerstone of Zion: "See, I lay a stone in Zion, a chosen and precious cornerstone, and the one who trusts in him will never be put to shame" (1 Peter 2:6).

Mount Zion as a geographical area is currently the center of much dispute. The Bible is clear that one day Zion will be the sole possession of the Lord Jesus, and Zion—the nation and the city—will be restored. "Awake, awake, clothe yourself in your strength, Zion; clothe yourself in your beautiful garments, Jerusalem, the holy city; for the uncircumcised and the unclean will no longer come into you" (Isaiah 52:1 NASB). And "the children of your oppressors will come bowing before you; all who despise you will bow down at your feet and will call you the City of the LORD, Zion of the Holy One of Israel" (Isaiah 60:14).

SECTION 7

Questions about the New Testament

57. Old Testament vs. New Testament— what are the differences?

While the Bible is a unified book, there are differences between the Old Testament and the New Testament. In many ways, they are complementary. The Old Testament is foundational; the New Testament builds on that foundation with further revelation from God. The Old Testament establishes principles that are seen to be illustrative of New Testament truths. The Old Testament contains many prophecies that are fulfilled in the New. The Old Testament provides the history of a *people*; the New Testament focus is on a *person*. The Old Testament shows the wrath of God against sin (with glimpses of His grace); the

New Testament shows the grace of God toward sinners (with glimpses of His wrath).

The Old Testament predicts a Messiah (see Isaiah 53), and the New Testament reveals who the Messiah is (John 4:25–26). The Old Testament records the giving of God's Law, and the New Testament shows how Jesus the Messiah fulfilled that Law (Matthew 5:17; Hebrews 10:9). In the Old Testament, God's dealings are mainly with His chosen people, the Jews; in the New Testament, God's dealings are mainly with His church (Matthew 16:18). Physical blessings promised under the old covenant (Deuteronomy 29:9) give way to spiritual blessings under the new covenant (Ephesians 1:3).

The Old Testament prophecies related to the coming of Christ, although incredibly detailed, contain a certain amount of ambiguity that is cleared up in the New Testament. For example, the prophet Isaiah spoke of the death of the Messiah (Isaiah 53) and of establishing the Messiah's kingdom (Isaiah 26) with no clues concerning the chronology of the two events—no hints that the suffering and the kingdom-building might be separated by millennia. In the New Testament, it becomes clear that the Messiah would have *two* advents: in the first He suffered and died (and rose again), and in the second He will establish His kingdom.

Because God's revelation in Scripture is progressive, the New Testament brings into sharper focus principles that were introduced in the Old Testament. The book of Hebrews describes how Jesus is the true High Priest and how His one sacrifice replaces all previous sacrifices, which were mere foreshadowings. The Passover lamb of the Old Testament (Ezra 6:20) becomes the Lamb of God in the New Testament (John 1:29). The Old Testament gives the Law. The New Testament clarifies that the Law was meant to show men their need of salvation and was never intended to be the means of salvation (Romans 3:19).

The Old Testament saw paradise lost for Adam; the New Testament shows how paradise is regained through the second Adam (Christ). The Old Testament declares that man was separated from

God through sin (Genesis 3), and the New Testament declares that man can be restored in his relationship to God (Romans 3–6). The Old Testament predicted the Messiah's life. The Gospels record Jesus' life, and the Epistles interpret His life and how we are to respond to all He has done.

In summary, the Old Testament lays the foundation for the coming of the Messiah who would sacrifice Himself for the sins of the world (1 John 2:2). The New Testament records the ministry of Jesus Christ and then looks back on what He did and how we are to respond. Both testaments reveal the same holy, merciful, and righteous God who condemns sin but desires to save sinners through an atoning sacrifice. In both testaments, God reveals Himself to us and shows us how we are to come to Him through faith (Genesis 15:6; Ephesians 2:8).

58. What is the new covenant?

The new covenant is the promise that God will forgive sin and restore fellowship with those whose hearts are turned toward Him. Jesus Christ is the mediator of the new covenant, and His death on the cross is the basis of the promise (Luke 22:20). The new covenant was predicted while the old covenant was still in effect—the prophets Moses, Jeremiah, and Ezekiel all allude to the new covenant.

The old covenant God had established with His people required strict obedience to the Mosaic law. Because the wages of sin is death (Romans 6:23), the Law required that Israel perform daily sacrifices in order to atone for sin. But Moses, through whom God established the old covenant, also anticipated the new covenant. In one of his final addresses to the nation of Israel, Moses looks forward to a time when Israel would be given "a heart to understand" (Deuteronomy 29:4 ESV). Moses predicts that Israel would fail in keeping the old covenant (verses 22–28), but he then sees a time of restoration (Deuteronomy 30:1–5). At that time, Moses says, "The LORD your God will circumcise your hearts and the hearts of your descendants, so that you may love him with all your heart and with all your soul, and live" (verse 6). The new covenant involves a total change of heart so that God's people are naturally pleasing to Him.

The prophet Jeremiah also predicted the new covenant. "'The days are coming,' declares the LORD, 'when I will make a new covenant with the people of Israel and with the people of Judah. . . . This is the covenant I will make with the people of Israel after that time,' declares the LORD. 'I will put my law in their minds and write it on their hearts. I will be their God, and they will be my people'" (Jeremiah 31:31, 33). Jesus Christ came to fulfill the law of Moses (Matthew 5:17) and to establish the new covenant between God and His people. The old covenant was written in stone, but the new covenant is written on hearts. Entering the new covenant is made possible only by faith in Christ, who shed His blood to take away the sins of the world (John 1:29). Luke 22:20 relates how Jesus, at the Last Supper, takes the cup and says, "This cup that is poured out for you is the new covenant in my blood" (ESV).

The new covenant is also mentioned in Ezekiel 36:26–27, "I will give you a new heart and put a new spirit in you; I will remove from you your heart of stone and give you a heart of flesh. And I will put my Spirit in you and move you to follow my decrees and be careful to keep my laws." Ezekiel lists several aspects of the new covenant here: a new heart, a new spirit, the indwelling Holy Spirit, and true holiness. The Mosaic law could provide none of these things (see Romans 3:20).

The new covenant was originally given to Israel and includes a promise of fruitfulness, blessing, and a peaceful existence in the Promised Land. In Ezekiel 36:28–30 God says, "Then you will live in the land I gave your ancestors; you will be my people, and I will be your God. . . . I will call for the grain and make it plentiful and will not bring famine upon you. I will increase the fruit of the trees and the crops of the field, so that you will no longer suffer disgrace among the nations because of famine." Deuteronomy 30:1–5 contains similar promises related to Israel under the new covenant. After the resurrection of

Christ, God in His grace brought the Gentiles into the blessing of the new covenant too (Acts 10; Ephesians 2:13–14). The fulfillment of the new covenant will be seen in two places: on earth during the millennial kingdom, and in heaven for all eternity.

We are no longer under the Law but under grace (Romans 6:14–15). The old covenant has served its purpose, and it has been replaced by "a better covenant" (Hebrews 7:22). "In fact the ministry Jesus has received is as superior to theirs as the covenant of which he is mediator is superior to the old one, since the new covenant is established on better promises" (Hebrews 8:6).

Under the new covenant, we are given the opportunity to receive salvation as a free gift (Ephesians 2:8–9). Our responsibility is to exercise faith in Christ, the One who fulfilled the Law on our behalf and brought an end to the Law's sacrifices through His own sacrificial death. Through the life-giving Holy Spirit who lives in all believers (Romans 8:9–11), we share in the inheritance of Christ and enjoy a permanent, unbroken relationship with God (Hebrews 9:15).

59. Who were the twelve disciples/apostles of Jesus Christ?

The word *disciple* refers to a learner or follower. The word *apostle* means one who is sent out. While Jesus was on earth, His twelve followers were called disciples. The twelve disciples followed Jesus Christ, learned from Him, and were trained by Him. After His resurrection and ascension, Jesus sent the disciples out to be His witnesses (Matthew 28:18–20; Acts 1:8). They were then referred to as the twelve apostles. However, even when Jesus was still on earth, the terms *disciples* and *apostles* were used somewhat interchangeably.

The original twelve disciples/apostles are listed in Matthew 10:2–4, "These are the names of the twelve apostles: first, Simon (who is called Peter) and his brother Andrew; James son of Zebedee, and his brother John; Philip and Bartholomew; Thomas and Matthew the tax collector;

James son of Alphaeus, and Thaddaeus; Simon the Zealot and Judas Iscariot, who betrayed him." The Bible also lists the twelve disciples/apostles in Mark 3:16–19 and Luke 6:13–16. A comparison of the three passages shows a couple of minor differences in the names. It seems that Thaddaeus was also known as "Judas son of James" (Luke 6:16) and Lebbaeus (Matthew 10:3 NKJV). Simon the Zealot was also known as Simon the Canaanite (Mark 3:18 NKJV). The Gospel of John uses the name Nathanael instead of Bartholomew, but Nathanael and Bartholomew were undoubtedly the same person. Judas Iscariot, who betrayed Jesus, was replaced as one of the twelve apostles by Matthias (see Acts 1:20–26). Some Bible teachers view Matthias as an "invalid" apostle and believe that Paul was God's choice to replace Judas Iscariot as the twelfth apostle.

The twelve disciples/apostles were ordinary men whom God used in an extraordinary manner. Among the twelve were fishermen, a tax collector, and a revolutionary. The Gospels record the constant failings, struggles, and doubts of these twelve men who followed Jesus Christ. After Jesus' resurrection and ascension into heaven, the Holy Spirit transformed the disciples/apostles into powerful men of God who turned the world upside down (Acts 17:6). What made the change? The twelve apostles/disciples had "been with Jesus" (Acts 4:13). May the same be said of us!

60. What are the differences between the Sadducees and the Pharisees?

The Gospels refer often to the Sadducees and Pharisees, as Jesus was in almost constant conflict with them. The Sadducees and Pharisees comprised the ruling class of Jews in Israel. There are some similarities between the two groups but important differences between them as well.

The Pharisees and the Sadducees were both religious sects within Judaism during the time of Christ. Both groups honored Moses and

the Law, and they both had a measure of political power. The Sanhedrin, the seventy-member supreme court of ancient Israel, had
members from both the Sadducees and the Pharisees.

The differences between the Pharisees and the Sadducees are
known to us through a couple of passages of Scripture and through
the extant writings of the Pharisees. Religiously, the Sadducees were
more conservative in one doctrinal area: they insisted on a literal
interpretation of the text of Scripture; if the Sadducees couldn't find
a command in the Tanakh, they dismissed it as manmade. The Pharisees, on the other hand, gave oral tradition equal authority to the
written Word of God.

Given the Pharisees' and the Sadducees' differing views of Scripture, it's no surprise that they argued over certain doctrines. The
Sadducees rejected a belief in the resurrection of the dead (Matthew
22:23; Mark 12:18; Acts 23:8), but the Pharisees did believe in the
resurrection. The Sadducees denied the afterlife, holding that the soul
perished at death, but the Pharisees believed in an afterlife and in an
appropriate reward and punishment for individuals. The Sadducees
rejected the idea of an unseen spiritual world, but the Pharisees taught
the existence of angels and demons in a spiritual realm.

The apostle Paul shrewdly used the theological differences between
the Pharisees and the Sadducees to escape their clutches. Paul had
been arrested in Jerusalem and was making his defense before the
Sanhedrin. Knowing that some of the court were Sadducees and the
others Pharisees, Paul called out, "My brothers, I am a Pharisee, descended from Pharisees. I stand on trial because of the hope of the
resurrection of the dead" (Acts 23:6). Paul's mention of the resurrection precipitated a dispute between the Pharisees and the Sadducees,
dividing the assembly, and causing "a great uproar" (verse 9). The
Roman commander who watched the proceedings sent troops into
the melee to rescue Paul from their violence (verse 10).

Socially, the Sadducees were more elitist and aristocratic than the
Pharisees. Sadducees tended to be wealthy and to hold more powerful
positions. The chief priests and high priest were Sadducees, and they

held the majority of the seats in the Sanhedrin. The Pharisees were more representative of the common working people and had the respect of the masses. The Sadducees' locus of power was the temple in Jerusalem; the Pharisees controlled the synagogues. The Sadducees were friendlier with Rome and more accommodating to the Roman laws than the Pharisees were. The Pharisees often resisted hellenization, but the Sadducees welcomed it.

Jesus had more run-ins with the Pharisees than with the Sadducees, probably because of the former's giving preeminence to oral tradition. "You ignore God's law and substitute your own tradition," Jesus told them (Mark 7:8 NLT; see also Matthew 9:14; 15:1–9; 23:5, 16, 23; Mark 7:1–23; and Luke 11:42). Because the Sadducees were often more concerned with politics than religion, they ignored Jesus until they began to fear He might bring unwanted Roman attention and upset the status quo. It was at that point that the Sadducees and Pharisees set aside their differences, united, and conspired to put Christ to death (John 11:48–50; Mark 14:53; 15:1).

The Sadducees as a group ceased to exist after the destruction of Jerusalem, but the Pharisees' legacy lived on. In fact, the Pharisees were responsible for the compilation of the Mishnah, an important document with reference to the continuation of Judaism beyond the destruction of the temple. In this way the Pharisees laid the groundwork for modern-day Rabbinic Judaism.

61. What does it mean to seek first the kingdom of God?

Jesus said to seek first the kingdom of God in His Sermon on the Mount (Matthew 6:33). The verse's meaning is as direct as it sounds. We are to seek the things of God as a priority over the things of the world. Primarily, it means we are to seek the salvation that is inherent in the kingdom of God because it is of greater value than all the world's riches. Does this mean that we should neglect the reasonable and daily duties that help sustain our lives? Certainly not. But for the Christian, there should be a difference in attitude toward them. If we are taking care of God's business as a priority—seeking His salvation, living in obedience to Him, and sharing the good news of the kingdom with others—then He will take care of our business as He promised—and if that's the arrangement, where is worrying?

But how do we know if we're truly seeking God's kingdom first? There are questions we can ask ourselves: "Where do I primarily spend my energies? Is all my time and money spent on goods and activities that will certainly perish, or in the service of God—the results of which live on for eternity?" Believers who have learned to truly put God first may then rest in this holy dynamic: ". . . and all these things will be given to you as well" (Matthew 6:33).

God has promised to provide for His own, supplying every need (Philippians 4:19), but His idea of what we need is often different from ours, and His timing will only occasionally meet our expectations. For example, we may see our need as riches or advancement, but perhaps God knows that what we truly need is a time of poverty, loss, or solitude. When this happens, we are in good company. God loved both Job and Elijah, but He allowed Satan to absolutely pound Job (all under His watchful eye), and He let that evil woman, Jezebel, break the spirit of His own prophet Elijah (Job 1–2; 1 Kings 18–19). In both cases, God followed these trials with restoration and sustenance.

These "negative" aspects of the kingdom run counter to a heresy that is gaining ground around the world, the so-called prosperity gospel. A growing number of false teachers are gathering followers under the message "God wants you to be rich!" But that philosophy is not the counsel of the Bible—and it is certainly not the counsel of Matthew 6:33, which is not a formula for gaining wealth. It is a description of how God works. Jesus taught that our focus should be shifted away from this world—its status and its lying allurements—and placed upon the things of God's kingdom.

62. What is the meaning of the parable of the prodigal son?

The parable of the prodigal son is found in Luke chapter 15, verses 11–32. The character of the forgiving father, who remains constant throughout the story, is a picture of God. In telling the story, Jesus identifies Himself with God in His loving attitude toward the lost, symbolized by the younger son (the tax collectors and sinners of Luke 15:1). The elder brother represents the self-righteous (the Pharisees and teachers of the law of Luke 15:2).

The major theme of this parable is not so much the conversion of the sinner, as in the previous two parables of Luke 15, but rather the restoration of a believer into fellowship with the Father. In the first two parables, the owner went out to look for what was lost (Luke 15:1–10), whereas in this story the father waits and watches eagerly for his son's return. We see a progression through the three parables from the relationship of one in a hundred (Luke 15:1–7), to one in ten (Luke 15:8–10), to one in one (Luke 15:11–32), demonstrating God's love for each individual and His personal attentiveness toward all humanity. We see in this story the graciousness of the father over-shadowing the sinfulness of the son, as it is the memory of the father's goodness that brings the prodigal son to repentance (Romans 2:4).

Jesus sets the scene for the parable of the prodigal son in Luke 15:11: "There was a man who had two sons."

The Younger Son

In Luke 15:12, the younger son asks his father for his share of his estate, which would have been half of what his older brother would receive (see Deuteronomy 21:17). In other words, the younger son asked for a third of the estate. Though it was perfectly within his rights to ask, it was not a loving thing to do, as it implied that he wished his father dead. Instead of rebuking his son, the father patiently grants him his request. This is a picture of God letting a sinner go his own way instead of choosing life (Deuteronomy 30:19).

Like the prodigal son, we all possess a foolish ambition to be independent, which is at the root of the sinner persisting in his sin (Genesis 3:6; Romans 1:28). A sinful state is a departure and distance from God (Romans 1:21). A sinful state is also a place of constant discontent. In Luke 12:15 Jesus says, "Watch out! Be on your guard against all kinds of greed; life does not consist in an abundance of possessions." The younger son in the parable learned the hard way that covetousness leads to a life of dissatisfaction and disappointment. He also learned that the most valuable things in life are the things we cannot buy or replace.

In Luke 15:13 the younger son travels to a distant country. It is evident from his previous actions he had already made that journey in his heart, and the physical departure was a display of his willful disobedience to all the goodness his father had offered (Proverbs 27:19; Matthew 6:21; 12:34). In the foreign land, the prodigal squanders all his inheritance on selfish, shallow fulfillment, losing everything. His financial disaster is followed by a natural disaster in the form of a famine, which he failed to plan for. At this point he hires himself out to a Gentile and finds himself feeding pigs, a detestable job to the Jewish people (Leviticus 11:7). Needless to say, the prodigal must have been incredibly desperate to willingly take such a loathsome position. He was paid so little and grew so hungry that he longed to eat the pigs' food. To top it off, he could find no mercy among the people he had chosen as his own: "No one gave him anything" (Luke 15:16). Apparently, once his wealth was gone, so were his friends. Even the unclean animals were better off than he was at that point.

The prodigal son toiling in the pigpen is a picture of the lost sinner or a rebellious Christian who has returned to a life of sin (2 Peter 2:19–21). The results of sin are never pretty (James 1:14–15).

The prodigal son begins to reflect on his miserable condition, and "he came to his senses" (Luke 15:17). He realizes that even his father's servants have it better. His painful circumstances help him to see his father in a new light. Hope begins to dawn in his heart (Psalm 147:11; Isaiah 40:30–31; 1 Timothy 4:10).

The prodigal's realization is reflective of the sinner's discovery that apart from God, there is no hope (Ephesians 2:12; 2 Timothy 2:25–26). When a sinner "comes to his senses," repentance follows, along with a longing to return to fellowship with God.

The son devises a plan of action, and it shows that his repentance was genuine. He will admit his sin (Luke 15:18), and he will give up his rights as a son and take on the position of a servant (verse 19). He realizes he has no right to a blessing from his father, and he has nothing to offer his father except a life of service. Returning home, the prodigal son is prepared to fall at his father's feet and beg for mercy.

In the same way, a repentant sinner coming to God is keenly aware of his own spiritual poverty. Laying aside all pride and feelings of entitlement, he brings nothing of value with him. The sinner's only thought is to cast himself at the mercy of God and beg for a position of servitude (1 John 1:9; Romans 6:6–18; 12:1).

The Father

The father in the parable of the prodigal son was waiting for his son to return. In fact, "while he was still a long way off, his father saw him and was filled with compassion for him" (Luke 15:20). He runs to his wayward son, embraces him, and kisses him. In Jesus' day, it was not customary for a grown man to run, yet the father runs to greet his son, breaking convention in his love and desire for restoration (verse 20). The returning son begins his prepared speech (verse 21), but his father cuts him off and begins issuing commands to honor his son—the best robe, the best ring, the best feast! The father does not question his son or lecture him; instead, he joyfully forgives him and receives him back into fellowship.

What a picture of God's love, condescension, and grace! God's heart is full of compassion for His children; He stands ready to welcome the returning sinner back home with joyous celebration.

The prodigal son was satisfied to return home as a slave, but to his surprise and delight he is restored back into the full privilege of being his father's son. The weary, gaunt, filthy sinner who trudged home was transformed into the guest of honor in a rich man's home. That is what God's grace does for a penitent sinner (Psalm 40:2; 103:4). Not only are we forgiven in Christ, but we receive the Spirit of "adoption to sonship" (Romans 8:15). We are His children, "heirs of God and co-heirs with Christ" (Romans 8:17).

The father's command to bring the best robe for the returned son is a sign of dignity and honor, proof of the prodigal's acceptance back into the family. The ring for the son's hand is a sign of authority and sonship. The sandals for his feet are a sign of his not being a servant, as servants did not wear shoes. The father orders the fattened calf to be prepared, and a party is held in honor of the returned son. Fatted calves in those times were saved for special occasions. This was not just any party; it was a rare and complete celebration.

All these things represent what we receive in Christ upon salvation: the robe of the Redeemer's righteousness (Isaiah 61:10), the privilege of partaking of the Spirit of adoption (Ephesians 1:5), and feet fitted with the readiness that comes from the gospel of peace, prepared to walk in the ways of holiness (Ephesians 6:15). The actions of the father in the parable show us that "[the LORD] does not treat us as our sins deserve or repay us according to our iniquities. For as high as the heavens are above the earth, so great is his love for those who fear him; as far as the east is from the west, so far has he removed our transgressions from us. As a father has compassion on his children, so the LORD has compassion on those who fear him" (Psalm 103:10–13). Instead of condemnation, there is rejoicing for a son who "was dead and is alive again; he was lost and is found" (Luke 15:32; cf. Romans 8:1; John 5:24). Those words—*dead* and *alive, lost* and *found*—are terms that also apply to one's state before and after conversion to Christ (Ephesians 2:1–5). The feast is a picture of what occurs in heaven over one repentant sinner (Luke 15:7, 10).

The Older Son

The final, tragic character in the parable of the prodigal son is the older son. As the older son comes in from the field, he hears music and dancing. He finds out from one of the servants that his younger brother has come home and what he hears is the sound of jubilation over his brother's safe return. The older brother becomes angry and refuses to go into the house. His father goes to his older son and pleads with him to come in. "But he answered his father, 'Look! All these years I've been slaving for you and never disobeyed your orders. Yet you never gave me even a young goat so I could celebrate with my friends. But when this son of yours who has squandered your property with prostitutes comes home, you kill the fattened calf for him!'" (Luke 15:29–30). The father answers gently: "My son, . . . you are always with me, and everything I have is yours. But we had to celebrate and be glad" (verses 31–32).

The older son's words and actions reveal several things about him: (1) His relationship with his father was based on works and merit. He points out to his father that he has always been obedient as he's been "slaving away"; thus, he deserves a party—he has earned it. (2) He despises his younger brother as undeserving of the father's favor. (3) He does not understand grace and has no room for forgiveness. In fact, the demonstration of grace toward his brother makes him angry. His brother does not *deserve* a party. (4) He has disowned the prodigal as a brother, referring to him as "this son of yours" (verse 30). (5) He thinks his father is stingy and unfair: "You never gave me even a young goat" (verse 29).

The father's words are corrective in several ways: (1) His older son should know that their relationship is not based on performance: "My son, . . . you are always with me, and everything I have is yours" (Luke 15:31). (2) His older son should accept his brother as part of the family. The father refers to the prodigal as "this brother of yours" (verse 32). (3) His older son could have enjoyed a party any time he wanted, but he never used the blessings at his disposal. (4) Grace is necessary and appropriate: "We had to celebrate" (verse 32).

The Pharisees and the teachers of the law, mentioned in Luke 15:1, are portrayed as the older brother in the parable. Outwardly, they lived blameless lives, but inwardly their attitudes were abominable

(Matthew 23:25–28). They saw their relationship with God as based on their performance, and they considered themselves deserving of God's favor—unlike the undeserving sinners around them. They did not understand grace and were, in fact, angered by it. They had no room for forgiveness. They saw no kinship between sinners and themselves. They viewed God as rather stingy in His blessings. And they considered that if God were to accept tax collectors and sinners into His family, then God would be unfair.

The older brother's focus was on himself and his own service; as a result, he had no joy in his brother's arrival home. He was so consumed with justice and equity (as he saw them) that he failed to see the value of his brother's repentance and return. The older brother had allowed bitterness to take root in his heart to the point that he was unable to show compassion toward his brother. The bitterness spilled over into other relationships, too, and he was unable to forgive the perceived sin of his father against him. Rather than enjoy fellowship with his father, brother, and community, the older brother stayed outside the house and nursed his anger. How sad to choose misery and isolation over restoration and reconciliation!

The older brother—and the religious leaders of Jesus' day—failed to realize that "anyone who claims to be in the light but hates a brother or sister is still in the darkness. Anyone who loves their brother and sister lives in the light, and there is nothing in them to make them stumble. But anyone who hates a brother or sister is in the darkness. They do not know where they are going, because the darkness has blinded them" (1 John 2:9–11).

The parable of the prodigal son is one of Scripture's most beautiful pictures of God's grace. We have all sinned and fallen short of the glory of God (Romans 3:23). We are all prodigals in that we have run from God, selfishly squandered our resources, and to some degree, wallowed in sin. But God is ready to forgive. He will save the contrite, not by works but by His grace, through faith (Ephesians 2:8–9; Romans 9:16). That is the core message of the parable of the prodigal son.

63. What did Jesus mean when He said, "Take up [your] cross and follow me" in Matthew 16:24?

In Matthew 16:24, Jesus told His disciples, "Whoever wants to be my disciple must deny themselves and take up their cross and follow me." Let's begin with what Jesus didn't mean in this verse. Many people interpret the "cross" to be taken up as some burden they must carry in their lives: a strained relationship, a thankless job, a physical illness, etc. With self-pitying pride, they look at their difficulty and say, "That's my cross I have to carry." Such an idea is not what Jesus meant when He said, "Take up [your] cross and follow me."

When a person carried a cross in Jesus' day, no one thought of it as a persistent annoyance or symbolic burden. To a person in the first century, the cross meant one thing and one thing only: death by crucifixion. To carry a cross was to face the most painful and humiliating means of death human beings could develop.

Two thousand years later, Christians view the cross as a cherished symbol of atonement, forgiveness, grace, and love. But in Jesus' day the cross represented a torturous death. The Romans forced convicted criminals to carry their own crosses to the place of crucifixion (see John 19:17). Bearing a cross meant one was about to die, and that one would face ridicule and disgrace along the way.

Therefore, Jesus' command to "take up [your] cross and follow me" is a call to self-abasement and self-sacrifice. One must be willing to die in order to follow Jesus. Dying to self is an absolute surrender to God.

After Jesus commanded cross-bearing, He said, "For whoever wants to save their life will lose it, but whoever loses their life for me will find it. What good will it be for someone to gain the whole world, yet forfeit their soul? Or what can anyone give in exchange for their soul?" (Matthew 16:25–26). Although the call to take up our cross is tough, the reward is matchless. Nothing in this world is worth passing up eternal life.

Wherever Jesus went, He drew crowds. Their view of who the Messiah really was—and what He would do—was often distorted. They thought the Christ would immediately usher in the restored kingdom (Luke 19:11). They believed He would free them from the oppressive rule of their Roman occupiers. Some hoped He would continue to provide free lunches for everyone (John 6:26). Jesus' statement that following Him required taking up a cross made people think twice about their motivation and level of commitment.

In Luke 9:57–62, three people seemed willing to follow Jesus. When Jesus pressed them, however, their commitment was shown to be halfhearted at best. They failed to count the cost of following Him. None were willing to take up their cross and crucify upon it their own interests.

Jesus' apparent attempts to dissuade people from following Him surely limited the number of false converts and insincere disciples (see John 6:66). But God seeks "true worshipers [who] will worship the Father in the Spirit and in truth" (John 4:23). Jesus' call to "take up [your] cross and follow me" serves to screen out the disingenuous, double-minded, and dissembling.

Are you ready to take up your cross and follow Jesus? Consider these questions:

- Are you willing to follow Jesus if it means losing your closest friends?
- Are you willing to follow Jesus if it means alienation from your family?
- Are you willing to follow Jesus if it means losing your reputation?
- Are you willing to follow Jesus if it means losing your job?
- Are you willing to follow Jesus if it means losing your life?

In some places of the world, these consequences are a reality. But notice the phrasing of the questions: "Are you willing?" Following

Jesus doesn't necessarily mean all these things will happen to you, but the disciple of Christ must be willing to suffer loss. Are you willing to take up your cross? If faced with a choice—Jesus or the comforts of this life—which will you choose?

Commitment to Christ means taking up your cross daily, giving up your hopes, dreams, possessions, and even your very life if need be for the cause of Christ. Only if you willingly take up your cross may you be called His disciple (Luke 14:27). The reward is worth the price. Remember that, as Jesus called His disciples to "take up [your] cross and follow me," He, too, bore a cross. Our Lord led the way.

64. What was the significance of Jesus washing the feet of the disciples?

Jesus washing the feet of the disciples (John 13:1–17) occurred in the upper room during the Last Supper and has significance in three ways. For Jesus, it was the display of His humility and servanthood in forgiving sinners. For the disciples, the washing of their feet displayed a mindset in direct contrast to their heart attitude at that time. For us, washing feet is symbolic of our role in the body of Christ.

Walking in sandals on the roads of Palestine in the first century made it imperative that feet be washed before a communal meal. People ate reclining at low tables, and feet were very much in evidence. When Jesus rose from the Last Supper and began to wash the feet of the disciples (John 13:4), He was doing the work of the lowliest of servants. The disciples must have been stunned at this act of humility and condescension—that Jesus, their Lord and Master, should wash the feet of His disciples. Washing feet was more properly *their* work, but no one had volunteered for the job. Jesus came to earth not as King and Conqueror but as the suffering Servant of Isaiah 53. As He revealed in Matthew 20:28, He came not "to be served, but to serve, and to give his life as a ransom for many." The humility expressed by Jesus' act with towel and basin foreshadowed His ultimate act of humility and love on the cross.

Jesus' attitude was in direct contrast to that of the disciples, who had recently been arguing among themselves as to which of them was the greatest (Luke 22:24). There was no servant present in the upper room to wash their feet, and it never occurred to them to wash one another's feet. When the Lord Himself stooped to this lowly task, they were stunned into silence. Peter was profoundly uncomfortable with the Lord washing his feet, and he protested: "You shall never wash my feet" (John 13:8).

Then Jesus said something that must have further shocked Peter: "Unless I wash you, you have no part with me" (John 13:8), prompting Peter, whose love for the Savior was genuine, to request a complete washing (verse 9). Then Jesus explained, "Those who have had a bath need only to wash their feet; their whole body is clean. And you are clean, though not every one of you" (verse 10). The disciples had "bathed," and they were all "clean" but one—Judas, who would betray Him (verse 11).

So, Jesus' act of washing the disciples' feet illustrated their spiritual cleansing. Jesus is the One who forgives. Peter and the rest had experienced the full cleansing of salvation and did not need to be bathed again in the spiritual sense. Salvation is a one-time act of justification by faith. What follows is the lifelong process of sanctification: a daily washing away of the stain of sin. As we walk through the world, some of the world's spiritual filth will cling to us, and that needs to be washed away—forgiven by Christ (see 1 John 1:9). Peter and the other disciples—all except Judas, who never belonged to Christ—needed only this minor cleansing.

When we come to Christ for salvation, He condescends to wash our sins away, and we can be sure that His forgiveness is permanent and complete (2 Corinthians 5:21). But, just as a bathed person needed to wash his feet periodically, we need periodic cleansing from the effects of living in the flesh in a sin-cursed world. This is sanctification, done by the power of the Holy Spirit who lives within us, through the "washing of water by the word" (Ephesians 5:26 NKJV), given to equip us for every good work (2 Timothy 3:16–17).

Further, when Jesus washed the disciples' feet, He told them (and us), "I have given you an example, that you should do as I have done to you" (John 13:15 NKJV). As His followers, we are to emulate Him, serving one another in lowliness of heart and mind, seeking to build one another up in humility and love. Part of that humble service is to forgive one another (Colossians 3:13). When we seek the pre-eminence, neglect to serve others, or refuse to forgive, we displease the Lord. True greatness in His kingdom is attained by those with a servant's heart (Mark 9:35; 10:44), and they will be greatly blessed (John 13:17).

65. What was the significance of the temple veil being torn in two when Jesus died?

During the lifetime of Jesus, the holy temple in Jerusalem was the center of Jewish religious life. The temple was the place where animal sacrifices were carried out and worship according to the law of Moses was followed faithfully. Hebrews 9:1–9 tells us that in the temple a veil separated the Holy of Holies—the earthly dwelling place of God's presence—from the rest of the temple, where men dwelt. This signi-fied that man was separated from God by sin (Isaiah 59:1–2). Only the high priest was permitted to pass beyond this veil once each year (Exodus 30:10; Hebrews 9:7) to enter God's presence for all of Israel and make atonement for their sins (Leviticus 16).

Solomon's temple was thirty cubits high (1 Kings 6:2), but Herod had increased the height to forty cubits, according to the writings of Josephus, a first-century Jewish historian. There is uncertainty as to the exact measurement of a cubit, but it is safe to assume that this veil was somewhere near sixty feet high. An early Jewish tradi-tion says that the veil was about four inches thick, but the Bible does not confirm that measurement. The book of Exodus teaches that this thick veil was fashioned from blue, purple, and scarlet material and fine twisted linen.

The size and thickness of the veil make the events occurring at the moment of Jesus' death on the cross so much more momentous. "And when Jesus had cried out again in a loud voice, he gave up his spirit. At that moment the curtain of the temple was torn in two from top to bottom" (Matthew 27:50–51).

So, what do we make of this? What significance does this torn veil have for us today? Above all, the tearing of the veil at the moment of Jesus' death dramatically symbolized that His sacrifice, the shedding of His own blood, was a sufficient atonement for sins. It signified that now the way into the Holy of Holies was open for all people, for all time, both Jew and Gentile.

When Jesus died, the veil was torn, and God moved out of that place never again to dwell in a temple made with human hands (Acts 17:24). God was through with that temple and its religious system, and the temple and Jerusalem were left "desolate" (destroyed by the Romans) in AD 70, just as Jesus prophesied in Luke 13:35. As long as the temple stood, it signified the continuation of the old covenant. Hebrews 9:8–9 refers to the age that was passing away as the new covenant was being established (Hebrews 8:13).

In a sense, the veil was symbolic of Christ Himself as the only way to the Father (John 14:6). This is indicated by the fact that the high priest had to enter the Holy of Holies through the veil. Now Christ is our superior High Priest, and as believers in His finished work, we partake of His better priesthood. We can now enter the Holy of Holies through Him. Hebrews 10:19–20 says, "We have confidence to enter the Most Holy Place by the blood of Jesus, by a new and living way opened for us through the curtain, that is, his body." Here we see the image of Jesus' flesh being torn for us just as He was tearing the veil for us.

The profound significance of the tearing of the veil is explained in glorious detail in Hebrews. The things of the temple were shadows of things to come, and they all ultimately point us to Jesus Christ. He was the veil to the Holy of Holies, and through His death the faithful now have free access to God.

The veil in the temple was a constant reminder that sin renders humanity unfit for the presence of God. The fact that the sin offering was offered annually and countless other sacrifices repeated daily showed graphically that sin could not truly be atoned for or erased by mere animal sacrifices. Jesus Christ, through His death, has removed the barriers between God and man, and now we may approach Him with confidence and boldness (Hebrews 4:14–16).

66. Why is the resurrection of Jesus Christ important?

The resurrection of Jesus is important for several reasons. First, the resurrection witnesses to the immense power of God Himself. To believe in the resurrection is to believe in God. If God exists, and if He created the universe and has power over it, then He has power to raise the dead. If He does not have such power, He is not worthy of our faith and worship. Only He who created life can resurrect it after death, only He can reverse the hideousness that is death itself, and only He can remove the sting of death and gain the victory over the grave (1 Corinthians 15:54–55). In resurrecting Jesus from the grave, God reminds us of His absolute sovereignty over life and death.

The resurrection of Jesus Christ is also important because it validates who Jesus claimed to be, namely, the Son of God and Messiah. According to Jesus, His resurrection was the "sign from heaven" that authenticated His ministry (Matthew 16:1–4). The resurrection of Jesus Christ, attested to by hundreds of eyewitnesses (1 Corinthians 15:3–8), provides irrefutable proof that He is the Savior of the world.

Another reason the resurrection of Jesus Christ is important is that it proves His sinless character and divine nature. The Scriptures said God's "Holy One" would never see corruption (Psalm 16:10 NKJV), and Jesus never saw corruption, even after He died (see Acts

13:32–37). It was on the basis of the resurrection of Christ that Paul preached, "Through Jesus the forgiveness of sins is proclaimed to you. Through him everyone who believes is set free from every sin" (Acts 13:38–39).

The resurrection of Jesus Christ not only validates His deity, but it also validates the Old Testament prophecies that foretold of Jesus' suffering and resurrection (see Acts 17:2–3). Christ's resurrection also authenticated His own claims that He would be raised on the third day (Mark 8:31; 9:31; 10:34). If Jesus Christ is not resurrected, then we have no hope that we will be either. In fact, apart from Christ's resurrection, we have no Savior, no salvation, and no hope of eternal life. As Paul said, our faith would be "useless," the gospel would be altogether powerless, and our sins would remain unforgiven (1 Corinthians 15:14–19).

Jesus said, "I am the resurrection and the life" (John 11:25), and in that statement claimed to be the source of both. There is no resurrection apart from Christ, no eternal life. Jesus does more than *give* life; He *is* life, and that's why death has no power over Him. Jesus confers His life on those who trust in Him, so that we can share His triumph over death (1 John 5:11–12). We who believe in Jesus Christ will personally experience resurrection because, having the life Jesus gives, we have overcome death. It is impossible for death to win (1 Corinthians 15:53–57).

Jesus is "the firstfruits of those who have fallen asleep" (1 Corinthians 15:20). In other words, Jesus led the way in life after death. The resurrection of Jesus Christ is important as a testimony to the resurrection of human beings, which is a basic tenet of the Christian faith. Unlike other religions, Christianity has a Founder who transcends death and promises that His followers will do the same. Every other religion was founded by men or prophets whose end was the grave. As Christians, we know that God became man, died for our sins, and was resurrected the third day. The grave could not hold Him. He lives, and He sits today at the right hand of the Father in heaven (Hebrews 10:12).

The Word of God guarantees the believer's resurrection at the coming of Jesus Christ for His church at the rapture. Such assurance results in a great song of triumph as Paul writes in 1 Corinthians 15:55, "Where, O death, is your victory? Where, O death, is your sting?" (cf. Hosea 13:14).

The importance of the resurrection of Christ has an impact on our service to the Lord now. Paul ends his discourse on resurrection with these words: "Therefore, my dear brothers and sisters, stand firm. Let nothing move you. Always give yourselves fully to the work of the Lord, because you know that your labor in the Lord is not in vain" (1 Corinthians 15:58). Because we know we will be resurrected to new life, we can endure persecution and danger for Christ's sake (verses 30–32), just as our Lord did. Because of the resurrection of Jesus Christ, thousands of Christian martyrs throughout history have willingly traded their earthly lives for everlasting life and the promise of resurrection.

The resurrection is the triumphant and glorious victory for every believer. Jesus Christ died, was buried, and rose the third day according to the Scriptures (1 Corinthians 15:3–4). And He is coming again! The dead in Christ will be raised up, and those who are alive at His coming will be changed and receive new, glorified bodies (1 Thessalonians 4:13–18). Why is the resurrection of Jesus Christ important? It proves who Jesus is. It demonstrates that God accepted Jesus' sacrifice on our behalf. It shows that God has the power to raise us from the dead. It guarantees that the bodies of those who believe in Christ will not remain dead but will be resurrected unto eternal life.

67. What is the full armor of God?

The phrase "full armor of God" comes from Ephesians 6:13–17: "Therefore put on the full armor of God, so that when the day of evil comes, you may be able to stand your ground, and after you have done everything, to stand. Stand firm then, with the belt of truth buckled around your waist, with the breastplate of righteousness in place, and with your feet fitted with the readiness that comes from the gospel of peace. In addition to all this, take up the shield of faith, with which you can extinguish all the flaming arrows of the evil one. Take the helmet of salvation and the sword of the Spirit, which is the word of God."

Ephesians 6:12 clearly indicates that the conflict with Satan is spiritual, and therefore no tangible weapons can be effectively employed against him and his minions. We are not given a list of specific tactics Satan will use. However, the passage is quite clear that when we follow all the instructions faithfully, we will be able to stand, and we will have victory regardless of Satan's strategy.

The first element of our armor is truth (Ephesians 6:14). This belt immediately sets the believer apart from the world, since Satan is the "father of lies" (John 8:44). Deception is high on the list of things God considers to be an abomination. A "lying tongue" is one of the things He describes as "detestable to him" (Proverbs 6:16–17). We are therefore exhorted to put on truth for our own sanctification and deliverance, as well as for the benefit of those to whom we witness.

Also in verse 14, we are told to put on the breastplate of righteousness. A breastplate shielded a warrior's vital organs from blows that would otherwise be fatal. This righteousness is not good works done by men. Rather, this is the righteousness of Christ, imputed by God and received by faith, which guards our hearts against the accusations and charges of Satan and secures our innermost being from his attacks.

Verse 15 speaks of the preparation of the feet for spiritual conflict. In warfare, sometimes an enemy places dangerous obstacles in the path of advancing soldiers. The idea of the preparation of the gospel of peace is that we need to advance into Satan's territory, aware that there will be traps. The message of grace is essential to winning souls to Christ, and we must be prepared with the gospel. Satan has many obstacles placed in the path to halt the propagation of the gospel.

The shield of faith in verse 16 "can extinguish all the flaming arrows of the evil one." When we bear the shield of faith, Satan can cast all the aspersions, doubt, and dismay he wants, but they will be ineffective. Our faith—of which Christ is "the author and perfecter" (Hebrews 12:2 NASB95)—is like a shield, solid and substantial.

The helmet of salvation in verse 17 is protection for the head, keeping safe a critical part of the body. We could say that our way of thinking needs preservation. The head is the seat of the mind, which, when it has laid hold of the sure hope of eternal life, will not receive false doctrine or give way to Satan's temptations. The unsaved person has no hope of warding off the blows of false doctrine because he is without the helmet of salvation and his mind is incapable of discerning between spiritual truth and spiritual deception.

Verse 17 interprets the sword of the Spirit as the Word of God. While all the other pieces of spiritual armor are for defense, the sword of the Spirit allows us to take the offense. The sword analogy speaks of the holiness and power of the Word of God. There is no greater spiritual weapon. In Jesus' temptations in the desert, the Word of God was always His overpowering response to Satan. What a blessing that the same Word is available to us!

In verse 18, we are told to pray in the Spirit (that is, with the mind of Christ, with His heart and His priorities) in addition to wearing the full armor of God. We cannot neglect prayer, as it is the means by which we draw spiritual strength from God. Without prayer, without reliance upon God, our efforts at spiritual warfare are empty and futile. The full armor of God—truth, righteousness, the gospel, faith, salvation, the Word of God, and prayer—are the tools God has given us, through which we can be spiritually victorious. Satan is a defeated foe.

SECTION 8

Questions about Religions, Cults, and Worldviews

68. What is the difference between Christianity and Judaism?

Of the major world religions, Christianity and Judaism are likely the most similar. Christianity and Judaism both believe in one God who is almighty, omniscient, omnipresent, eternal, and infinite. Both religions believe in a God who is holy, righteous, and just, while at the same time loving, forgiving, and merciful. Christianity and Judaism share the Hebrew Scriptures (the Old Testament) as the authoritative Word of God, although Christianity includes the New Testament as well. Both Christianity and Judaism believe in the existence of heaven, the eternal dwelling place of the righteous, and hell, the eternal dwelling place of the wicked (although not all Christians and not all Jews believe in the eternality of hell). Christianity and Judaism have basically the same ethical code, commonly known today as Judeo-Christian. Both Judaism and Christianity teach that God has a special plan for the nation of Israel and the Jewish people.

The all-important difference between Christianity and Judaism is the doctrine of Jesus Christ. Christianity teaches that Jesus Christ is the fulfillment of the Old Testament prophecies of a coming Messiah/Savior (Isaiah 7:14; 9:6–7; Micah 5:2). Judaism often recognizes Jesus as a good teacher and perhaps even a prophet of God. Judaism does not believe that Jesus was the Messiah. Taking it a step further, Christianity teaches that Jesus is God in the flesh (John 1:1, 14; Hebrews 1:8). Christianity teaches that God became a human being in the person of Jesus Christ so He could lay down His life to pay the price for our sins (Romans 5:8; 2 Corinthians 5:21). Judaism strongly denies that Jesus is God or that such a sacrifice was necessary.

Jesus Christ is the all-important distinction between Christianity and Judaism. The person and work of Jesus Christ is the one primary issue that Christianity and Judaism cannot agree upon. In Matthew 15:24, Jesus declared, "I was sent only to the lost sheep of Israel." The religious leaders of Israel in Jesus' time asked Him, "Are you the Messiah, the Son of the Blessed One?" Jesus replied, "I am, . . . And you will see the Son of Man sitting at the right hand of the Mighty One and coming on the clouds of heaven" (Mark 14:61–62). But they didn't believe His words or accept Him as the Messiah.

Jesus Christ is the fulfillment of the Hebrew prophecies of a coming Messiah. Psalm 22:14–18 describes an event undeniably similar to Jesus' crucifixion: "I am poured out like water, and all my bones are out of joint. My heart has turned to wax; it has melted within me. My mouth is dried up like a potsherd, and my tongue sticks to the roof of my mouth; you lay me in the dust of death. Dogs surround me; a pack of villains encircles me, they pierce my hands and my feet. All my bones are on display; people stare and gloat over me. They divide my clothes among them and cast lots for my garment." Clearly, this messianic prophecy speaks of Jesus Christ, whose crucifixion fulfilled each of these details (Luke 23; John 19).

There is an amazing description of Jesus in Isaiah 53:3–6, "He was despised and rejected by mankind, a man of suffering, and familiar with pain. Like one from whom people hide their faces he was despised, and we held him in low esteem. Surely he took up our pain and bore our suffering, yet we considered him punished by God, stricken by him, and afflicted. But he was pierced for our transgressions, he was crushed for our iniquities; the punishment that brought us peace was on him, and by his wounds we are healed. We all, like sheep, have gone astray, each of us has turned to our own way; and the LORD has laid on him the iniquity of us all."

The apostle Paul, a Jew and a strict adherent of Judaism, encountered Jesus Christ in a vision (Acts 9:1–9) and proceeded to become a great witness for Christ and the author of almost half of the New Testament. Paul understood the difference between Christianity and Judaism more than anyone else. What was Paul's message? "I am not ashamed of the gospel, because it is the power of God that brings salvation to everyone who believes: first to the Jew, then to the Gentile" (Romans 1:16).

69. What is the difference between Catholics and Protestants?

There are several important differences between Catholics and Protestants. While there have been many attempts in recent years to find common ground between the two groups, the fact is that the differences remain, and they are just as important today as they were at the beginning of the Protestant Reformation. The following is a brief summary of some of the more important differences:

One of the major differences between Catholicism and Protestantism is the issue of the sufficiency and authority of Scripture.

Protestants believe that the Bible alone is the source of God's special revelation to mankind and teaches us all that is necessary for our salvation from sin. Protestants view the Bible as the standard by which all Christian behavior must be measured. This belief is commonly referred to as *sola scriptura* and is one of the five *solas* (*sola* is Latin for "alone") that came out of the Protestant Reformation.

There are many verses in the Bible that establish its authority and claim it to be sufficient for all matters of faith and practice. One of the clearest is 2 Timothy 3:16–17, where we see that "all Scripture is inspired by God and profitable for teaching, for rebuking, for correction, for training in righteousness, so that the man of God may be complete, equipped for every good work" (CSB).

Catholics reject the doctrine of *sola scriptura* and do not believe that the Bible alone is sufficient. They believe that both the Bible and sacred Roman Catholic tradition are equally binding upon the Christian. Many Roman Catholic doctrines, such as purgatory, praying to the saints, worship or veneration of Mary, etc., have little or no basis in Scripture but are based solely on Roman Catholic traditions. The Roman Catholic Church's insistence that the Bible and tradition are equal in authority undermines the sufficiency, authority, and completeness of the Bible. The view of Scripture is at the root of many, if not all, of the differences between Catholics and Protestants.

Another disagreement between Catholicism and Protestantism is over the office and authority of the Pope. According to Catholicism the Pope is the "Vicar of Christ" (a vicar is a substitute) and represents Jesus as the head of the Church. As such, the Pope has the ability to speak *ex cathedra* (literally "from the chair," that is, with authority on matters of faith and practice). His pronouncements made from the seat of authority are infallible and binding upon all Christians. On the other hand, Protestants believe that no human being is infallible and that Christ alone is the Head of the Church. Catholics rely on apostolic succession as a way of establishing the Pope's authority. Protestants believe that the church's authority comes not from apostolic succession but from the Word of

God. Catholicism teaches that only the Catholic Church can properly interpret the Bible, but Protestants believe that the Bible teaches God sent the Holy Spirit to indwell all born-again believers, enabling all believers to understand the message of the Bible (John 14:16–17, 26; 1 John 2:27).

A third major difference between Catholicism and Protestantism is how one is saved. Another of the five *solas* of the Reformation is *sola fide* ("faith alone"), which affirms the biblical doctrine of justification by grace alone through faith alone because of Christ alone (Ephesians 2:8–10). However, Catholics teach that the Christian must rely on faith plus "meritorious works" in order to be saved. Essential to the Roman Catholic doctrine of salvation are the Seven Sacraments, which are baptism, confirmation, the Eucharist, penance, anointing of the sick, holy orders, and matrimony. Protestants believe that on the basis of faith in Christ alone, believers are justified by God, as all their sins are paid for by Christ on the cross and His righteousness is imputed to them. Catholics, on the other hand, believe that Christ's righteousness is imparted to the believer by grace through faith but that in itself is not sufficient to justify the believer. The believer must supplement the righteousness of Christ imparted to him or her with meritorious works.

Catholics and Protestants also disagree on what it means to be justified before God. To the Catholic, justification involves being made righteous and holy. He believes that faith in Christ is only the beginning of salvation and that the individual must build upon that with good works because God's grace of eternal salvation must be merited. This view of justification contradicts the clear teaching of Scripture in passages such as Romans 4:1–12 and Titus 3:3–7. Protestants distinguish between the one-time act of justification (when we are declared righteous by God based on our faith in Christ's atonement on the cross) and the process of sanctification (the development of righteousness that continues throughout our lives on earth). Protestants recognize that works are important, but they believe the works are the result or fruit of salvation—never the means to it. Catholics blend justification and sanctification into one ongoing process, which leads to confusion about how one is saved.

A fourth major difference between Catholics and Protestants has to do with what happens after death. Both groups teach that unbelievers will spend eternity in hell, but there are significant differences about what happens to believers. From their church traditions and their reliance on noncanonical books, the Catholics have developed the doctrine of purgatory. Purgatory, according to the *Catholic Encyclopedia*, is a "place or condition of temporal punishment for those who, departing this life in God's grace, are not entirely free from venial faults, or have not fully paid the satisfaction due to their transgressions."[1] On the other hand, Protestants believe that we are justified by faith in Christ alone and that Christ's righteousness is imputed to us; therefore, when we die, we will go straight to heaven to be in the presence of the Lord (2 Corinthians 5:6–10; Philippians 1:23).

One disturbing aspect about the Catholic doctrine of purgatory is the belief that man can and must pay for his own sins. This results in a low view of the sufficiency and efficiency of Christ's atonement on the cross. Simply put, the Roman Catholic view of salvation implies that Christ's atonement on the cross was insufficient payment for the sins of those who believe in Him and that even a believer must pay for his own sins, either through acts of penance or time in purgatory. Yet the Bible teaches that it is Christ's death alone that can satisfy or propitiate God's wrath against sinners (Romans 3:25; Hebrews 2:17; 1 John 2:2; 1 John 4:10). Our works of righteousness cannot add to what Christ has already accomplished.

The differences between Catholicism and evangelical Protestants are important and significant. Paul wrote Galatians to combat the Judaizers (Jews who said that Gentile Christians had to obey the Old Testament Law to be saved). Like the Judaizers, Catholics make human works necessary for one to be justified by God, and they end up with a completely different gospel.

It is our prayer that God will open the eyes of those who are putting their faith in the teachings of the Catholic Church. It is our hope that everyone will understand that "righteous acts" cannot justify or sanctify a person (Isaiah 64:6). We pray that all will put their faith solely in Christ and the fact that we are "justified freely by [God's] grace through the redemption that came by Christ Jesus. God presented Christ as a sacrifice of atonement, through the shedding of his blood—to be received by faith" (Romans 3:24–25). God saves us "not because of righteous things we had done, but because of his mercy. He saved us through the washing of rebirth and renewal by the Holy Spirit, whom he poured out on us generously through Jesus Christ our Savior, so that, having been justified by his grace, we might become heirs having the hope of eternal life" (Titus 3:5–7).

70. What is Islam, and what do Muslims believe?

Islam is a religious system begun in the seventh century by Muhammad. Muslims follow the teachings of the Qur'an, their holy book, and strive to keep the Five Pillars, the basic tenets of their religion.

The History of Islam

In the seventh century, Muhammad claimed the angel Gabriel visited him. During these angelic visitations, which continued for about twenty-three years until Muhammad's death, the angel purportedly revealed to Muhammad the words of Allah (the Arabic word for "God" used by Muslims). These dictated revelations compose the Qur'an, Islam's holy book. *Islam* means "submission," deriving from a root word that means "peace." The word *Muslim* means "one who submits to Allah."

The Doctrine of Islam

Muslims summarize their doctrine in six articles of faith:

1. Belief in one Allah: Muslims believe Allah is one, eternal, creator, and sovereign.

2. Belief in the angels.

3. Belief in the prophets: the prophets include the biblical
   prophets but end with Muhammad as Allah's final prophet.

4. Belief in the revelations of Allah: Muslims accept certain portions of the Bible, such as the Torah and the Gospels. They
   believe the Qur'an is the preexistent, perfect word of Allah.

5. Belief in the last day of judgment and the hereafter: everyone
   will be resurrected for judgment into either paradise or hell.

6. Belief in predestination: Muslims believe Allah has decreed
   everything that will happen. Muslims testify to Allah's sovereignty with their frequent phrase, *inshallah*, meaning "if God
   wills."

The Five Pillars of Islam

These five tenets compose the framework of obedience for Muslims:

1. The testimony of faith (*shahada*): "*la ilaha illa allah. Muhammad rasul Allah.*" This means, "There is no deity but
   Allah. Muhammad is the messenger of Allah." A person can
   convert to Islam by stating this creed. The *shahada* shows
   that a Muslim believes in Allah alone as deity and believes
   that Muhammad reveals Allah.

2. Prayer (*salat*): five ritual prayers must be performed every
   day.

3. Giving (*zakat*): this almsgiving is a certain percentage given
   once a year.

4. Fasting (*sawm*): Muslims fast during Ramadan in the ninth
   month of the Islamic calendar. They must not eat or drink
   from dawn until sunset.

5. Pilgrimage (*hajj*): If physically and financially possible, a
   Muslim must make the pilgrimage to Mecca in Saudi Arabia
   at least once. The *hajj* is performed in the twelfth month of
   the Islamic calendar.

A Muslim's entrance into paradise hinges on obedience to these Five Pillars. Still, Allah may reject them. Even Muhammad was not sure whether Allah would admit him to paradise (Surah 46:9; Hadith 5.266).

An Evaluation of Islam

Compared to Christianity, Islam has some similarities but significant differences as well. Like Christianity, Islam is monotheistic. However, Muslims reject the Trinity—that God has revealed Himself as one in three Persons: Father, Son, and Holy Spirit.

Muslims claim that Jesus was one of the most important prophets—not God's Son. Islam asserts that Jesus, though born of a virgin, was created like Adam. Muslims do not believe Jesus died on the cross. They do not understand why Allah would allow His prophet Isa (the Islamic word for "Jesus") to die a torturous death. Yet the Bible shows how the death of the perfect Son of God was essential to pay for the sins of the world (Isaiah 53:5–6; John 3:16; 14:6; 1 Peter 2:24).

Islam teaches that the Qur'an is the final authority and the last revelation of Allah. The Bible, however, was completed in the first century with the book of Revelation. The Bible warns against anyone adding to or subtracting from God's Word (Deuteronomy 4:2; Proverbs 30:6; Galatians 1:6–12; Revelation 22:18). The Qur'an, as a claimed addition to God's Word, directly disobeys God's command.

Muslims believe that paradise can be earned through keeping the Five Pillars. The Bible, in contrast, reveals that sinful man can never measure up to the holy God (Romans 3:23; 6:23). Only by God's grace may sinners be saved through repentant faith in Jesus (Acts 20:21; Ephesians 2:8–9).

Because of these essential differences and contradictions, Islam and Christianity cannot both be true. The Bible and Qur'an cannot both be God's Word. The truth has eternal consequences.

"Beloved, do not believe every spirit, but test the spirits to see whether they are from God, because many false prophets have gone out into the world. By this you know the Spirit of God: every spirit that confesses that Jesus Christ has come in the flesh is from God; and every spirit that does not confess Jesus is not from God; this is the spirit of the antichrist, of which you have heard is coming, and now it is already in the world" (1 John 4:1–4 NASB; see also John 3:35–36).

71. Why do Jews and Arabs/Muslims hate each other?

First, it is important to understand that not all Arabs are Muslims, and not all Muslims are Arabs. While a majority of Arabs are Muslims, there are many non-Muslim Arabs. Further, there are significantly more non-Arab Muslims in areas such as Indonesia and Malaysia than there are Arab Muslims. Second, it is important to remember that not all Arabs hate Jews, not all Muslims hate Jews, and not all Jews hate Arabs and Muslims. We must be careful to avoid stereotyping people. However, generally speaking, Arabs and Muslims have a dislike of and distrust for Jews, and vice versa.

If there is an explicit biblical explanation for this animosity, it goes all the way back to Abraham. The Jews are descendants of Abraham's son Isaac. The Arabs are descendants of Abraham's son Ishmael. With Ishmael being the son of a slave woman (Genesis 16:1–16) and Isaac being the promised son who would inherit the blessings of Abraham (Genesis 21:1–3), naturally there would be some animosity between the two sons. As a result of Ishmael's mocking Isaac (Genesis 21:9), Sarah talked Abraham into sending Hagar and Ishmael away (Genesis 21:11–21). Likely, this caused even more contempt in Ishmael's heart toward Isaac. An angel told Hagar that Ishmael would be the father of a great nation (Genesis 21:18) and, interestingly, that Ishmael would be "a wild donkey of a man; his hand will be against everyone and everyone's hand against him, and he will live in hostility toward all his brothers" (Genesis 16:12).

However, the ancient root of bitterness between Isaac and Ishmael does not explain all the hostility between Jews and Arabs today.

The religion of Islam, which a majority of Arabs follow, has made the hostility predicted of Ishmael more profound. The Qur'an contains somewhat contradictory instructions for Muslims regarding Jews. At one point it seems to consider Jews as brothers (Surah 2:136), and in other places seems to forbid Muslims from having Jewish friends (Surah 5:51) and to command Muslims to attack Jews who refuse to convert to Islam (Surah 9:29–30). The Qur'an also introduces a conflict as to which son of Abraham was truly the son of promise. The Hebrew Scriptures say it was Isaac (Genesis 21:12; 26:3–5). The Qur'an says it was Ishmael. The Qur'an implies that it was Ishmael whom Abraham almost sacrificed to the Lord, not Isaac (see Surah 37:100–112, in contradiction to Genesis 22). This debate over who was the son of promise further contributes to today's hostility.

Another root of the conflict between Jews and Arabs is political. After World War II, when the United Nations gave a portion of the land of Israel to the Jewish people, the land was ruled by the British and primarily inhabited by Arabs (although one third of the population was Jewish). Most Arabs protested vehemently against the new Israeli state, even as they refused an Arab Palestinian state offered as part of the UN plan. Arab nations including Egypt, Jordan, Iraq, and Syria attacked Israel in an attempt to drive them into the sea, but they were defeated. The defeat of the Arab forces soon became a human tragedy when the surrounding Arab nations refused to absorb the Arab refugees from Palestine.

Ever since 1948, there has been great hostility between Israel and its Arab neighbors. The tensions have been stoked by political rhetoric and the existence of groups such as Hamas with their continuing obsession with wiping out the so-called "Zionist entity."

Israel exists on one tiny piece of land surrounded by much larger Arab nations such as Jordan, Syria, Saudi Arabia, Iraq, and Egypt. It is our viewpoint that, biblically speaking, Israel has a right to exist as a nation in its own land that God gave to the descendants of Jacob, grandson of Abraham (Genesis 12:7). While there is no easy solution to the conflict in the Middle East, Psalm 122:6 declares, "Pray for the peace of Jerusalem: 'May those who love you be secure.'"

72. What is Mormonism? What do Mormons believe?

The Mormon religion (Mormonism), whose followers are known as Mormons and as members of the Church of Jesus Christ of Latter-Day Saints (LDS), was founded less than two hundred years ago by a man named Joseph Smith. He claimed to have received a personal visit from God the Father and Jesus Christ (*Articles of Faith*, p. 35) who told him that all churches and their creeds were an abomination (1 Nephi 13:28; *Pearl of Great Price, Joseph Smith—History* 1:18–19). Joseph Smith then set out to "restore true Christianity" and claimed his church to be the "only true church on earth"[2] (1 Nephi 14:10). The problem with Mormonism is that it contradicts, modifies, and expands on the Bible. Christians have no reason to believe that the Bible is not true and adequate. To truly believe in and trust God means to believe in His Word, and all Scripture is inspired by God, which means it comes from Him (2 Timothy 3:16).

Mormons believe that there are in fact four sources of divinely inspired words, not just one: (1) the Bible "as far as it is translated correctly" (*Eighth Article of Faith*). Which verses are considered incorrectly translated is not always made clear. (2) The Book of Mormon, which was "translated" by Smith and published in 1830. Smith claimed it is the "most correct book" on earth and that a person can get closer to God by following its precepts "than by any other book" (*History of the Church* 4:461). (3) *Doctrine and Covenants*, containing a collection of modern revelations regarding the "Church of Jesus Christ as it has been restored."[3] (4) *The Pearl of Great Price*, which is considered by Mormons to "clarify" doctrines and teachings that were lost from the Bible (*Articles of Faith*, p. 182–185) and adds its own information about the earth's creation.

Mormons believe the following about God: He has not always been the Supreme Being of the universe[4] but attained that status through righteous living and persistent effort.[5] They believe God the Father has a "body of flesh and bones as tangible as man's" (*Doctrine and Covenants* 130:22). Brigham Young taught that Adam actually was God and the father of Jesus Christ—although this teaching has been abandoned by modern Mormon leaders.

In contrast, Christians know this about God: There is only one true God (Deuteronomy 6:4; Isaiah 43:10; 44:6–8). He always has existed and always will exist (Deuteronomy 33:27; Psalm 90:2; 1 Timothy 1:17). He was not created but is the Creator (Genesis 1; Psalm 24:1; Isaiah 37:16). He is perfect, and no one else is equal to Him (Psalm 86:8; Isaiah 40:25). God the Father is not a man, nor was He ever (Numbers 23:19; 1 Samuel 15:29; Hosea 11:9). He is Spirit (John 4:24), and Spirit is not made of flesh and bone (Luke 24:39).

Mormons, or Latter-Day Saints, believe that there are different levels or kingdoms in the afterlife: the celestial kingdom, the terrestrial kingdom, the telestial kingdom, and outer darkness.[6] Where mankind will end up depends on what they believe and do in this life (2 Nephi 25:23; *Articles of Faith*, p. 79).

In contrast, the Bible tells us that after death we go to heaven or hell based on whether or not we had faith in Jesus Christ as our Lord and Savior. To be absent from our bodies means, as believers, we are with the Lord (2 Corinthians 5:6–8). Unbelievers are sent to hell or the place of the dead (Luke 16:22–23). When Jesus comes the second time, we will receive resurrected, glorified bodies (1 Corinthians 15:50–54). There will be a new heaven and new earth for believers (Revelation 21:1), and unbelievers will be thrown into an everlasting lake of fire (Revelation 20:11–15). There is no second chance for redemption after death (Hebrews 9:27).

Mormon leaders have taught that Jesus' incarnation was the result of a physical relationship between God the Father and Mary (*Journal of Discourses*, 8:115).[7] Mormons believe Jesus is a god and that any human can also become a god (*Doctrine and Covenants* 132:20).[8]

Mormonism teaches that salvation can be earned by a combination of faith and good works.[9]

Contrary to this, Christians historically have taught that no one can achieve the status of God—only He is holy (1 Samuel 2:2). We can only be made holy in God's sight through faith in Him (1 Corinthians 1:2). Jesus is the only begotten Son of God (John 3:16), is the only one ever to have lived a sinless life, and now has the highest place of honor in heaven (Hebrews 7:26). Jesus and God are one in essence, Jesus being the only man who existed before physical birth (John 1:1–8; 8:56). Jesus gave Himself as a sacrifice, God raised Him from the dead, and one day everyone will confess that Jesus Christ is Lord (Philippians 2:6–11). Jesus tells us it is impossible to get to heaven by our own works and that only by faith in Him is it possible (Matthew 19:26). We all deserve eternal punishment for our sins, but God's infinite love and grace have allowed us a way out. "For the wages of sin is death, but the gift of God is eternal life in Christ Jesus our Lord" (Romans 6:23).

Clearly, there is only one way to receive salvation, and that is to know God and His Son, Jesus (John 17:3). Receiving salvation is not done by works but by faith (Romans 1:17; 3:28). We can receive this gift no matter who we are or what we have done (Romans 3:22). "Salvation is found in no one else, for there is no other name under heaven given to mankind by which we must be saved" (Acts 4:12).

Although Mormons are usually friendly, loving, and kind people, they are deceived by a false religion that distorts the nature of God, the person of Jesus Christ, and the means of salvation.

73. Who are the Jehovah's Witnesses, and what are their beliefs?

The sect known today as the Jehovah's Witnesses started out in Pennsylvania in 1870 as a Bible class led by Charles Taze Russell. Russell named his group the "Millennial Dawn Bible Study," and those who followed him were called "Bible students." Charles T. Russell began writing a series of books he called *Millennial Dawn*, which stretched to six volumes before his death and contained much of the theology Jehovah's Witnesses now hold.

The Watchtower Bible and Tract Society was founded in 1886 and quickly became the vehicle through which the Millennial Dawn movement began distributing their views. Group members were sometimes disparagingly called Russellites. After Russell's death in 1916, Judge Joseph Franklin Rutherford, Russell's successor, wrote the seventh and final volume of the Millennial Dawn series, *The Finished Mystery*, in 1917. That was also the year that the organization split. Those who followed Rutherford began calling themselves Jehovah's Witnesses.

What do Jehovah's Witnesses believe? Close scrutiny of their doctrinal position on such subjects as the deity of Christ, salvation, the Trinity, the Holy Spirit, and the atonement shows beyond a doubt that they do not hold to orthodox Christian positions on these subjects. Jehovah's Witnesses believe Jesus is Michael the archangel, the highest created being. This contradicts many passages of Scripture that clearly declare Jesus to be God (John 1:1, 14; 8:58; 10:30). Jehovah's Witnesses believe salvation is obtained by a combination of faith, good works, and obedience. This contradicts Scripture, which declares salvation to be received by grace through faith (John 3:16; Ephesians 2:8–9; Titus 3:5). Jehovah's Witnesses reject the doctrine of the Trinity, believing Jesus to be a created being and the Holy Spirit to essentially be the inanimate power of God. Jehovah's Witnesses reject the concept of Christ's substitutionary atonement and instead hold to a ransom theory, that Jesus' death was a ransom payment for Adam's sin.

How do the Jehovah's Witnesses justify these unbiblical doctrines? First, they claim that the church has corrupted the Bible over the centuries; thus, they have re-translated the Bible to reflect their unique doctrines—the result is the New World Translation. The New World Translation has gone through numerous editions, as the Jehovah's

Witnesses discover more and more passages of Scripture that contradict their doctrines.

The Watchtower bases its beliefs and doctrines on the original and expanded teachings of Charles Taze Russell, Judge J. F. Rutherford, and their successors. The governing body of the Watchtower Bible and Tract Society claims sole authority to interpret Scripture. In other words, what the governing body says concerning any scriptural passage is viewed as the last word, and independent thinking is strongly discouraged. This is in direct opposition to Paul's admonition to Timothy (and to us as well) to study to be approved by God, so that we need not be ashamed as we correctly handle the Word of God (2 Timothy 2:15). God's children are to be like the Berean Christians, who searched the Scriptures daily to see if the things they were being taught lined up with the Word (Acts 17:11).

There is probably no religious group that is more faithful than the Jehovah's Witnesses at spreading their message. Unfortunately, the message is full of distortions, deceptions, and false doctrine. May God open the eyes of the Jehovah's Witnesses to the truth of the gospel and the true teaching of God's Word.

74. What is Free Masonry, and what do Free Masons believe?

Freemasonry, Eastern Star, and other similar "secret" organizations seem to be harmless fellowship gatherings. Many of them appear to promote belief in God. However, Freemasonry, also sometimes called the Craft, does not have belief in the one true God; rather, each man must "act with courage, fidelity, and devotion to *his* God."[10] Freemasonry teaches the existence of a "Supreme Being," whoever that may be: the god of Islam, Hinduism, or any other religion will do. The unbiblical beliefs of Masonry are partially hidden by a supposed compatibility with the Christian faith. The following is a comparison of what the Bible says with what Freemasonry teaches:

Salvation from Sin

The Bible's view: Jesus became the sinner's sacrifice before God when He shed His blood and died as the payment for the sins of all those who believe in Him (Ephesians 2:8–9, Romans 5:8, John 3:16).

Masonry's view: The very process of joining the Lodge requires Christians to ignore the exclusivity of Jesus Christ as Lord and Savior. According to Freemasonry, a person will be saved and go to heaven as a result of their good works and personal self-improvement.

The View of the Bible

The Bible's view: The supernatural and plenary inspiration of the Scriptures—that they are inerrant and that their teachings and authority are absolute, supreme, and final. The Bible is the Word of God (2 Timothy 3:16; 1 Thessalonians 2:13).

Masonry's view: The Bible is only one of several "Volume(s) of Sacred Law," all of which are deemed to be equally important in Freemasonry. The Bible is an important book, only as far as those members who claim to be Christians are concerned, just as the Qur'an is important to Muslims. The Bible is not considered to be the exclusive Word of God, nor is it considered to be God's sole revelation of Himself to humankind. It is only one of many religious sourcebooks. It is a good guide for morality. The Bible is used primarily as a symbol of God's will, which can also be captured in other sacred texts like the Qur'an or Rigveda.

The Doctrine of God

The Bible's view: There is one God. The various names of God refer to the God of Israel and reveal certain attributes of God. To worship other gods or to call upon other deities is idolatry (Exodus 20:3). Paul spoke of idolatry as a heinous sin (1 Corinthians 10:14), and John said that idolaters will perish in hell (Revelation 21:8).

Masonry's view: All members must believe in a deity. Different religions (Christianity, Judaism, Islam, etc.) acknowledge the same God, but they call Him different names. Freemasonry invites people of all faiths, but even if they use different names for the "Nameless One of a hundred names," they are yet praying to the one God and Father of all.

The Doctrine of Jesus and the Trinity

The Bible's view: Jesus was God in human form (Matthew 1:18–24; John 1:1). Jesus is the second person of the Trinity (Matthew 28:19; Mark 1:9–11). He is fully human (Mark 4:38; Matthew 4:2) and fully divine (John 20:28; John 1:1–2; Acts 4:10–12). Christians should pray in Jesus' name and proclaim Him before others, regardless of offense to non-Christians (John 14:13–14; 1 John 2:23; Acts 4:18–20).

Masonry's view: There is no exclusivity in Jesus Christ or the Triune God who is the Father, Son, and Holy Spirit; therefore, there is no doctrine of the deity of Jesus Christ. It is deemed to be un-Masonic to invoke the name of Jesus when praying or to mention His name in the Lodge. Suggesting that Jesus is the only way to God contradicts the principle of tolerance. Jesus is on the same level as other religious leaders.

Human Nature and Sin

The Bible's view: All humans are born with a sinful nature, are totally depraved, and need a Savior from sin (Romans 3:23; 5:12; Psalm 51:5; Ephesians 2:1). Because of the fall, humanity has within itself no capacity for moral perfection (1 John 1:8–10; Romans 1:18–25).

Masonry's view: Through symbols and emblems, Masons teach that man is not sinful, just "rude and imperfect by nature."[11] Human beings are able to improve their character and behavior in various ways, including acts of charity, moral living, and voluntary performance of civic duty. Humanity possesses the ability of moving from imperfection toward total perfection. Moral and spiritual perfection lies within men and women.

When a Christian takes the oath of Freemasonry, he is swearing to the following doctrines that God has pronounced false and sinful:

1. Salvation can be gained by man's good works.
2. Jesus is just one of many equally revered prophets.
3. He will remain silent in the Lodge and not talk of Christ.
4. He is approaching the Lodge in spiritual darkness and ignorance, whereas the Bible says Christians are already in the light, children of the light, and are indwelt by the Light of the World—Jesus Christ.
5. The G.A.O.T.U. (Great Architect of the Universe) is representative of all gods in all religions.

By demanding that Christians take the Masonic oath, Masonry leads Christians into blasphemy and taking the name of the Lord in vain. Masonry makes Christians take a universalist approach in their prayers, demanding a generic name be used so as not to offend nonbelievers who are Masonic "brothers."

By swearing the Masonic oath and participating in the doctrines of the Lodge, Christians are perpetuating a false gospel to other Lodge members, who look only to Masonry's plan of salvation to get to heaven. By their very membership in such a syncretistic organization, they have severely compromised their witness as Christians.

By taking the Masonic obligation, the Christian agrees to allow the pollution of his or her mind, spirit, and body by those who serve false gods and believe false doctrines.

Masonry denies and contradicts the clear teaching of Scripture on numerous issues. Masonry also requires people to engage in activities that the Bible condemns. As a result, a Christian should not be a member of any secret society or organization that has any connection with Freemasonry.

75. What is the Illuminati conspiracy?

The Illuminati conspiracy is a conspiracy theory that holds there is a society of the "global elite" that is either in control of the world or is seeking to take control of the world. As with most conspiracy theories, beliefs regarding the Illuminati conspiracy vary widely, and so it is virtually impossible to give a synopsis of the Illuminati conspiracy. Popularized in recent books and movies, the Illuminati conspiracy has reached "cult fiction" status.

If one were to attempt to summarize the Illuminati conspiracy, it would go something like this: The Illuminati began as a secret society under the direction of Jesuit priests. Later, a council of five men, one for each of the points on the pentagram, formed what was called "The Ancient and Illuminated Seers of Bavaria." They were high order Luciferian Freemasons, thoroughly immersed in mysticism and Eastern mental disciplines, seeking to develop the superpowers of the mind. Their alleged plan and purpose is world domination for their lord (who precisely this lord is varies widely). The Illuminati are alleged to be the primary motivational forces encouraging global governance, a one-world religious ethic, and centralized control of the world's economic systems. Organizations such as the United Nations, the International Monetary Fund, the World Bank, and the International Criminal Court are seen as tentacles of the Illuminati. According to the Illuminati conspiracy, the Illuminati are the driving force behind efforts to brainwash the gullible masses through thought control and manipulation of beliefs, through the press, the educational curriculum, and the political leadership of nations.

The Illuminati supposedly have a private board of elite, interlocking delegates who control the world's major banks. They create inflations, recessions, and depressions and manipulate the world markets, supporting certain leaders and undermining others to achieve their overall goals. The supposed goal behind the Illuminati conspiracy is to create and then manage crises that will eventually convince the masses that globalism, with its centralized economic control and one-world religious ethic, is the necessary solution to the world's woes. This structure, usually known as the "New World Order," will, of course, be ruled by the Illuminati.

Does the Illuminati conspiracy have any basis from a Christian/ biblical perspective? Perhaps. There are many end-times prophecies in the Bible that are interpreted as pointing to an end-times, one-world government, a one-world monetary system, and a one-world religion. Many Bible prophecy interpreters see this New World Order as being controlled by the Antichrist, the end-times false messiah. If the Illuminati conspiracy and the New World Order have any validity and are indeed occurring, there is one fact that Christians must remember: God has sovereignly allowed all these developments, and they are not outside of His overall plan. God is in control, not the Illuminati. No plan or scheme the Illuminati develop could in any way prevent, or even hinder, God's sovereign plan for the world.

If there is indeed some truth to the Illuminati conspiracy, the Illuminati are nothing but pawns in the hands of Satan, tools to be manipulated in his conflict with God. The fate of the Illuminati will be the same as the fate of their lord, Satan/Lucifer, who will be cast into the lake of fire to "be tormented day and night, for ever and ever" (Revelation 20:10). In John 16:33 Jesus declared, "In this world you will have trouble. But take heart! I have overcome the world." Christians do not fear the Illuminati conspiracy, having this promise in 1 John 4:4: "You, dear children, are from God and have overcome them, because the one who is in you is greater than the one who is in the world."

76. What is cultural relativism?

Cultural relativism is the view that all beliefs, customs, and ethics are relative to the individual within his or her own social context. In other words, "right" and "wrong" are culture specific; what is considered moral in one society may be considered immoral in another, and, since no universal standard of morality exists, no one has the right to judge another society's customs.

Cultural relativism is widely accepted in modern anthropology. Cultural relativists believe that all cultures are worthy in their own right and are of equal value. Diversity of cultures, even those with conflicting moral beliefs, is not to be considered in terms of right and wrong or good and bad. Today's anthropologist considers all cultures to be equally legitimate expressions of human existence, to be studied from a purely neutral perspective.

Cultural relativism is closely related to ethical relativism, which views truth as variable and not absolute. What constitutes right and wrong is determined solely by the individual or by society. Since truth is not objective, there can be no objective standard that applies to all cultures. No one can say if someone else is right or wrong; it is a matter of personal opinion, and no society can pass judgment on another society.

Cultural relativism sees nothing inherently wrong (and nothing inherently good) with any cultural expression. So, the ancient Mayan practices of self-mutilation and human sacrifice are neither good nor bad; they are simply cultural distinctives, akin to the American custom of shooting fireworks on the Fourth of July. Human sacrifice and fireworks—both are simply different products of separate socialization.

In January 2002, when President Bush referred to terrorist nations as an "axis of evil,"[12] the cultural relativists were mortified. That any society would call another society "evil" is anathema to the relativist. The current movement to "understand" radical Islam—rather than to fight it—is a sign that relativism is making gains. The cultural relativist believes Westerners should not impose their ideas on terrorists, including the idea that the suicide bombing of civilians is evil. Islamic belief in the necessity of jihad is just as valid as any belief in Western civilization, the relativists assert, and America is as much to blame for the attacks of 9/11 as are the terrorists.

Cultural relativists are generally opposed to missionary work. When the gospel penetrates hearts and changes lives, some cultural change always follows. For example, when Don and Carol Richardson evangelized the Sawi tribe of the Netherlands New Guinea in 1962, the Sawi changed: specifically, they gave up their long-held customs of cannibalism and immolating widows on their husbands' funeral pyres. The cultural relativists may accuse the Richardsons of cultural imperialism, but most of the world would agree that ending cannibalism is a good thing.[13]

As Christians, we value all people, regardless of culture, because we recognize that all people are created in the image of God (Genesis 1:27). We also recognize that diversity of culture is a beautiful thing and differences in food, clothing, language, etc., should be preserved and appreciated. At the same time, we know that because of sin, not all beliefs and practices within a culture are godly or culturally beneficial. Truth is not subjective (John 17:17); truth is absolute, and there does exist a moral standard to which all people of every culture will be held accountable (Revelation 20:11–12).

Our goal as missionaries is not to westernize the world. Rather, it is to bring the good news of salvation in Christ to the world. The gospel message will kindle social reform to the extent that any society whose practices are out of step with God's moral standard will change— idolatry, polygamy, and slavery, for example, will come to an end as the Word of God prevails (see Acts 19). In amoral issues, missionaries seek to preserve and honor the culture of the people they serve.

SECTION 9

Questions about Sin

77. What is the definition of *sin*?

Sin is described in the Bible as transgression of the law of God (1 John 3:4) and rebellion against God (Deuteronomy 9:7; Joshua 1:18). Sin had its beginning with Lucifer, probably the most beautiful and powerful of the angels. Not content with his position, he desired to be higher than God, and that was his downfall, the beginning of sin (Isaiah 14:12–15). Renamed Satan, he brought sin to the human race in the garden of Eden, where he tempted Adam and Eve with the same enticement, "you will be like God" (Genesis 3:5). Genesis 3 describes Adam and Eve's rebellion against God and against His command. Since that time, sin has been passed down through all the generations of mankind and we, Adam's descendants, have inherited sin from him. Romans 5:12 tells us that through Adam sin entered the world, and so death was passed on to all men because "the wages of sin is death" (Romans 6:23).

Through Adam, the inherent inclination to sin entered the human race, and human beings became sinners by nature. When Adam sinned, his inner nature was transformed by his sin of rebellion, bringing to him spiritual death and depravity that would be passed on to all who came after him. We are sinners because we sin, *and* we sin because we are sinners. This passed-on depravity is known as inherited sin. Just as we inherit physical characteristics from our parents, we inherit our sinful natures from Adam. King David lamented this condition of fallen human nature in Psalm 51:5: "Surely I was sinful at birth, sinful from the time my mother conceived me."

Another type of sin is known as imputed sin. Used in both financial and legal settings, the Greek word translated "impute" means "to take something that belongs to someone and credit it to another's account." Before the law of Moses was given, sin was not imputed to man, although men were still sinners because of inherited sin. After the Law was given, sins committed in violation of the Law were imputed (accounted) to them (Romans 5:13). Even before transgressions of the law were imputed to men, the ultimate penalty for sin (death) continued to reign (Romans 5:14). All humans, from Adam to Moses, were subject to death, not because of their sinful acts against the Mosaic law (which they did not have), but because of their own inherited sinful nature. After Moses, humans were subject to death both because of inherited sin from Adam and imputed sin from violating the laws of God.

God used the principle of imputation to benefit mankind when He imputed the sin of believers to the account of Jesus Christ, who paid the penalty for that sin—death—on the cross. Imputing our sin to Jesus, God treated Him as if He were a sinner, though He was not, and had Him die for the sins of the entire world (1 John 2:2). It is important to understand that sin was imputed to Him, but He did not inherit it from Adam. He bore the penalty for sin, but He never became a sinner. His pure and perfect nature was untouched by sin. He was treated as though He were guilty of all the sins ever committed by the human race, even though He committed none. God then imputed the righteousness of Christ to believers and credited our accounts with His righteousness, just as He had credited our sins to Christ's account (2 Corinthians 5:21).

A third type of sin is personal sin, that which is committed every day by every human being. Because we have inherited a sin nature from Adam, we commit individual, personal sins, everything from seemingly innocent untruths to murder. Those who have not placed their faith in Jesus Christ must pay the penalty for these personal sins, as well as inherited and imputed sin. However, believers have been freed from the eternal penalty of sin—hell and spiritual death. We also have the power to resist sinning. Now we can choose whether or not to commit personal sins because we have the sanctifying power of the Holy Spirit who dwells within us. When we do sin, the Spirit convicts us (Romans 8:9–11). Once we confess our personal sins to God and ask forgiveness for them, we are restored to perfect fellowship and communion with Him. "If we confess our sins, He is faithful and just to forgive us our sins and cleanse us from all unrighteousness" (1 John 1:9 NKJV).

We are three times condemned due to inherited sin, imputed sin, and personal sin. The only just penalty for this sin is death (Romans 6:23), not just physical death but eternal death (Revelation 20:11–15). Thankfully, inherited sin, imputed sin, and personal sin have all been crucified on the cross of Jesus, and now by faith in Jesus Christ as the Savior "we have redemption through His blood, the forgiveness of sins, according to the riches of His grace" (Ephesians 1:7 NKJV).

78. Will God continue to forgive you if you commit the same sin over and over again?

One of the most effective tricks Satan plays on Christians is to convince us that our sins aren't really forgiven, despite the promise of

God's Word. If we've received Jesus as Savior by faith and still feel uneasy about whether we have true forgiveness, that worry may have a demonic source. Demons hate it when people are delivered from their grasp, and they try to plant seeds of doubt in our minds about the reality of our salvation. In his vast arsenal of tricks, one of Satan's biggest tools is to constantly remind us of our past transgressions. He is "the accuser" (Revelation 12:10), and he tries to use past sins to prove that God couldn't possibly forgive or restore us. The devil's attacks make it a real challenge for us to simply rest in the promises of God and trust His love.

To allay fear, we will look at two powerful passages of Scripture. The first is found in the book of Psalms: "As far as the east is from the west, so far has he removed our transgressions from us" (Psalm 103:12). God not only forgives our sins but removes them completely from His presence. This is a profound thing! Without question, this removal of sin is a difficult concept to grasp, which is why it's so easy for us to worry and wonder about forgiveness instead of just accepting it. The key lies in giving up our doubts and our feelings of guilt and resting in God's promises of forgiveness.

Another helpful passage is 1 John 1:9, "If we confess our sins, he is faithful and just and will forgive us our sins and purify us from all unrighteousness." What an incredible promise! God cleanses His children of their sin. All we must do is come to Him and confess our sins to Him. We will stumble in this world, but in Christ we can always find cleansing.

In Matthew 18:21–22, "Peter came to Jesus and asked, 'Lord, how many times shall I forgive my brother or sister who sins against me? Up to seven times?' Jesus answered, 'I tell you, not seven times, but seventy-seven times.'" Peter was probably thinking that he was being generous in asking the question. Rather than repay a sin in kind, Peter suggested giving the brother some leeway, say, forgiving him up to seven times. But the eighth time, forgiveness and grace would run out. Christ challenged the rules of Peter's suggested economy of grace by saying that forgiveness is infinite for those who are truly seeking it. Such forgiveness is only possible because of the infinite grace of God shown by the shed blood of Christ on the cross. Because of Christ's forgiving power, we are His children, and we can always be made clean—even after a repeated sin—if we humbly seek God's forgiveness.

At the same time, we should note that a believer will not pursue a lifestyle of habitual and continual sin (1 John 3:8–9). Paul admonishes, "Examine yourselves to see whether you are in the faith; test yourselves. Do you not realize that Christ Jesus is in you—unless, of course, you fail the test?" (2 Corinthians 13:5). As Christians, we do stumble, but we do not live a lifestyle of continued, unrepentant sin. All of us have weaknesses and can fall into sin, even if we don't want to. Even the apostle Paul did what he didn't want to do because of the sin at work in his body (Romans 7:15). Like Paul, the response of the believer is to hate the sin, repent of it, and ask for divine grace to overcome it (Romans 7:24–25). When our faith grows weak and, like Peter, we deny our Lord in word or in deed, even then there is a chance to repent and be forgiven of our sin.

Satan would have us think that there is no hope, that there is no possibility that we can be forgiven, healed, and restored. He will try to get us to feel trapped by guilt so that we do not feel worthy of God's forgiveness any longer. But since when were we ever worthy of God's grace? Grace is, by definition, extended to the unworthy. God loved us and chose us to be in Christ before the foundation of the world (Ephesians 1:4–6), not because of anything we did, but "in order that we, who were the first to put our hope in Christ, might be for the praise of his glory" (Ephesians 1:12). There is no place we can go that God's grace cannot reach, and there is no depth to which we can sink that God is no longer able to pull us out. His grace is greater than all our sin. Whether we are just starting to wander off course or we are already sinking and drowning in our sin, grace can be received.

Grace is a gift from God (Ephesians 2:8). When we sin, the Spirit will convict us of sin such that a godly sorrow will result (2 Corinthians 7:10–11). He will not condemn our souls as if there is no hope, for there is no longer any condemnation for those who are in Christ Jesus (Romans 8:1). The Spirit's conviction within us is a movement of love and grace. Grace is not an excuse to sin (Romans 6:1–2), and it dare not be abused. Sin must be faced honestly; it must be called "sin," and it cannot be treated as if it were harmless or inoffensive. Unrepentant believers need to be lovingly confronted and guided to freedom, and unbelievers need to be told of their need to repent. Yet let us also emphasize the remedy, for we have been given grace upon grace (John 1:16). Grace is how we live, how we are saved, how we are sanctified, and how we will be kept and glorified. Let us receive grace when we sin by repenting and confessing our sin to God. Why live a sinful life when Christ offers to make us whole and right in the eyes of God?

79. What does the Bible say about drinking alcohol/wine? Is it a sin for a Christian to drink alcohol/wine?

Scripture has much to say regarding the drinking of alcohol (Leviticus 10:9; Numbers 6:3; Deuteronomy 29:6; Judges 13:4, 7, 14; Proverbs 20:1; 31:4; Isaiah 5:11, 22; 24:9; 28:7; 29:9; 56:12). However, Scripture does not necessarily forbid a Christian from drinking beer, wine, or any other drink containing alcohol. In fact, some passages of Scripture discuss alcohol in positive terms. Ecclesiastes 9:7 instructs, "Drink your wine with a merry heart" (ESV). Psalm 104:14–15 states that God gives wine "that makes glad the heart of man" (NKJV). Amos 9:14 discusses drinking wine from your own vineyard as a sign of God's blessing. Isaiah 55:1 encourages, "Come, buy wine and milk."

What God commands Christians regarding alcohol is to avoid drunkenness (Ephesians 5:18). The Bible condemns drunkenness and its effects (Proverbs 23:29–35). Christians are also commanded to not allow their bodies to be "mastered" by anything (1 Corinthians 6:12; 2 Peter 2:19). Drinking alcohol in excess is undeniably addictive. Scripture also forbids a Christian from doing anything that might offend other Christians or encourage them to sin against their conscience (1 Corinthians 8:9–13). In light of these principles, it would be extremely difficult for any Christian to say they are drinking alcohol in excess to the glory of God (1 Corinthians 10:31).

Jesus changed water into wine. It even seems that Jesus drank wine on occasion (Matthew 26:29; John 2:1–11). In New Testament times, the water was not very clean. Without modern sanitation, the water was often filled with bacteria, viruses, and all kinds of contaminants. The same is true in many third world countries today. As a result, people often drank wine (or grape juice) because it was far less likely to be contaminated. In 1 Timothy 5:23, Paul instructed Timothy to stop drinking water exclusively (which was probably causing his stomach problems) and instead drink wine. In that day, wine was fermented (containing alcohol), but not necessarily to the degree it is today. It is incorrect to say it was grape juice, but it is also incorrect to say it was the same thing as the wine commonly used today. Again, Scripture does not forbid Christians from drinking beer, wine, or any other drink containing alcohol. Alcohol is not, in and of itself, tainted by sin. It is drunkenness and addiction to alcohol that a Christian must absolutely refrain from (Ephesians 5:18; 1 Corinthians 6:12).

Alcohol, consumed in small quantities, is neither harmful nor addictive. In fact, some doctors advocate drinking small amounts of red wine for its health benefits, especially for the heart. Consumption of small quantities of alcohol is a matter of Christian freedom. Drunkenness and addiction are sin. However, due to the biblical concerns regarding alcohol and its effects, due to the easy temptation to consume alcohol in excess, and due to the possibility of causing a brother or sister to stumble, it is often best for a Christian to abstain from drinking alcohol.

80. What does the Bible say about tattoos?

Tattoos are more popular than ever in many parts of the world. The number of people with tattoos has increased dramatically in recent years. Tattoos are not just for delinquents or rebels anymore. The edginess of rebellion historically associated with tattoos has worn off.

The New Testament does not say anything about whether or not a believer in Jesus Christ should get a tattoo. Therefore, we cannot say that getting a tattoo is a sin. Because of Scripture's silence, getting inked falls under the category of a gray area, and believers should follow their convictions in the matter, respecting those who may have different convictions.

Here are some general biblical principles that may apply to getting a tattoo:

- Children are to honor and obey their parents (Ephesians 6:1–2). For a minor to get a tattoo in violation of his or her parents' wishes is biblically unsupportable. Tattoos born of rebellion are sinful.

- "Outward adornment" is not as important as the development of the "inner self" and should not be the focus of a Christian (1 Peter 3:3–4). A person who desires a tattoo to garner attention or draw admiration has a vain, sinful focus on self.

- God sees the heart, and our motivation for anything we do should be to glorify God (1 Corinthians 10:31). Motivations for getting a tattoo such as to fit in, to stand out, etc., fall short of the glory of God. The tattoo itself may not be a sin, but the motivation in getting it might be.

- Our bodies, as well as our souls, have been redeemed and belong to God. The believer's body is the temple of the Holy Spirit (1 Corinthians 6:19–20). How much modification of that temple is appropriate? Is there a line that should not be crossed? Is there a point at which the proliferation of tattoos on one body ceases to be art and starts becoming sinful mutilation? This should be a matter of individual reflection and honest prayer.

- We are Christ's ambassadors, delivering God's message to the world (2 Corinthians 5:20). What message does the tattoo send, and will it aid or detract from representing Christ and sharing the gospel?

- Whatever does not come from faith is sin (Romans 14:23), so the person getting the tattoo should be fully convinced that it is God's will for him or her.

We cannot leave the discussion of tattoos without looking at the Old Testament law that prohibited tattoos: "Do not cut your bodies for the dead or put tattoo marks on yourselves. I am the LORD" (Leviticus 19:28). The reason for the prohibition of tattoos in this passage is not stated, but it is likely that tattooing was a pagan practice connected with idolatry and superstition. It was probably common for the pagans to mark their skin with the name of a false god or with a symbol honoring some idol. God demanded that His children be different. As He reminded them in the same verse, "I am the LORD." The Israelites belonged to Him; they were His workmanship, and they should not bear the name of a false god on their bodies. While New Testament believers are not under the Mosaic law, we can take from this command the principle that if a Christian chooses to get a tattoo, it should never be for superstitious reasons or to promote worldly philosophy. The bottom line is that getting a tattoo is not a sin, per se. It is a matter of Christian freedom and should be guided by biblical principles and rooted in love.

81. Is gambling a sin? What does the Bible say about gambling?

The Bible does not specifically condemn gambling, betting, or the lottery. The Bible does warn us, however, against the love of money

(1 Timothy 6:10; Hebrews 13:5). Scripture also encourages us to avoid attempts to get rich quick (Proverbs 13:11; 23:5; Ecclesiastes 5:10); we are to work hard and earn a living (Proverbs 14:23; 2 Thessalonians 3:10). Gambling focuses on the love of money and tempts people with the promise of quick and easy riches.

Gambling, if done in moderation and only on occasion, is a waste of money but not necessarily evil. People waste money on all sorts of activities. Gambling is no more or less wasteful than seeing a movie (in many cases), eating an unnecessarily expensive meal, or purchasing a worthless item. Of course, the fact that money is wasted on other things does not justify gambling. Money should not be wasted. By cutting wasteful spending, one can save money for future needs or give more to the Lord's work. Gambling only adds to the waste.

While the Bible does not explicitly mention gambling, it does mention events of luck or chance. For example, casting lots was God's prescribed method of choosing between the sacrificial goat and the scapegoat (Leviticus 16:8). Joshua cast lots to determine the allotment of land to the various tribes, and the results were accepted as God's will (Joshua 18:10). Nehemiah cast lots to determine who would live inside the walls of Jerusalem (Nehemiah 11:1). The apostles cast lots to determine the replacement for Judas (Acts 1:26). Each of these occasions proved the truth of Proverbs 16:33, which says, "The lot is cast into the lap, but its every decision is from the LORD." With the exception of the Roman soldiers' gambling at the foot of the cross (John 19:24), none of the instances of casting lots in the Bible have to do with betting or the transfer of goods. The apostles' casting lots in Acts 1 is no justification for playing craps in Vegas.

Gambling, by nature, takes advantage of the misfortune of others. In order for one person to win, someone else—usually multiple others—must lose. For a Christian to risk money on the off chance that he will gain even more is foolish. But to actively seek financial benefit from someone else's loss is more than foolish; it is unethical.

What about casinos and lotteries? Casinos use all sorts of marketing schemes to entice gamblers to risk as much money as possible.

They often offer inexpensive or even free alcohol, which encourages drunkenness—and a decreased ability to make wise decisions. Everything in a casino is perfectly rigged for taking money in large sums and giving nothing in return but momentary thrills and empty pleasures.

State and national lotteries are a form of gambling. Lotteries tempt people with the possibility of quick riches and are marketed as a way to fund education and/or social programs. However, it seems that those the lottery is touted to help are actually being hurt. A recent study showed that households in the lowest income bracket spend 13 percent of their annual household income on the lottery, in contrast to the highest earners, who spend just 1 percent of their income on the lottery.[1] In other words, those who can least afford to spend money on lottery tickets are often the ones buying them. With the chances of winning the lottery being infinitesimal, the whole system preys upon the poor.

First Timothy 6:10 provides wisdom that directly relates to gambling: "For the love of money is a root of all kinds of evil. Some people, eager for money, have wandered from the faith and pierced themselves with many griefs." Those who gamble cannot follow the admonition of Hebrews 13:5: "Keep your lives free from the love of money and be content with what you have, because God has said, 'Never will I leave you; never will I forsake you'" (Hebrews 13:6). Serving God and serving money are incompatible (Matthew 6:24).

In summary, gambling is poor stewardship of one's God-given resources, it attempts to bypass honest work, it promotes greed and covetousness, and it rejoices in the misfortune of others. A Christian should not be involved in gambling or in other forms of materialism.

82. What is the Christian view of suicide? What does the Bible say about suicide?

The Bible mentions six specific people who committed suicide: Abimelech (Judges 9:54), Saul (1 Samuel 31:4), Saul's armor-bearer

(1 Samuel 31:4–6), Ahithophel (2 Samuel 17:23), Zimri (1 Kings 16:18), and Judas (Matthew 27:5). Five of these men were noted for their wickedness (the exception is Saul's armor-bearer—nothing is said of his character). Some consider Samson's death an instance of suicide because he knew his actions would lead to his death (Judges 16:26–31), but Samson's goal was to kill Philistines, not himself.

The Bible views suicide as equal to murder, which is what it is— self-murder. God is the only one who is to decide when and how a person should die. We should say with the psalmist, "My times are in your hands" (Psalm 31:15).

God is the giver of life. He gives, and He takes away (Job 1:21). Suicide, the taking of one's own life, is ungodly because it rejects God's gift of life. No man or woman should presume to take God's authority upon themselves to end his or her own life.

Some people in Scripture felt deep despair in life. Solomon, in his pursuit of pleasure, reached the point where he "hated life" (Ecclesiastes 2:17). Elijah was fearful and depressed and yearned for death (1 Kings 19:4). Jonah was so angry at God that he wished to die (Jonah 4:8). Even the apostle Paul and his missionary companions at one point "were under great pressure, far beyond our ability to endure, so that we despaired of life itself" (2 Corinthians 1:8).

However, none of these men committed suicide. Solomon learned to "fear God and keep his commandments, for this is the duty of all mankind" (Ecclesiastes 12:13). Elijah was comforted by an angel, allowed to rest, and given a new commission. Jonah received admonition and rebuke from God. Paul learned that although the pressure he faced was beyond his ability to endure, the Lord can bear all things: "This happened that we might not rely on ourselves but on God, who raises the dead" (2 Corinthians 1:9).

So, according to the Bible, suicide is a sin. It is not the greatest sin—it is no worse than other evils, in terms of how God sees it, and it does not determine a person's eternal destiny. However, suicide definitely has a deep and lasting impact on those left behind. The painful scars left by a suicide do not heal easily. May God grant His grace to each one who is facing trials today (Psalm 67:1). And may each of us take hope in the promise "Everyone who calls on the name of the Lord will be saved" (Romans 10:13).

If you are considering suicide, please seek help now. If you are in the United States, call 1-800-273-8255, the national hotline, get yourself to a hospital if you can, call 911, or go alert someone in your home, apartment, or workplace, or wherever you are. Do whatever it takes to get help.

National Hopeline Network: 1-800-422-HOPE (4673)

National Suicide Prevention Lifeline: 1-800-273-TALK (8255)

To Write Love on Her Arms: http://twloha.com/find-help

Befrienders.org: http://www.befrienders.org/directory

Suicide hotlines available in most countries: http://www.suicide .org/international-suicide-hotlines.html

83. What does the Bible say about abortion?

The Bible never specifically addresses the issue of abortion. However, there are numerous teachings in Scripture that make it abundantly clear what God's view of abortion is.

Jeremiah 1:5 tells us that God knows us before He forms us in the womb. Psalm 139:13–16 speaks of God's active role in our creation and formation in the womb. Exodus 21:22–25 prescribes the same penalty—death—for someone who causes the death of a baby in the womb as for someone who commits murder. This law and its punishment clearly indicate that God considers a baby in the womb to be just as much a human being as a full-grown adult. For the Christian, abortion is not a matter of a woman's right to choose to have a baby. The baby is already present and living. Abortion is a matter of the life or death of a human being made in God's image (Genesis 1:26–27; 9:6).

What does the Bible say about abortion? Simply put, abortion is murder. It is the killing of a human being created in the image of God.

A common argument against the Christian stance on abortion is, What about cases of rape and/or incest? As difficult as it would be to become pregnant as a result of rape or incest, is the murder of a baby the solution? Two wrongs do not make a right. Intentionally killing the unborn child is not the answer. Also, keep in mind that having an abortion is a traumatic experience. It seems nonsensical to add an additional trauma to the woman. Too, abortion can be a means of rapists covering up their crimes. For example, if a minor is molested and becomes pregnant and then is taken to have an abortion, the molestation could continue without penalty. Abortion will never erase the pain of rape or incest, but it very well may add to it.

A child who is conceived through rape or incest is made in the image of God the same as any other human. That child's life should be protected just as much as the life of any other human being. The circumstances of conception never determine the worth of a person or that person's future. The baby in this situation is completely innocent and should not be punished for the evil act of his or her father. Depending on the situation, the mother might choose to raise the child. If she does not already have a community of support, she can turn to many organizations and local churches prepared to walk alongside her. Or she might place the child for adoption. There are many families, some unable to have children on their own, who stand ready to receive and love a child from any background.

It's also important to keep in mind that abortions due to rape or incest account for a very small percentage of total abortions: only 1 percent of abortions can be traced to cases of rape or incest.[2]

Another argument often used against the Christian stance on abortion is "What about when the life of the mother is at risk?" Honestly, this is the most difficult question to answer on the issue of abortion. First, let's remember that such a situation is exceedingly rare. Dr. Landrum Shettles, a pioneer in the field of in vitro fertilization, wrote, "Less than 1 percent of all abortions are performed to save the mother's life."[3] Dr. Irving Cushner, professor of obstetrics at the UCLA School of Medicine, when testifying before the US Senate, was asked how often abortions are necessary to save the life of the mother or to preserve her physical health. His response: "In this country, about 2 percent."[4]

Other medical professionals go further, stating that abortion is *never* necessary to save the mother's life. Over one thousand OB-GYNs and maternal healthcare experts signed a statement in 2012, saying, in part, "As experienced practitioners and researchers in obstetrics and gynaecology, we affirm that direct abortion—the purposeful destruction of the unborn child—is not medically necessary to save the life of a woman."[5] Further, in 2019, "medical leaders representing more than 30,000 doctors said intentionally killing a late-term unborn baby in an abortion is never necessary to save a mother's life."[6]

Second, let's remember that God is a God of miracles. He can preserve the life of a mother and her child despite all the medical odds being against them. Third, even in the small percentage of abortions performed to save the life of the mother, most of those abortions can be prevented by an early induced delivery of the baby or a C-section. It is extremely rare that a baby must be actively aborted in order to save the life of the mother. Ultimately, if the life of the mother is genuinely at risk, the course of action can only be decided by the woman, her doctor, oftentimes the father of the child, and God. Any woman facing this extremely difficult situation should pray to the Lord for wisdom (James 1:5) as to what He would have her do.

The overwhelming majority of abortions performed today involve women who simply do not want to have the baby. As indicated above, just 2 percent of abortions are for the reason of rape, incest, or the mother's life being at risk. Even in these more difficult 2 percent of instances, abortion should never be the first option. The life of a human being in the womb is worth every effort to preserve.

For those who have had an abortion, remember that the sin of abortion is no less forgivable than any other sin. Through faith in Christ, all sins can be forgiven (John 3:16; Romans 8:1; Colossians

1:14). A woman who has had an abortion, a man who has encouraged an abortion, and a doctor who has performed an abortion—all can be forgiven and find healing and restoration by faith in Jesus Christ.

84. What is blasphemy against the Holy Spirit?

The concept of blasphemy against the Spirit is mentioned in Mark 3:22–30 and Matthew 12:22–32. Jesus had just performed a miracle. A demon-possessed man was brought to Jesus, and the Lord cast the demon out, healing the man of blindness and muteness. The eyewitnesses to this exorcism began to wonder if Jesus was indeed the Messiah they had been waiting for. A group of Pharisees, hearing the talk of the Messiah, quickly quashed any budding faith in the crowd: "It is only by Beelzebul, the prince of demons, that this fellow drives out demons," they said (Matthew 12:24).

Jesus rebuts the Pharisees with some logical arguments for why He is not casting out demons in the power of Satan (Matthew 12:25–29). Then He speaks of the blasphemy against the Holy Spirit: "I tell you, every kind of sin and slander can be forgiven, but blasphemy against the Spirit will not be forgiven. Anyone who speaks a word against the Son of Man will be forgiven, but anyone who speaks against the Holy Spirit will not be forgiven, either in this age or in the age to come" (verses 31–32).

The term *blasphemy* may be generally defined as defiant irreverence. The term can be applied to such sins as cursing God or willfully degrading things relating to God. Blasphemy is also attributing some evil to God or denying Him some good that we should attribute to Him. This particular case of blasphemy, however, is called "blasphemy against the Spirit" in Matthew 12:31. The Pharisees, having witnessed irrefutable proof that Jesus was working miracles in the power of the Holy Spirit, claimed instead that the Lord was possessed by a demon (Matthew 12:24). Notice in Mark 3:30 Jesus is very specific about what the Pharisees did to commit blasphemy against the Holy Spirit: "He said this because they were saying, 'He has an impure spirit.'"

Blasphemy against the Holy Spirit has to do with accusing Jesus Christ of being demon-possessed instead of Spirit-filled. This particular type of blasphemy cannot be duplicated today. The Pharisees were in a unique moment in history: they had the Law and the Prophets, they had the Holy Spirit stirring their hearts, they had the Son of God Himself standing right in front of them, and they saw with their own eyes the miracles He did. Never before in the history of the world (and never since) had so much divine light been granted to men; if anyone should have recognized Jesus for who He was, it was the Pharisees. Yet they chose defiance. They purposely attributed the work of the Spirit to the devil, even though they knew the truth and had the proof. Jesus declared their willful blindness to be unpardonable. Their blasphemy against the Holy Spirit was their final rejection of God's grace. They had set their course, and God was going to let them sail into perdition unhindered.

Jesus told the crowd that the Pharisees' blasphemy against the Holy Spirit "will not be forgiven, either in this age or in the age to come" (Matthew 12:32). This is another way of saying that their sin would never be forgiven, ever. Not now, not in eternity. As Mark 3:29 puts it, "They are guilty of an eternal sin."

The immediate result of the Pharisees' public rejection of Christ (and God's rejection of them) is seen in the next chapter. Jesus, for the first time, "told them many things in parables" (Matthew 13:3; cf. Mark 4:2). The disciples were puzzled at Jesus' change of teaching method, and Jesus explained His use of parables: "Because the knowledge of the secrets of the kingdom of heaven has been given to you, but not to them. . . . Though seeing, they do not see; though hearing, they do not hear or understand" (Matthew 13:11, 13). Jesus began to veil the truth with parables and metaphors as a direct result of the Jewish leaders' official denunciation of Him.

Again, the blasphemy of the Holy Spirit cannot be repeated today, although some people try. Jesus Christ is not on earth—He is seated at the right hand of God. No one can personally witness Jesus performing a miracle and then attribute that power to Satan instead of the Spirit.

The unpardonable sin today is the state of continued unbelief. The Spirit currently convicts the unsaved world of sin, righteousness, and judgment (John 16:8). To resist that conviction and willfully remain unrepentant is to blaspheme the Spirit. There is no pardon, either in this age or in the age to come, for a person who rejects the Spirit's promptings to trust in Jesus Christ and then dies in unbelief. The love of God is evident: "For God so loved the world that he gave his one and only Son, that whoever believes in him shall not perish but have eternal life" (John 3:16). And the choice is clear: "Whoever believes in the Son has eternal life, but whoever rejects the Son will not see life, for God's wrath remains on him" (John 3:36).

85. What does the Bible say about breaking generational curses?

The Bible mentions generational curses in several places (Exodus 20:5; 34:7; Numbers 14:18). God warns that He is "a jealous God, punishing the children for the sin of the parents to the third and fourth generation of those who hate me" (Deuteronomy 5:9).

It sounds unfair for God to punish children for the sins of their parents. However, there is more to it than that. The effects of sin are naturally passed down from one generation to the next. When a father has a sinful lifestyle, his children are likely to practice the same sinful lifestyle. Implied in the warning of Exodus 20:5 is the fact that the children will choose to repeat the sins of their parents. A Jewish Targum (a Jewish Aramaic translation of the Hebrew Bible) specifies that this passage refers to "ungodly fathers" and "rebellious children." So, it is not unjust for God to punish sin to the third or fourth generation—those generations are committing the same sins their ancestors did.

There is a trend in the church today to try to blame every sin and problem on some sort of generational curse. This is not biblical. God's warning to visit iniquity on future generations is part of the Old Testament law. A generational curse was a consequence for a specific nation (Israel) for a specific sin (idolatry). The history books of the Old Testament (especially Judges) contain the record of this divine punishment meted out.

The cure for a generational curse has always been repentance. When Israel turned from idols to serve the living God, the curse was broken and God saved them (Judges 3:9, 15; 1 Samuel 12:10–11). Yes, God promised to visit Israel's sin upon the third and fourth generations, but in the very next verse He promised that He would show "love to a thousand generations of those who love me and keep my commandments" (Exodus 20:6). In other words, God's grace lasts a thousand times longer than His wrath.

For someone worried about a generational curse, the answer is salvation through Jesus Christ. A Christian is a new creation (2 Corinthians 5:17). How can a child of God still be under God's curse (Romans 8:1)? The cure for a "generational curse" is repentance of the sin in question, faith in Christ, and a life consecrated to the Lord (Romans 12:1–2).

86. What is sanctification? What is the definition of Christian sanctification?

Sanctification is God's will for us (1 Thessalonians 4:89). The word *sanctification* is related to the word *saint*; both words have to do with holiness. To sanctify something is to set it apart for special use; to sanctify a person is to make him holy.

Jesus had a lot to say about sanctification in John 17. In verse 16 the Lord says, "They are not of the world, even as I am not of it," and this is before His request: "Sanctify them by the truth; your word is truth" (verse 17). In Christian theology, sanctification is a state of separation unto God; all believers enter into this state when they are born of God: "You are in Christ Jesus, who became to us wisdom from God, righteousness and sanctification and redemption" (1 Corinthians 1:30 ESV). The sanctification mentioned in this verse is a once-for-all separation of believers unto God. It is a work God performs, an integral part of our salvation and our connection with Christ (Hebrews 10:10). Theologians sometimes refer to this state of holiness before God as "positional" sanctification; it is related to justification.

While we are *positionally* holy ("set free from every sin" by the blood of Christ, Acts 13:39), we know that we still sin (1 John 1:10). That's why the Bible also refers to sanctification as a practical experience of our separation unto God. "Progressive" or "experiential" sanctification, as it is sometimes called, is the effect of obedience to the Word of God in one's life. It is the same as growing in the Lord (2 Peter 3:18) or spiritual maturity. God started the work of making us like Christ, and He is continuing it (Philippians 1:6). This type of sanctification is to be pursued by the believer earnestly (1 Peter 1:15; Hebrews 12:14) and is effected by the application of the Word (John 17:17). Progressive sanctification has in view the setting apart of believers for the purpose for which they are sent into the world: "As you sent me into the world, I have sent them into the world. For them I sanctify myself, that they too may be truly sanctified" (John 17:18–19). That Jesus set Himself apart for God's purpose is both the basis and the condition of our being set apart (see John 10:36). We are sanctified and sent because Jesus was. Our Lord's sanctification is the pattern of and power for our own. The sending and the sanctifying are inseparable. On this account we are called *saints* (*hagioi* in the Greek), or *sanctified ones*. Prior to salvation, our behavior bore witness to our standing in the world in separation from God, but now our behavior should bear witness to our standing before God in separation from the world. Little by little, every day, "those who are being sanctified" (Hebrews 10:14 ESV) are becoming more like Christ.

There is a third sense in which the word *sanctification* is used in Scripture—a complete or ultimate sanctification. This is the same as glorification. Paul prays in 1 Thessalonians 5:23, "May the God of peace himself sanctify you completely, and may your whole spirit and soul and body be kept blameless at the coming of our Lord Jesus Christ" (ESV). Paul speaks of Christ as "the hope of glory" (Colossians 1:27) and links the glorious appearing of Christ to our personal glorification: "When Christ, who is your life, appears, then you also will appear with him in glory" (Colossians 3:4). This glorified state will be our ultimate separation from sin, a total sanctification in every regard. "We know that when Christ appears, we shall be like him, for we shall see him as he is" (1 John 3:2).

To summarize, *sanctification* is a translation of the Greek word *hagiasmos*, meaning "holiness" or "a separation." In the past, God granted us justification, a once-for-all, positional holiness in Christ. In the present, God guides us to maturity, a practical, progressive holiness. In the future, God will give us glorification, a permanent, ultimate holiness. These three phases of sanctification separate the believer from the penalty of sin (justification), the power of sin (maturity), and the presence of sin (glorification).

87. What does the Bible mean when it says "Do not judge"?

Jesus' command not to judge others could be the most widely quoted of His sayings, even though it is almost invariably quoted in complete disregard of its context. Here is Jesus' statement: "Do not judge, or you too will be judged" (Matthew 7:1). Many people use this verse in an attempt to silence their critics, interpreting Jesus' meaning as "You don't have the right to tell me I'm wrong." Taken in isolation, Jesus' command "Do not judge" does indeed seem to preclude all negative assessments. However, there is much more to the passage than those three words.

The Bible's command that we not judge others does not mean we cannot show discernment. Immediately after Jesus says, "Do not judge," He says, "Do not give dogs what is sacred; do not throw your pearls to pigs" (Matthew 7:6). A little later in the same sermon, He says, "Watch out for false prophets. . . . By their fruit you will recognize them" (verses 15, 20). How are we to discern who are the "dogs" and "pigs" and "false prophets" unless we have the ability to make a judgment call on doctrines and deeds? Jesus is giving us permission to tell right from wrong.

Also, the Bible's command that we not judge others does not mean all actions are equally moral or truth is relative. The Bible clearly teaches that truth is objective, eternal, and inseparable from God's character. Anything that contradicts the truth is a lie—but, of course, to call something a lie is to pass judgment. To call adultery or murder a sin is likewise to pass judgment—but it's also to agree with God. When Jesus said not to judge others, He did not mean that no one can identify sin for what it is, based on God's definition of *sin*.

And the Bible's command that we not judge others does not mean there should be no mechanism for dealing with sin. The Bible has a whole book entitled Judges. The judges in the Old Testament were raised up by God Himself (Judges 2:18). The modern judicial system, including its judges, is a necessary part of society. In saying, "Do not judge," Jesus was not saying, "Anything goes."

Elsewhere, Jesus gives a direct command to judge: "Stop judging by mere appearances, but instead judge correctly" (John 7:24). Here we have a clue as to the right type of judgment versus the wrong type. Taking this verse and some others, we can put together a description of the sinful type of judgment:

Superficial judgment is wrong. Passing judgment on someone based solely on appearances is sinful (John 7:24). It is foolish to jump to conclusions before investigating the facts (Proverbs 18:13). Simon the Pharisee passed judgment on a woman based on her appearance and reputation, but he could not see the woman had been forgiven; Simon thus drew Jesus' rebuke for his unrighteous judgment (Luke 7:36–50).

Hypocritical judgment is wrong. Jesus' command not to judge others in Matthew 7:1 is preceded by comparisons to hypocrites (Matthew 6:2, 5, 16) and followed by a warning against hypocrisy (Matthew 7:3–5). When we point out the sin of others while we ourselves commit the same sin, we condemn ourselves (Romans 2:1).

Harsh, unforgiving judgment is wrong. We are "always to be gentle toward everyone" (Titus 3:2). It is the merciful who will be shown mercy (Matthew 5:7), and as Jesus warned, "In the same way you judge others, you will be judged, and with the measure you use, it will be measured to you" (Matthew 7:2).

Self-righteous judgment is wrong. We are called to humility, and "God opposes the proud" (James 4:6). In Jesus' parable of the Pharisee and the tax collector, the Pharisee was confident in his own righteousness and from that proud position judged the publican; however, God sees the heart and refused to forgive the Pharisee's sin (Luke 18:9–14).

Untrue judgment is wrong. The Bible clearly forbids bearing false witness (Proverbs 19:5). "Slander no one" (Titus 3:2).

Christians are often accused of judging or intolerance when they speak out against sin. But opposing sin is not wrong. Holding aloft the standard of righteousness naturally defines unrighteousness and draws the slings and arrows of those who choose sin over godliness. John the Baptist incurred the ire of Herodias when he spoke out against her adultery with Herod (Mark 6:18–19). She eventually silenced John, but she could not silence the truth (Isaiah 40:8).

Believers are warned against judging others unfairly or unrighteously, but Jesus commends "right judgment" (John 7:24 ESV). We are to be discerning (Colossians 1:9; 1 Thessalonians 5:21). We are to preach the whole counsel of God, including the Bible's teaching on sin (Acts 20:27; 2 Timothy 4:2). We are to gently confront erring brothers or sisters in Christ (Galatians 6:1). We are to practice church discipline (Matthew 18:15–17). We are to speak the truth in love (Ephesians 4:15).

SECTION 10

Questions about Sexuality

88. What is sexual immorality?

In the New Testament, the word most often translated "sexual immorality" is *porneia*. This word is also translated as "whoredom," "fornication," and "idolatry." It means a surrendering of sexual purity, and it is primarily used to describe premarital sexual relations. From this Greek word we get the English word *pornography*, stemming from the concept of "selling off." Sexual immorality is the "selling off" of sexual purity and involves any type of sexual expression outside the boundaries of a biblically defined marriage relationship (Matthew 19:4–5).

The connection between sexual immorality and idolatry is best understood in the context of 1 Corinthians 6:18, which says, "Flee from sexual immorality. All other sins a person commits are outside the body, but whoever sins sexually sins against their own body." The bodies of believers are "temples of the Holy Spirit" (1 Corinthians 6:19). Pagan idol worship often involved perverse and immoral sexual acts performed in the temple of a false god. When we use our physical bodies for immoral purposes, we are imitating pagan worship by profaning God's holy temple with acts He calls detestable (1 Corinthians 6:9–11).

Biblical prohibitions against sexual immorality are often coupled with warnings against "impurity" (Romans 1:24; Galatians 5:19; Ephesians 4:19). This word in the Greek is *akatharsia*, which means "defiled, foul, ceremonially unfit." It connotes actions that render a person unfit to enter God's presence. Those who persist in unrepentant immorality and impurity cannot come into the presence of God. Jesus said, "Blessed are the pure of heart, for they will see God" (Matthew 5:8; cf. Psalm 24:3–4). It is impossible to maintain a healthy intimacy with God when our bodies and souls are given over to impurities of any kind.

Sexuality is God's design. He alone can define the parameters for its use. The Bible is clear that sex was created to be enjoyed between one man and one woman who are in a covenant marriage until one of them dies (Matthew 19:6). Sexuality is His sacred wedding gift to human beings. Any expression of it outside those parameters constitutes an abuse of God's gift. Adultery, premarital sex, pornography, and homosexual relations are all contrary to God's design for sex. That makes those things sinful.

The following are some common objections to God's commands against sexual immorality:

1. **It's not wrong if we love each other.** The Bible makes no distinction between loving and unloving sexual relations. The only biblical distinction is between married and unmarried people. Sex within marriage is blessed (Genesis 1:28); sex outside of marriage is fornication or "sexual immorality" (1 Corinthians 7:2–5).

2. **Times have changed, and what was wrong in biblical times is no longer considered sin.** Most of the passages condemning sexual immorality also include evils such as greed, lust, stealing, etc. (1 Corinthians 6:9–10; Galatians 5:19–21). We have no problem understanding that these other things are still sin. God's character does not change with culture's opinion (Numbers 23:19; Malachi 3:6; Hebrews 13:8).

3. **We're married in God's eyes.** The fallacy of this idea is that the God who created marriage in the first place would retract His own command to accommodate what He has called sin. God declared marriage to be one man and one woman united for life (Mark 10:6–9). The Bible often uses the imagery of a wedding and a covenant marriage as a metaphor to teach spiritual truth (Matthew 22:2; Revelation 19:9). God takes marriage seriously, and He sees immorality for what it is, regardless of how cleverly we have redefined it.

4. **I can still have a good relationship with God because He understands.** Proverbs 28:9 says, "If one turns away his ear from hearing the law, even his prayer is an abomination" (ESV). We fool ourselves when we think that we can stubbornly choose sin and God does not care. First John 2:3–4 contains a serious challenge for those who persist in this line of thinking: "We know that we have come to know him if we keep his commands. Whoever says, 'I know him,' but does not do what he commands is a liar, and the truth is not in that person."

Hebrews 13:4 makes God's expectation for His children crystal clear: "Let marriage be held in honor among all, and let the marriage bed be undefiled, for God will judge the sexually immoral and adulterous" (ESV). Sexual immorality is wrong. The blood of Jesus can cleanse us from every type of impurity when we repent and receive His forgiveness (1 John 1:7–9). But that cleansing means our old nature and all its practices, including sexual immorality, are put to death (Romans 6:12–14; 8:13). Ephesians 5:3 says, "But among you there must not be even a hint of sexual immorality, or of any kind of impurity, or of greed, because these are improper for God's holy people."

89. What constitutes marriage according to the Bible?

The Bible nowhere explicitly states at what point God considers a man and a woman to be married. Due to the Bible's silence on this matter, identifying the precise moment a man and woman are married in God's eyes is a complex undertaking. Here are the three most common viewpoints: (1) God only considers a man and a woman married when they are legally married—that is, when they become husband and wife in the eyes of the law. (2) A man and a woman are married in God's eyes when they have completed some kind of formal wedding ceremony involving covenantal vows. (3) God considers a man and a woman to be married at the moment they engage in sexual intercourse. Let's look at each of the three views and evaluate the strengths and weaknesses of each.

1. God only considers a man and a woman married when they are legally married. The scriptural support typically given for this view is the command to obey the government's laws (Romans 13:1–7; 1 Peter 2:17). The argument is that, if the government requires certain procedures and paperwork to be completed before a marriage is recognized, then a couple should submit themselves to that process. It is definitely biblical for a couple to submit to the government as long as the requirements do not contradict God's Word and are reasonable. Romans 13:1–2 tells us, "Let everyone be subject to the governing authorities, for there is no authority except that which God has established. The authorities that exist have been established by God. Consequently, whoever rebels against the authority is rebelling

against what God has instituted, and those who do so will bring judgment on themselves."

However, there are some weaknesses and potential problems with this view. First, marriage existed before any government was organized. For thousands of years, people were getting married with no such thing as a marriage license. Second, even today, there are some countries that have no governmental recognition of marriage, and/or no legal requirements for marriage. Third, there are some governments that place unbiblical requirements on a marriage before it is legally recognized. As an example, some countries require weddings to be held in a Catholic church, according to Catholic teachings, and overseen by a Catholic priest. Obviously, for those who have strong disagreements with the Catholic Church and the Catholic understanding of marriage as a sacrament, it would be unbiblical to submit to being married in the Catholic Church. Fourth, to make the legitimacy of the marriage union solely dependent on government statutes is to indirectly sanction the statutory definition of marriage, which may fluctuate.

2. A man and a woman are married in God's eyes when they have completed some kind of formal wedding ceremony. Some interpreters understand God's bringing Eve to Adam (Genesis 2:22) as God's overseeing the first wedding "ceremony"—the modern practice of a father giving away his daughter at a wedding reflects God's action in Eden. In John chapter 2, Jesus attended a wedding ceremony. Jesus would not have attended such an event if He did not approve of what was occurring. Jesus' presence at a wedding ceremony by no means indicates that God requires a wedding ceremony, but it does indicate that a wedding ceremony is acceptable in God's sight. Nearly every culture in the history of humanity has observed some kind of formal wedding ceremony. In every culture there is an event, action, covenant, vow, or proclamation that is recognized as declaring a man and woman to be married.

3. God considers a man and a woman to be married at the moment they engage in sexual intercourse. There are some who take this to

mean that a married couple is not truly married in God's eyes until they have consummated the marriage physically. Others argue that if any man and woman have sex, God considers the two of them to be married. The basis for this view is the fact that sexual intercourse between a husband and wife is the ultimate fulfillment of the "one flesh" principle (Genesis 2:24; Matthew 19:5; Ephesians 5:31). In this sense, sexual intercourse is the final "seal" on a marriage covenant. However, the view that intercourse constitutes marriage is not biblically sound. If a couple is legally and ceremonially married but for some reason is unable to engage in sexual intercourse, that couple is still considered married.

We know that God does not equate sexual intercourse with marriage based on the fact that the Old Testament often distinguishes a wife from a concubine. For example, 2 Chronicles 11:21 describes one king's family life: "Rehoboam loved Maakah daughter of Absalom more than any of his other wives and concubines. In all, he had eighteen wives and sixty concubines." In this verse, concubines who had sexual intercourse with King Rehoboam are not considered wives and are mentioned as a separate category.

Also, 1 Corinthians 7:2 indicates that sex before marriage is immorality. If sexual intercourse causes a couple to become married, it could not be considered immoral, as the couple would be considered married the moment they engaged in sexual intercourse. There is no biblical basis for an unmarried couple to have sex and then declare themselves to be married, thereby declaring all future sexual relations to be moral and God-honoring.

Some point to Genesis 24 and the story of Isaac and Rebekah as an example of a couple being married solely by sexual intercourse, without any type of ceremony. But the details that lead up to the marriage reveal that a formal process was followed. Isaac's father, Abraham, gave his servant a list of things to do to find Isaac a wife (Genesis 24:1–10). The servant did all his master asked, plus he prayed to God for guidance and confirmation (verses 12–14). God did guide him, and He also confirmed all of the servant's "tests" to show that the marriage of Isaac and Rebekah was indeed God-approved (verses 15–27). So convinced was the servant of God's will that he immediately related to Rebekah's brother, Laban, all the details confirming God's choice (verses 32–49). By the time dinner was served, everyone knew that this was of God, that both Isaac and Rebekah should be married (verses 50–51). Then a dowry was paid, and verbal contracts were pledged between them (verses 52–59). Thus, the marriage mentioned in verse 67 was hardly based on a mere sexual act. Cultural procedures and dowry traditions were fulfilled, conditions were met, answers to prayer were seen, and the obvious blessing by God was upon the entire scenario.

So, what constitutes marriage in God's eyes? It would seem that the following principles should be followed: (1) As long as the requirements are reasonable and not against the Bible, a man and a woman should seek whatever formal governmental recognition is available. (2) A man and a woman should follow whatever cultural, familial, and covenantal practices are typically employed to recognize a couple as "officially married." (3) If possible, a man and a woman should consummate the marriage sexually, fulfilling the physical aspect of the "one flesh" principle.

90. What does the Bible say about homosexuality?

In some people's minds, being homosexual is as much outside one's control as the color of your skin and your height. On the other hand, the Bible clearly and consistently declares that homosexual activity is a sin (Genesis 19:1–13; Leviticus 18:22; 20:13; Romans 1:26–27; 1 Corinthians 6:9; 1 Timothy 1:10). This disconnect leads to much controversy, debate, and even hostility.

When examining what the Bible says about homosexuality, it is important to distinguish between homosexual *behavior* and homosexual *inclinations* or *attractions*. It is the difference between active sin and the passive condition of being tempted. Homosexual behavior is sinful, but the Bible never says it is a sin to be tempted. Simply stated, a struggle with temptation may lead to sin and may come as a result of sin from the fall, but the struggle itself is not a sin.

Romans 1:26–27 teaches that homosexuality is a result of denying and disobeying God. When people continue in sin and unbelief, God gives them over to even more wicked and depraved sin to show them the futility and hopelessness of life apart from God. One of the fruits of rebellion against God is homosexuality. First Corinthians 6:9 proclaims that those who practice homosexuality, and therefore transgress God's created order, are not saved.

A person may be born with a greater susceptibility to homosexuality, just as some people are born with a tendency to violence and other sins. That does not excuse the person's choosing to sin by giving in to sinful desires. Just because a person is born with a greater susceptibility to fits of rage doesn't make it right for them to give in to those desires and explode at every provocation. The same is true with a susceptibility to homosexuality.

No matter our proclivities or attractions, we cannot continue to define ourselves by the very sins that crucified Jesus—and at the same time assume we are right with God. Paul lists many of the sins that the Corinthians once practiced (homosexuality is on the list). But in 1 Corinthians 6:11, he reminds them, "That is what some of you *were*. But you were washed, you were sanctified, you were justified in the name of the Lord Jesus Christ and by the Spirit of our God" (emphasis added). In other words, some of the Corinthians, before they were saved, lived homosexual lifestyles; but no sin is too great for the cleansing power of Jesus. Once cleansed, we are no longer defined by sin.

The problem with homosexual attraction is that it is an attraction to something God has forbidden, and any desire for something sinful ultimately has its roots in sin. The pervasive nature of sin causes us to see the world and our own actions through a warped perspective. Our thoughts, desires, and dispositions are all affected. So, homosexual attraction does not always result in active, willful sin—there may not be a conscious choice to sin—but it springs from the sinful nature. Same-sex attraction is always, on some basic level, an expression of the fallen nature.

As sinful human beings living in a sinful world (Romans 3:23), we are beset with weaknesses, temptations, and inducements to sin. Our world is filled with lures and entrapments, including the enticement to practice homosexuality.

The temptation to engage in homosexual behavior is very real to many. Those who struggle with homosexual attraction often report suffering through years of wishing things were different. People may not always be able to control how or what they feel, but they *can* control what they do with those feelings (1 Peter 1:5–8). We all have the responsibility to resist temptation (Ephesians 6:13). We must all be transformed by the renewing of our minds (Romans 12:2). We must all "walk by the Spirit" so as not to "gratify the desires of the flesh" (Galatians 5:16).

Finally, the Bible does not describe homosexuality as a greater sin than any other. All sin is offensive to God. Without Christ, we are lost, no matter the type of sin that has entangled us. According to the Bible, God's forgiveness is available to the homosexual just as it is to the adulterer, idol worshiper, murderer, and thief. God promises the strength for victory over sin, including homosexuality, to all those who will believe in Jesus Christ for their salvation (1 Corinthians 6:11; 2 Corinthians 5:17; Philippians 4:13).

91. What does the Bible say about gay marriage/same sex marriage?

While the Bible does address homosexuality, it does not explicitly mention gay marriage/same sex marriage. It is clear, however, that the Bible condemns homosexuality as an immoral and unnatural sin. Leviticus 18:22 identifies homosexual sex as an abomination, a detestable sin. Romans 1:26–27 declares homosexual desires and actions to be "shameful" and "unnatural." First Corinthians 6:9 states that homosexuals are "wrongdoers" who will not inherit the kingdom of God. Since homosexuality is condemned in the Bible, it follows that homosexuals marrying is not God's will and would be, in fact, sinful.

Every mention of marriage in the Bible refers to the union of a male and a female. The first mention of marriage, Genesis 2:24, describes it as a man leaving his parents and being united to his wife. In passages that contain instructions regarding marriage, such as 1 Corinthians 7:2–16 and Ephesians 5:23–33, the Bible clearly identifies marriage as being between a man and a woman. Biblically speaking, marriage is the lifetime union of a man and a woman, primarily for the purpose of building a family and providing a stable environment for that family.

The biblical understanding of marriage as the union of a man and a woman is found in every human civilization in world history. History thus argues against gay marriage. Modern secular psychology recognizes that men and women are psychologically and emotionally designed to complement one another. In regard to the family, psychologists contend that a union between a man and woman in which both spouses serve as good gender role models is the best environment in which to raise well-adjusted children. So, psychology also argues against gay marriage. Anatomically, men and women were clearly designed to fit together sexually. The "natural" purpose of sexual intercourse is procreation, and only a sexual relationship between a man and a woman can fulfill this purpose. In this way, nature argues against gay marriage.

So, if the Bible, history, psychology, and nature all argue for marriage being between a man and a woman, why is there such a controversy today? Why are those who are opposed to gay marriage/same sex marriage labeled as hateful people or intolerant bigots, no matter how respectfully the opposition is presented? Why is the gay rights movement so aggressively pushing for gay marriage/same sex marriage when most people, religious and non-religious, are supportive of gay couples having the same legal rights as married couples through some form of civil union?

The answer, according to the Bible, is that everyone inherently knows that homosexuality is immoral and unnatural. Romans 1:18–32 says that God has made the truth plain. But the truth is rejected and replaced with a lie. The lie is then promoted, and the truth suppressed. One way to suppress the truth is to normalize homosexuality and marginalize those who oppose it. And a good way to normalize homosexuality is to place gay marriage/same sex marriage on an equal plane with traditional opposite-gender marriage.

To sanction gay marriage/same sex marriage is to approve of the homosexual lifestyle, which the Bible clearly and consistently labels as sinful. Christians should stand firmly against the idea of gay marriage/same sex marriage. Further, there are strong, logical arguments against gay marriage/same sex marriage from contexts apart from the Bible. One does not have to be an evangelical Christian to recognize that marriage is between a man and a woman.

According to the Bible, marriage is ordained by God as the lifetime union of a man and a woman (Genesis 2:21–24; Matthew 19:4–6). Gay marriage/same sex marriage is a perversion of the institution of marriage and an offense to the God who created marriage. As Christians, we do not condone or ignore sin. Rather, we share the love of God and act as ministers of reconciliation (2 Corinthians 5:18). We point to the forgiveness of sins that is available to all, including homosexuals, through Jesus Christ. We speak the truth in love (Ephesians 4:15) and contend for truth with "gentleness and respect" (1 Peter 3:15).

92. What is a Christian couple allowed to do in sex?

The Bible says that "marriage should be honored by all, and the marriage bed kept pure, for God will judge the adulterer and all the sexually immoral" (Hebrews 13:4). Scripture never says what a husband and wife are or are not allowed to do sexually, so how can we know if something is sexually permissible between a husband and wife? The Bible gives us general principles regarding sex within marriage:

1. *Sex is to be God-honoring*—Our bodies are meant to glorify the Lord, not to be controlled by our passions and not to be used for sexual immorality (1 Corinthians 6:12–13). "Therefore honor God with your bodies" (1 Corinthians 6:20).

2. *Sex is to be exclusive*—Sex is between a husband and wife only (1 Corinthians 7:2).

3. *Sex is to be loving and other-oriented*—First Corinthians 7:3–4 instructs, "The husband should fulfill his marital duty to his wife, and likewise the wife to her husband. The wife does not have authority over her own body but yields it to her husband. In the same way, the husband does not have authority over his own body but yields it to his wife." Each spouse lovingly yields his or her body to the other.

4. *Marital sex happens regularly*—"Do not deprive each other except perhaps by mutual consent and for a time, so that you may devote yourselves to prayer. Then come together again so that Satan will not tempt you because of your lack of self-control" (1 Corinthians 7:5).

5. *Marital sex unifies*—Sexual intimacy unites a husband and wife (1 Corinthians 7:5) and solidifies the "one flesh" aspect of marriage, not just physically but emotionally, intellectually, spiritually, and in every other way.

If the sexual act in question satisfies these principles, and both the husband and wife are agreeable to loving each other in that way, there is no biblical case for declaring it to be a sin. The principle of "mutual consent" applies to abstaining from sex (1 Corinthians 7:5) and to whatever is done sexually within a marriage. Neither spouse should be coerced into doing something he or she is not completely comfortable with or thinks is wrong. If a husband and wife both agree that they want to try something (e.g., oral sex, different positions, sex toys, etc.), then the Bible does not give any reason why they cannot.

There are a few things, though, that are never allowable for a married couple. The practice of "swapping," "swinging," or "bringing in an extra" (threesomes, foursomes, etc.) is adultery (Galatians 5:19; Ephesians 5:3; Colossians 3:5; 1 Thessalonians 4:3). Adultery is sin even if one's spouse allows, approves, or even participates in it. Viewing pornography is another practice that should be off-limits for a married couple. Porn appeals to the "lust of the flesh" and "the lust of the eyes" (1 John 2:16) and is therefore condemned by God.

Scripture provides great freedom in the bedroom for a husband and wife. As long as a married couple's sexual practices are God-honoring, exclusive, loving, other-oriented, unifying, and mutually agreed upon, they carry God's blessing.

93. What does the Bible say about interracial marriage?

The Old Testament Law commanded the Israelites not to engage in interracial marriage (Deuteronomy 7:3–4). However, the reason for this command was not skin color or ethnicity. Rather, it was religious. God commanded against interracial marriage for the Jews because foreign people were worshipers of false gods. The Israelites would be led astray if they intermarried with idol worshipers, pagans, or heathens. This is exactly what happened in Israel, according to Malachi 2:11.

A similar principle of spiritual purity is laid out in the New Testament, but it has nothing to do with race: "Do not be yoked together with unbelievers. For what do righteousness and wickedness have in common? Or what fellowship can light have with darkness?" (2 Corinthians 6:14). Just as the Israelites (believers in the one true God) were commanded not to marry idolaters, so Christians (believers in the one true God) are commanded not to marry unbelievers. The Bible never says that interracial marriage is wrong. Anyone who forbids interracial marriage is doing so without biblical authority.

As Martin Luther King, Jr., noted, a person should be judged by his or her character, not by skin color. There is no place in the life of the Christian for favoritism based on race (James 2:1–10). In fact, the biblical perspective is that there is only one "race"—the human race—with everyone having descended from Adam and Eve. When selecting a mate, a Christian should first find out if the potential spouse is born again by faith in Jesus Christ (John 3:3–5). Faith in Christ, not skin color, is the biblical standard for choosing a spouse. Interracial marriage is not a matter of right or wrong but of prayer and personal choice.

A couple considering marriage needs to weigh many factors. While a difference in skin color or ethnicity should not be ignored, it absolutely should not be the determining factor in whether a couple should marry. An interracial couple may face discrimination and ridicule, and they should be prepared to respond to such prejudice in a biblical manner. But marriage is honorable among all (Hebrews 13:4). Also, "there is no difference between Jew and Gentile—the same Lord is Lord of all and richly blesses all who call on him" (Romans 10:12). A Christian interracial marriage can be a powerful illustration of our equality and oneness in Christ.

94. What does the Bible say about divorce and remarriage?

First of all, no matter what view one takes on the issue of divorce, it is important to remember Malachi 2:16: "'I hate divorce,' says the LORD, the God of Israel" (AMP). According to the Bible, marriage is a lifetime commitment. "So they are no longer two, but one flesh. Therefore what God has joined together, let no one separate" (Matthew 19:6). God realizes, though, that since marriages involve two sinful human beings, divorces are going to occur. In the Old Testament, He laid down some laws to protect the rights of divorcées (Deuteronomy 24:1–4). Jesus pointed out that these laws were given because of the hardness of people's hearts, not because such laws were God's desire (Matthew 19:8).

The controversy over whether divorce and remarriage are allowed according to the Bible revolves primarily around Jesus' words in Matthew 5:32 and 19:9. The phrase "except for sexual immorality" is the only thing in Scripture that possibly gives God's permission for divorce and remarriage. Many interpreters understand this "exception clause" as referring to marital unfaithfulness during the betrothal period. In Jewish custom, a man and a woman were considered married even while they were still engaged or betrothed. According to this view, immorality during this betrothal period would be the only valid reason for a divorce.

However, the Greek word translated "marital unfaithfulness" is a word that can mean any form of sexual immorality. It can refer to fornication, prostitution, adultery, etc. Jesus is possibly saying that divorce is permissible if sexual immorality is committed. Sexual relations are an integral part of the marital bond: "the two will become one flesh" (Genesis 2:24; Matthew 19:5; Ephesians 5:31). Therefore, any breaking of that bond by sexual relations outside of marriage might be a permissible reason for divorce. If so, Jesus also has remarriage in mind in this passage. The phrase "and marries another" (Matthew 19:9) indicates that divorce and remarriage are allowed in an instance of the exception clause, whatever it is interpreted to be. It is important to note that only the innocent party is allowed to remarry. Although not stated in the text, it would seem the allowance for remarriage after divorce is God's mercy for the one who was sinned against, not for the one who committed the sexual immorality. There may be instances where the guilty party is allowed to remarry, but they are not evident in this text.

Some understand 1 Corinthians 7:15 as another "exception," allowing remarriage if an unbelieving spouse divorces a believer. However, the context does not mention remarriage but only says a believer is not bound to continue a marriage if an unbelieving spouse wants to leave. Others claim that abuse (spousal or child) is a valid reason for divorce even though it is not listed as such in the Bible. While this may very well be the case, it is never wise to presume upon the Word of God.

Sometimes lost in the debate over the exception clause is the fact that whatever "marital unfaithfulness" means, it is an allowance for divorce, not a requirement for it. Even when adultery is committed, a couple can, through God's grace, learn to forgive and begin rebuilding their marriage. God has forgiven us so much more. Surely, we can follow His example and even forgive the sin of adultery (Ephesians 4:32). However, in many instances a spouse is unrepentant and continues in sexual immorality. That is where Matthew 19:9 can possibly be applied. Many also look to quickly remarry after a divorce when God might desire them to remain single. God sometimes calls people to be single so that their attention is not divided (1 Corinthians 7:32–35). Remarriage after a divorce may be an option in some circumstances, but that does not mean it is the only option.

The Bible makes it abundantly clear that God hates divorce (Malachi 2:16) and that reconciliation and forgiveness should mark a believer's life (Luke 11:4; Ephesians 4:32). However, God recognizes that divorce will occur, even among His children. A divorced and/or remarried believer should not feel any less loved by God, even if the divorce and/or remarriage is not covered under the possible exception clause of Matthew 19:9.

95. What is the difference between dating and courting?

Dating and courtship are two methods of beginning relationships with the opposite sex. While there are non-Christians who date with the intention of having a series of intimate physical relationships, for the Christian this is not acceptable and should never be the reason for dating. Many Christians see dating as little more than friendship and maintain the friendship aspect of their dating until both people are ready to commit to each other as potential marriage partners. First and foremost, dating is a time when a Christian finds out if his or her potential marriage partner is also a believer in Christ. The Bible warns that believers and unbelievers should not marry each other, because those living in the light (of Christ) and those living in the darkness cannot live in harmony (2 Corinthians 6:14–15). Christians who date should limit their physical contact with each other to avoid temptation (1 Corinthians 6:18–20).

Those who advocate courtship instead of dating take the position that the couple should have no physical contact at all (no touching, no handholding, no kissing) until marriage. Many in a courtship relationship will not spend any time together unless family members, preferably parents, are also present. In addition, courting couples state up front that their intentions are to see if they are suitable marriage partners. Courtship advocates claim that courtship allows for two people to truly get to know each other in a platonic setting without the pressures of physical intimacy or emotions clouding their view.

There are problems inherent with both relationship approaches. For daters, spending time alone with a member of the opposite sex whom they find attractive can present hard-to-resist temptations. The Christian dating couple must have boundaries in place and be committed to not crossing them. If they find this hard to do, they must take steps to ensure that Christ will always be honored during their time together and that sin is never given a chance to take hold in their relationship. If the dating couple are still under parental authority, then the parents should be involved, knowledgeable, and available.

The courtship style presents its own set of difficulties. While many courtship advocates see it as the only choice for finding a mate, others find it oppressive and overly controlling. In addition, it can be hard to find the "real" person behind the public face presented in front of the entire family. No one is the same in a group setting as he or she is one-on-one. If a couple is never alone together, they never have that one-on-one opportunity to relate and get to know one another in emotional and spiritual intimacy. In addition, some courtship situations have led to something akin to an arranged marriage, which can foster resentment in the couple.

Neither dating nor courtship is mandated in Scripture. In the end, the Christian character and spiritual maturity of the couple are far more important than the exact nature of how and when they spend time together. The result of the process—whatever method is used— should be godly Christian men and women marrying and raising families that honor God. "Therefore, whether you eat or drink, or whatever you do, do all to the glory of God" (1 Corinthians 10:31 NKJV).

Believing one's personal preference—dating or courting—is the only way is a pitfall. Looking down on those who make the opposite choice is prideful. The unity of the body of Christ is something we should strive for, regardless of personal choices others make pertaining to relationship issues on which the Bible is silent.

96. What does the Bible say about sex before marriage?

The Bible clearly condemns sexual sins: adultery (consensual sex between a married person and someone other than his or her spouse) (Proverbs 6:32; cf. 1 Corinthians 6:18 and Hebrews 13:4) and fornication (sexual immorality in general) are specified (Matthew 15:19; Romans 1:29; 1 Corinthians 5:1). Sex before marriage, or premarital sex, is not addressed in that exact term, but it does fall within the scope of sexual immorality.

The Bible teaches that sex before marriage is immoral in a couple of different passages. One is 1 Corinthians 7:2, which says, "But since sexual immorality is occurring, each man should have sexual relations with his own wife, and each woman with her own husband." In this verse, marriage is presented as the protection against sexual immorality. Sexual union within marriage, which is commended, is set against immorality, which is to be avoided. Thus, any sex out-side of marriage is considered immoral. This would have to include premarital sex.

Another verse that presents sex before marriage as immoral is Hebrews 13:4, "Marriage should be honored by all, and the marriage bed kept pure, for God will judge the adulterer and all the sexually im-moral." Here, we have both adultery and fornication contrasted with what happens in the marriage bed. Marriage (and sexual intercourse within marriage) is honorable; all other types of sexual activity are condemned as immoral and bring God's judgment.

Based on these passages, a biblical definition of sexual immorality would have to include sex before marriage. That means that all the Bible verses that condemn sexual immorality in general also con-demn sex before marriage. These include Acts 15:20; 1 Corinthians 5:1; 6:13, 18; 10:8; 2 Corinthians 12:21; Galatians 5:19; Ephesians 5:3; Colossians 3:5; 1 Thessalonians 4:3; Jude 1:7; and Revelation 21:8.

God designed sex, and the Bible honors marriage. Part of honor-ing marriage is the Bible's promotion of complete abstinence before marriage. When two unmarried people engage in sexual intercourse, they are defiling God's good gift of sex. Before marriage, a couple has no binding union, and they've entered no sacred covenant; without the marriage vows, they have no right to exploit the culmination of such vows.

Too often, we focus on the "recreation" aspect of sex without recog-nizing that there is another aspect—procreation. Sex within marriage is pleasurable, and God designed it that way. God wants men and women to enjoy sexual activity within the confines of marriage. Song of Solomon 4 and several other Bible passages (such as Proverbs 5:19) describe the pleasure of sex. However, God's intent for sex includes producing children. Thus, for a couple to engage in sex before mar-riage is doubly wrong—they are enjoying pleasures not intended for them, and they are taking a chance of creating a human life outside of the family structure God intended for every child.

While practicality does not determine right from wrong, following the Bible's instructions concerning sex before marriage would greatly benefit society. If the Bible's message on sex before marriage were obeyed, there would be far fewer sexually transmitted diseases, far fewer abortions, far fewer unwed mothers and unwanted pregnancies, and far fewer children growing up without both parents in their lives. Abstinence saves lives, protects babies, gives sexual relations their proper value, and most importantly, honors God. Sex between a husband and wife is the only form of sexual relations of which God approves.

97. What does the Bible say about oral sex?

Oral sex, also known as *cunnilingus* when performed on females and *fellatio* when performed on males, is not mentioned in the Bible. There are two primary questions asked in regard to oral sex: (1) "Is oral sex a sin if done before marriage?" and (2) "Is oral sex a sin if done within a marriage?" While the Bible does not specifically address either question, there are biblical principles that apply.

Is oral sex a sin if done before or outside of marriage?

This question is becoming increasingly common as young people are told that oral sex is not really sex, and as oral sex is promoted as a safer alternative to sexual intercourse (no risk of pregnancy, less risk of sexually transmitted diseases).[1] What does the Bible say? Ephesians 5:3 declares, "But among you there must not be even a hint of sexual immorality, or of any kind of impurity . . . because these are improper for God's holy people." The biblical definition of *immorality* is any form of sexual contact outside of marriage (see 1 Corinthians 7:2). According to the Bible, all sex is to be reserved for marriage (Hebrews 13:4). Period. So, yes, oral sex is always a sin if done before or outside of marriage.

Is oral sex a sin if done within a marriage?

Many Christian married couples have had this question. The Bible
nowhere says what specifically is allowed or disallowed sexually between a husband and wife. Of course, any sexual activity involving
another person (swapping, threesomes, etc.) or lust for someone else
(pornography) is sinful. Apart from those two restrictions, how can we
know if something is sexually permissible between a husband and wife?

1. *Sex is to be God-honoring*—Our bodies are meant to glorify
   the Lord, not to be controlled by our passions and not to be
   used for sexual immorality (1 Corinthians 6:12–13). "Therefore honor God with your bodies" (1 Corinthians 6:20).
2. *Sex is to be exclusive*—Sex is between a husband and wife
   only (1 Corinthians 7:2).
3. *Sex is to be loving and other-oriented*—1 Corinthians 7:3–4
   instructs, "The husband should fulfill his marital duty to his
   wife, and likewise the wife to her husband. The wife does not
   have authority over her own body but yields it to her husband. In the same way, the husband does not have authority
   over his own body but yields it to his wife." Each spouse lovingly yields his or her body to the other.
4. *Marital sex happens regularly*—"Do not deprive each other
   except perhaps by mutual consent and for a time, so that you
   may devote yourselves to prayer. Then come together again
   so that Satan will not tempt you because of your lack of self-
   control" (1 Corinthians 7:5).
5. *Marital sex unifies*—Sexual intimacy unites a husband and
   wife (1 Corinthians 7:5) and solidifies the "one flesh" aspect
   of marriage, not just physically but emotionally, intellectually,
   spiritually, and in every other way.

Oral sex before marriage is absolutely a sin. It is immoral. It is not
a biblically acceptable alternative to sexual intercourse for unmarried
couples. Within the confines of marriage, oral sex is free from sin if

it is God-honoring, exclusive, loving, other-oriented, unifying, and mutually agreed upon.

98. Masturbation—is it a sin according to the Bible?

The Bible does not mention masturbation or self-gratification or "solo sex," as it is sometimes called. In its silence on the subject, the Bible does not state whether or not masturbation is a sin.

A passage frequently associated with masturbation is the story of Onan in Genesis 38:9–10. Some interpret this passage to say that "spilling seed"—squandering semen—is a sin. However, that is not what the passage is saying. God condemned Onan not for spilling his seed but because Onan was rebellious. Onan refused to fulfill his duty to provide an heir for his deceased brother. The passage is not about masturbation but about fulfilling a family obligation.

A second passage sometimes used as evidence that masturbation is a sin is Matthew 5:27–30. Jesus speaks against having lustful thoughts and then says, "If your right hand causes you to stumble, cut it off and throw it away." While there is often a connection between lustful thoughts and masturbation, it is unlikely that Jesus was alluding to the specific sin of masturbation in this passage.

Though the Bible nowhere explicitly addresses masturbation, it does outline the purpose of sex. According to 1 Corinthians 7:2–5, "Each man should have sexual relations with his own wife, and each woman with her own husband. The husband should fulfill his marital duty to his wife, and likewise the wife to her husband. The wife does not have authority over her own body but yields it to her husband. In the same way, the husband does not have authority over his own body but yields it to his wife. Do not deprive each other except perhaps by mutual consent and for a time, so that you may devote yourselves to prayer. Then come together again so that Satan will not tempt you because of your lack of self-control." Implicit in this passage are these truths:

- God's plan for sex requires relationship, namely, that of a husband and wife (verse 2). Masturbation is sex disconnected from relationship.
- Foundational to God's plan for sex is giving one's body to another (verse 4). Masturbation is the keeping of one's body to oneself.
- The solution to a time of deprivation is to "come together" (verse 5). Masturbation is done alone, not together.

First Corinthians 7:9 identifies the proper outlet for single people who struggle with sexual desire: "If they cannot control themselves, they should marry, for it is better to marry than to burn with passion." Paul suggests that self-control is the best avenue. To singles who lack self-control, Paul does not say, "Let them masturbate"; he says, "Let them marry." Again, marriage is the God-given outlet for sexual yearnings.

Those who believe that masturbation has no moral or ethical import argue that masturbation is a "need" akin to the need to eat or the need to scratch an itch. However, the Bible never presents sexual fulfillment as a need. On the contrary, Paul says to the unmarried, "It's better to stay unmarried" (1 Corinthians 7:8 NLT).

Certain actions often associated with masturbation are sinful and should be dealt with: lustful thoughts, inappropriate sexual stimulation, and pornography use, for example. If these problems are tackled, masturbation becomes less of a temptation. Many people struggle with guilt concerning masturbation, when in reality, they would be better off repenting of the sins that lead them to masturbate.

So, is masturbation a sin? The Bible does not directly answer this question, but there definitely are some biblical principles to apply:

1. "So whether you eat or drink or whatever you do, do it all for the glory of God" (1 Corinthians 10:31). If we cannot give God glory for something, we should not do it.

2. "Everything that does not come from faith is sin" (Romans 14:23). If we are not fully convinced that an activity is honoring to God, it is a sin.

3. "I will not be mastered by anything" (1 Corinthians 6:12). Christians have a responsibility to avoid anything that might enslave them.

4. "I discipline my body and keep it under control" (1 Corinthians 9:27 ESV). Self-denial is difficult, but self-discipline is worth it.

5. "The fruit of the Spirit is . . . self-control" (Galatians 5:22–23). Masturbation is almost always a sign of a *lack* of self-control.

6. Do "not gratify the desires of the flesh. For the flesh desires what is contrary to the Spirit, and the Spirit what is contrary to the flesh. They are in conflict with each other, so that you are not to do whatever you want" (Galatians 5:16–17). We are called to self-denial, not to self-gratification.

These truths should have an impact on what we do with our bodies. In light of the above principles, it is doubtful that masturbation can be a God-honoring activity. If masturbation could be done with

- no lust in the heart
- no immoral thoughts
- no pornography
- no self-gratification of the flesh
- full assurance that it is good and right
- thanks given to God

then perhaps it would be allowable. But those qualifiers seem to negate the very meaning and purpose of masturbation.

99. What does the Bible say about pornography?

By far, the most searched-for terms on the internet are related to pornography. Pornography is rampant in the world today. Satan has succeeded in perverting God's gift of sex perhaps more than any other of God's good gifts. Satan has taken what is good and right (loving sex between a husband and wife) and replaced it with lust, pornography, and other sins. Pornography can be the first step on a slippery slope of sexual addiction and ungodly desires (see Romans 6:19). The addictive nature of pornography is well documented.

The three main categories of sin are the lust of the flesh, the lust of the eyes, and the pride of life (1 John 2:16). Pornography causes users to lust after the flesh, and it is undeniably a lust of the eyes. Pornography does not qualify as one of the things we are to think about, according to Philippians 4:8. Pornography is addictive, and we are not to be mastered by anything (1 Corinthians 6:12; 2 Peter 2:19). Lusting in the mind, which is the essence of pornography, is offensive to God (Matthew 5:28) and destructive (see Proverbs 6:25–28; Ephesians 4:19).

For those involved in pornography, God can and will give the victory to those who seek Him. Are you involved with pornography and desire freedom from it? Here are some steps to victory:

1. Confess your sin to God (1 John 1:9).
2. Ask God to cleanse, renew, and transform your mind (Romans 12:2).
3. Ask God to fill your mind with things that are true, honorable, just, pure, lovely, and commendable (Philippians 4:8)—and consume media that can be described that way.
4. Learn to possess your body in holiness (1 Thessalonians 4:3–4).
5. Understand the proper meaning of sex and rely on your spouse alone to meet that need (1 Corinthians 7:1–5).

6. Realize that if you walk in the Spirit, you will not fulfill the lusts of the flesh (Galatians 5:16).

7. Take practical steps to reduce your exposure to pornographic images. Install pornography blockers on your computer, limit television and video usage, and find another Christian who will pray for you and help keep you accountable.

You can find freedom from the bondage of pornography. God's plan for your life, including His design for your sexuality, is far better than anything sin entices you with.

100. What is agape love?

The Greek word *agape* is often translated "love" in the New Testament. How is "agape love" different from other types of love? The essence of agape love is goodwill, benevolence, and willful delight in the object of love. Unlike our English word *love*, *agape* is not used in the New Testament to refer to romantic or sexual love. Nor does it refer to close friendship or brotherly love, for which the Greek word *philia* is used. Agape love involves faithfulness, commitment, and an act of the will. It is distinguished from the other types of love by its lofty moral nature and strong character. Agape love is beautifully described in 1 Corinthians 13.

Outside of the New Testament, the word *agape* is used in a variety of contexts, but in the vast majority of instances in the New Testament, it carries distinct meaning. *Agape* is almost always used to describe the love that is of and from God, whose very nature is love itself: "God is love" (1 John 4:8). God does not merely love; He *is* love. Everything God does flows from His love. *Agape* is also used to describe our love for God (Luke 10:27), a servant's faithful respect to his master (Matthew 6:24), and a man's attachment to things (John 3:19).

The type of love that characterizes God is not a sappy, sentimental feeling such as we often hear portrayed. God loves because that is

His nature and the expression of His being. He loves the unlovable and the unlovely, not because we deserve to be loved or because of any excellence we possess but because it is His nature to love and He must be true to His nature.

Agape love is always shown by what it does. God's love is displayed most clearly at the cross. "God, being rich in mercy, because of the great love with which he loved us, even when we were dead in our trespasses, made us alive together with Christ—by grace you have been saved" (Ephesians 2:4–5 ESV). We did not deserve such a sacrifice, "but God demonstrates his own love for us in this: While we were still sinners, Christ died for us" (Romans 5:8). God's agape love is unmerited, gracious, and constantly seeking the benefit of the ones He loves. The Bible says we are the undeserving recipients of His lavish agape love (1 John 3:1). God's demonstration of agape love led to the sacrifice of the Son of God for those He loves.

We are to love others with agape love, whether they are fellow believers (John 13:34) or bitter enemies (Matthew 5:44). Jesus gave the parable of the Good Samaritan as an example of sacrifice for the sake of others, even for those who may care nothing at all for us. Agape love as modeled by Christ is not based on a feeling; rather, it is a determined act of the will, a joyful resolve to put the welfare of others above our own.

Agape love does not come naturally to us. Because of our fallen nature, we are incapable of producing such a love. If we are to love as God loves, that love—that *agape*—can only come from its Source. This is the love that "has been poured out into our hearts through the Holy Spirit, who has been given to us" when we became His children (Romans 5:5; cf. Galatians 5:22). "This is how we know what love is: Jesus Christ laid down his life for us. And we ought to lay down our lives for our brothers and sisters" (1 John 3:16). Because of God's love toward us, we are able to love one another.

Notes

Section 2 Questions about Salvation

1. *C. H. Spurgeon's Autobiography*, ed. W. J. Harrald, vol. 1, *1834–1854* (London: Passmore and Alabaster, 1897), 175.

Section 4 Questions about Theology

1. William Smith, *Smith's Bible Dictionary*, rev. ed. (United States: Thomas Nelson Incorporated, 2004).

Section 6 Questions about the Old Testament

1. Marco Polo, *The Travels of Marco Polo*, ed, Milton Rugoff, trans. William Marsden (New York: Signet Classics, 1961), 158–159.

2. Frederick Buechner, *The Magnificent Defeat* (San Francisco: HarperOne, 1985), 18.

Section 8 Questions about Religions, Cults, and Worldviews

1. Edward J. Hanna, "Purgatory," in *The Catholic Encyclopedia,* eds. Charles G. Herbermann et al. (New York: Robert Appleton Company, 1913), 12:575.

2. Bruce R. McConkie, *Mormon Doctrine* (Salt Lake City, UT: Bookcraft, 1966), 670.

3. "Scriptures," in Church of Jesus Christ of Latter-day Saints, *Gospel Principles* (Salt Lake City, UT: Church of Jesus Christ of Latter-day Saints, 2011).

4. McConkie, *Mormon Doctrine*, 321.

5. Joseph Smith, *Teachings of the Prophet Joseph Smith* (Salt Lake City, UT: Deseret Book Company, 1977), 345.

6. McConkie, *Mormon Doctrine*, 348.

7. See also McConkie, *Mormon Doctrine*, 547.

8. See also Teachings of the Prophet Joseph Smith, 345–354.

9. Robert J. Matthews, *Bible Dictionary*, 697.

10. "Master Mason," The Grand Lodge of Ohio, accessed November 15, 2022, www.freemason.com/master-mason.

11. R. W. Donald Gardner Hicks, Jr., "Masonry: Faith, Hope and Charity," *Proceedings*, 2004–2094.

12. "Text of President Bush's 2002 State of the Union Address," *The Washington Post*, January 29, 2002, https://www.washingtonpost.com/wp-srv/onpolitics/transcripts/sou012902.htm.

13. For the complete story of the Sawis' conversion as well as an exposition of cultural reform as it relates to missions, see Don Richardson's book *Peace Child*.

Section 9 Questions about Sin

1. Amanda Dixon, "Vices like drinking, smoking and gambling cost Americans more than $2,400 per year," Bankrate, December 12, 2019, https://www.bankrate.com/surveys/financial-vices-december-2019/.

2. John C. Willke, "Fact #8: Less than 1% of all abortions are performed to save the life of a mother," AbortionFacts.com, accessed May 24, 2023, https://www.abortionfacts.com/facts/8#cite-1. (See the table titled "Why Women Choose Abortion.")

3. Landrum Shettles and David Rorvik, *Rites of Life* (Grand Rapids, MI: Zondervan Publishing House, 1983), 129.

4. Dr. Irving Cushner, "Testimony before the Senate Judiciary Committee's Subcommittee on the Constitution of the United States on October 14, 1981," as quoted in *The Village Voice*, July 16, 1985.

5. "Dublin Declaration on Maternal Healthcare," Dublin Declaration on Maternal Health, September 2012, https://www.dublindeclaration.com/.

6. Micaiah Bilger, "30,000 Doctors Say: 'Abortion is Never Medically Necessary to Save a Mother's Life,'" LifeNews, March 5, 2019, https://www.lifenews.com/2019/03/05/30000-doctors-say-abortion-is-never-medically-necessary-to-save-a-mothers-life/.

Section 10 Questions about Sexuality

1. While oral sex is *safer* than sexual intercourse in regard to sexually transmitted diseases, it is definitely not safe. Chlamydia, gonorrhea, herpes, HIV/AIDS, and other STDs can be transmitted through oral sex.

Acknowledgments

This book is dedicated to the staff of Got Questions Ministries. Without their hard work, commitment, and passion, this ministry would not be possible. So, thank you to MeLissa Houdmann, Elizabeth DeVore, Kevin Stone, Gwen Sellers, Dianna Merrill, Jeff Laird, Athalia Bufano, Robin Bower, Tiffany Shelton, and Nelson Domingues. Thank you, also, to the more than eight hundred individuals who have served as volunteer question answerers for GotQuestions.org in the past twenty-two years. The Got Questions Ministries staff and volunteers have contributed greatly to this book in writing and editing. GotQuestions.org never has been, and never will be, a one-man show. Above all, to God be the glory—great things He has done!

> "For from him and through him and for him are all things. To him be the glory forever! Amen."

> —Romans 11:36

Shea Michael Houdmann is the president, CEO, and founder of Got Questions Ministries, the parent organization of GotQuestions .org, one of the most frequently visited Christian websites in the world, with over 1.6 billion visits in 22 years. With GotQuestions.org having received over one million questions from people around the world, Shea has tremendous insights into the questions people are actually asking. He has earned a master of arts in Christian theology from Calvary Theological Seminary and a master of theology with an emphasis in apologetics from Dallas Theological Seminary. He is also currently pursuing a doctor of ministry degree from Dallas Theological Seminary. In his limited free time, Shea loves sports, hiking, off-roading, movies, and hanging out with his German Shepherd.

NOTES

NOTES

NOTES

NOTES

NOTES

NOTES